FESTIVALS OF SHARING

IMMIGRANT COMMUNITIES & ETHNIC MINORITIES IN THE UNITED STATES & CANADA: No. 53

ISSN 0749-5951

Series Editor: Robert J. Theodoratus
Department of Anthropology, Colorado State University

1. James G. Chadney. *The Sikhs of Vancouver.*
2. Paul Driben. *We Are Metis: The Ethnography of a Halfbreed Community in Northern Alberta.*
3. A. Michael Colfer. *Morality, Kindred, and Ethnic Boundary: A Study of the Oregon Old Believers.*
4. Nanciellen Davis. *Ethnicity and Ethnic Group Persistance in an Acadian Village in Maritime Canada.*
5. Juli Ellen Skansie. *Death Is for All: Death and Death-Related Beliefs of Rural Spanish-Americans.*
6. Robert Mark Kamen. *Growing Up Hasidic: Education and Socialization in the Bobover Hasidic Community.*
7. Liucija Baskauskas. *An Urban Enclave: Lithuanian Refugees in Los Angeles.*
8. Manuel Alers-Montalvo. *The Puerto Rican Migrants of New York City.*
9. Wayne Wheeler. *An Analysis of Social Change in a Swedish-Immigrant Community: The Case of Lindsborg, Kansas.*
10. Edwin B. Almirol. *Ethnic Identity and Social Negotiation: A Study of a Filipino Community in California.*
11. Stanford Neil Gerber. *Russkoya Celo: The Ethnography of a Russian-American Community.*
12. Peter Paul Jonitis. *The Acculturation of the Lithuanians of Chester, Pennsylvania.*
13. Irene Isabel Blea. *Bessemer: A Sociological Perspective of a Chicano Bario.*
14. Dorothy Ann Gilbert. *Recent Portuguese Immigrants to Fall River, Massachusetts: An Analysis of Relative Economic Success.*
15. Jeffrey Lynn Eighmy. *Mennonite Architecture: Diachronic Evidence for Rapid Diffusion in Rural Communities.*
16. Elizabeth Kathleen Briody. *Household Labor Patterns among Mexican Americans in South Texas: Buscando Trabajo Seguro.*
17. Karen L. S. Muir. *The Strongest Part of the Family: A Study of Lao Refugee Women in Columbus, Ohio.*
18. Judith A. Nagate. *Continuity and Change Among the Old Order Amish of Illinois.*
19. Mary G. Harris. *Cholas: Latino Girls and Gangs.*
20. Rebecca B. Aiken. *Montreal Chinese Property Ownership and Occupational Change, 1881—1981.*
21. Peter Vasiliadis. *Dangerous Truths: Interethnic Competition in a Northeastern Ontario Goldmining Community.*
22. Bruce La Brack. *The Sikhs of Northern California, 1904—1975: A Socio—Historical Study.*
23. Jenny K. Phillips. *Symbol, Myth, and Rhetoric: The Politics of Culture in an Armenian-American Population.*
24. Stacy G. H. Yap. *Gather Your Strength, Sisters: The Emerging Role of Chinese Women Community Workers.*
25. Phyllis Cancilla Martinelli. *Ethnicity In The Sunbelt: Italian-American Migrants in Scottsdale, Arizona.*
26. Dennis L. Nagi. *The Albanian-American Odyssey: A Pilot Study of the Albanian Community of Boston, Massachusetts.*
27. Shirley Ewart. *Cornish Mining Families of Grass Valley, California.*
28. Marilyn Preheim Rose. *On the Move: A Study of Migration and Ethnic Persistence among Mennonites from East Freeman, South Dakota.*
29. Richard H. Thompson. *Toronto's Chinatown: The Changing Social Organization of an Ethnic Community.*
30. Bernard Wong. *Patronage, Brokerage, Entrepreneurship and the Chinese Community of New York.*

FESTIVALS OF SHARING

Family Reunions in America

Greta E. Swenson

AMS Press
New York

Library of Congress Cataloging-in-Publication Data

Swenson, Grerta E.
  Festivals of sharing : Family Reunions in America
  p. c.m. — (Immigrant communities & ethnic minorities in the
United States & Canada ; 53)
  Bibliography: p.
  Includes index.
  ISBN 0-404-19463-X
  1. Family reunions-United States.
  2. United States—Social life and customs.
  I. Title.
  GT2423.S96 1989 394.2   88-35126

All AMS books are printed on acid-free paper that meets
the guidelines for performance and durability of the Committee on Production Guidelines for Book Longevity of the
Council on Library Resources.

AMS PRESS
56 East 13th Street
New York, N.Y. 10003, U.S.A.

MANUFACTURED IN THE UNITED STATES OF AMERICA

CONTENTS

ACKNOWLEDGEMENTS

It is difficult to find words adequate enough to express gratitude to those without whom this work could not have been completed. Thank you must suffice, first of all, to Dr. Linda Dégh, whose constant encouragement and good will have worked miracles; her solid scholarship has always been a model. Drs. Felix J. Oinas, Warren E. Roberts, and Roger Janelli have guided me through many of my folkloric wanderings, and continued their support and aid throughout my research and writing.

To the Swenson family, my family, anything I say will be inadequate. Their interest, support, cooperation, and lives are this book. Norman Swenson's careful documentation of the reunion process formed an important tool for my research. The Swensons in and around Hettinger, North Dakota, took me under wing and guided me through my in-field stage of research. Other Swensons and Swenson spouses have been more than generous with their time, stories, and ideas. I have learned a great deal from them and with them; theirs is blood I am fortunate to share.

Numerous other families and family members included herein have openly shared their time and experiences with me. Their reunions have served as a base of information for understanding

vii

this important American event. The citizens of Adams County, North Dakota also gave me much of themselves in the course of this research. I am grateful to them all.

Friends and colleagues too numerous to name have willingly listened to and discussed my thoughts about reunions and families. A special thank you goes to Lois, Sue, and Maco, for their willing ears. Photographic advice and aid from Elsa Frettem enabled me to more thoroughly document the reunion, and I am also grateful for a small doctoral research grant-in-aid from Indiana University, with which I was able to purchase some field tapes.

This work is dedicated to the memory of my grandparents, Erik and Johanna Swenson, and to the vibrant lives of my parents, Christian and Anna Marie Swenson.

PREFACE

HOW THE STUDY STARTED

During the summer of 1976, I participated in a discussion
which began the planning of a reunion of the Swenson family to be
held sometime during the summer of 1978. In the fall of 1976 I
became interested in documenting the development of this event--an
event rooted in the basic grouping of the family and, as far as I
could determine, distinct to America. I discussed the possibility
of my research with the family member in charge of organizing the
Swenson reunion, indicating that I had no idea what would come of
it, or if I would do anything at all, but that I would at least
document the event in some form or other. He agreed to keep all
correspondence concerning the reunion, and a record of reactions,
suggestions, and interchanges from various family members.

My explorations developed into a full proposal sometime during
the early winter of 1977 and were solidified in early spring 1978.
By that time, I had begun to interview people whose families have
had or now have reunions, and to pay attention to all mention I
heard of family events. I found that reunions are a frequent

topic of conversation, directly or indirectly, in these United
States. When the topic of family comes up, it is often attached
to a comment on, an anecdote from, or a complaint about the family
reunion. The reunions, by all indications, are certainly not
rare, and not recent occurrences.

Facing the possibility of taking on the entire United States
with all of its subtly differing cultures, I realized that I must
first have a close look at a reunion within which I could immerse
myself with its full background, including knowledge of the family
involved. Thus developed my use of the Swenson family reunion as
a case study. Further, I concentrated on families in the north
central states of the United States--an area which has received
little attention from folklorists.

FIELD PREPARATION

Research from 1976 to the spring of 1978 involved interviewing
a wide range of people whose families currently held or had in the
past held family reunions. During that time I also contacted
organizations such as Kiwanis International and followed media
coverage of the American family and family events.

In the spring of 1978, I devised a questionnaire for the
Swenson family which was coded for generations and blood relations. These were mailed, with self-addressed, stamped return
envelopes, to each member of the family. The questionnaires were
intended as a means to obtain vital data and attributes of the

family, not as a substitute for personal contact. The questionnaires also served as a means for me to introduce the project to
the entire kin network for their comments and/or objections.
There were no objections.

After my preliminary inquiries in September of 1976, I had
been officially designated historian of the reunion; this designation seemed to carry implications which allowed me to gather
such information. Many of the Swensons, in fact, were intensely
interested in what I was doing. Separate questionnaires were
prepared and answered for blood relations, affines, and children
at home. Affines were also asked about reunions in their own
blood relationships. Results of this questionnaire are discussed
in Chapter 5, concerning the Swenson family itself.

Previous to the Swenson reunion, more than 80 percent of the
persons eligible to attend the reunion had returned their questionnaires. The remaining 20 percent dribbled in during and, with
some coaxing, for several months following the event--some as
results of Christmas card correspondence.

FIELD METHODS

I spent the spring of 1978 in Minnesota where the Swenson
family was originally rooted (immediately after immigration).
During that time I continued to interview families who have
reunions and prepared background information for the event I was
to document. In May 1978 I moved to Hettinger, North Dakota, the

site of the Swenson family homestead. I resided in Hettinger previous to and following the reunion. My time there was spent as a participant-observer in the community and with the various Swensons yet located in the vicinity. I conducted family and personal history interviews, developing an understanding of the historical development of the county and the Swenson family. The summer months were also spent interviewing members of families in the county who also had reunions and observing family reunions which took place in Hettinger.

Over the course of discussions with Swenson family members leading up to the reunion, some of my cousins and a sister had expressed enough interest in my research that I requested aid from them in documenting the event. This request was an attempt to remedy a logistical problem I had been considering for some time: as planned, the three-day reunion would take place over a relatively large area and include any number of simultaneously occurring activities. I could not be in on all conversations and activities. In an effort to aid volunteers for this supplementary information program, I designed a set of guidelines intended as a type of fieldworker's guide to help the users determine what type of behavior should be noted. I also supplied notebooks.

A similar attempt at guidelines was prepared for camera carriers. At some point during the planning stages, I had requested that a first cousin of mine on my non-Swenson side be allowed to attend and supply free photographic services. Since this idea was discouraged (see page 30), I prepared to enlist the aid of

numerous cousins and in-laws who I knew would be well armed with
photographic equipment. I requested that they keep an index and
take double shots with 35mm color slide film which I would supply
and develop.

The results of these two endeavors proved to be unfruitful on
the surface, but in fact constitute invaluable information concerning family interaction. Initial reactions to one or two
people sitting around with notebooks was one of amusement. "We
don't have to talk to each other, we can just write notes," one
volunteer commented. Another noted the intrusive effect of the
guidelines--they caused her to be more aware of whom she spent
time with, she wrote after the reunion.

By and large, however, the notebooks were forgotten as the
reunion swung into gear and everyone swung into full participation. With the exception of two second-generation affines,
photographers were more interested in getting their own slides as
soon as possible after the reunion than they were in free film and
developing. Due to interaction with Swensons in North Dakota,
Minnesota, and Kansas after the reunion, however, I was able to
see the majority of photographs taken during the weekend.

I myself arrived at the reunion site two days early in order
to orient myself to the layout and meet my parents. I armed
myself throughout the weekend with tape-recorder, notebook, and
cameras. Relying upon the other photographers for color slides, I
took black and white 35mm prints. The tape-recorder was used
infrequently, primarily due to an overloaded sound environment. I

took notes throughout each day and kept journal entries each
night. My notebook became a point of humor, particularly for my
godfather (father's sister's husband), who would caution: "Be
careful, she's writing everything down," or would turn to me and
ask, "Did you get all of that?" Other family members took either
no or little notice of what I was doing. No one at any time
objected to notebook, tape-recorder, or camera.

Following the reunion I continued to reside in Hettinger,
North Dakota, observing family reaction to the reunion and interviewing more Adams County families. Interviews, family participant-observation, and attention to media coverage continued
through 1979. Due to the paucity of scholarly research concerning
family reunions, comparative material has been gleaned from interviews, media coverage, and magazine and newspaper articles.

CHAPTER 1

INTRODUCTION

STATEMENT OF PURPOSE

The purpose of this investigation is to explore the American
family as a viable group of identity and transmission, and to
explore the American family reunion as a manifestation of family
identity in a mobile society. This exploration will be undertaken
through a close look at the organized, planned family reunion,
beginning with a general overview, then specifically focusing upon
family reunions in one area of the United States and the reunion
of one family.

When Carl Wilhelm von Sydow set forth his theory of bearers
of tradition, he noted that tradition was "bound up with certain
social circles,"[1] and that "inheritance from the home" was the
simplest way to become an active bearer.[2] Von Sydow early on
called attention to the importance of the family "circle" as the
primary group of transmission of traditions. This importance has
been recognized by folklorists, anthropologists, psychologists,
and sociologists.[3] Barre Toelken, for instance, tells us that we
are taught to see by family, as the earliest group--a group which

1

extends across groups since religious and ethnic identities are all shared within the family.[4] Indeed, the importance of shared identity for folklore transmission has been discussed or assumed throughout the history of the discipline, especially in the realm of ethnic identity studies.[5] Yet, in Alan Dundes' index to folk-lore theses, there is to be found no category for "family," and until recent times, few scholars other than sociologists have looked at the American family as a structured group of identity and transmission.[6]

A reluctance to deal with the family is understandable. It is an emotional concern wrought with subjective involvement in one's own culture, and "family" is nearly impossible to fully comprehend or "belong to" in another. Family study has been approached in a round-about way. Within personality studies, done particularly in Eastern Europe, the family has been considered an effective force upon particular bearers.[7] These bearers, however, can also be located in a small-group community involving a wide variety of shared identities and social relations.

For families in America, space and mobility do not often allow a small group, community approach to investigation. In most instances of "family folklore" study, however, folklorists in America have collected from and interacted with families who also were social communities interacting on a daily basis. Folklorists have approached these families as small groups from which to collect a corpus of narratives or songs. Laurel Doucette's study of her Canadian family pinpoints the importance of the daily

interaction of family members to the transmission of narratives.[8]

In the case of her family, the two sibling members who live at a

great distance from the others are not active bearers--they do not

actively interact with their sisters and brothers in tale-telling

situations and have not retained the narratives.

Karen Baldwin's study of the Solley family also demonstrates

this aspect of narrative sharing.[9] This family is also a

geographically located community, as is the Copper family of

Sussex,[10] the Ritchie family of the Kentucky Cumberlands,[11] or the

Hammons family recorded by Carl Fleischhauer and Alan Jabbour.[12]

And yet, a large portion of American families do not live

anywhere near one another; the nuclear residential units may be

scattered from sea to shining sea and beyond. Except upon

specific occasions such as Christmas or for funerals, members of

American families seemingly have little to do with one another.

For this reason, I have focused on the organized, planned family

reunion--the one event which serves for American families as a

gathering point. Family reunions emerge on the American landscape

as the most visible demonstration of the family as a viable group

of identity. They stand out as events with which most of us are

familiar, whether or not we attend one. The acceptance of

reunions as a normal, regular aspect of our lives was revealed in

a comment made to me when I began this study.

One summer morning, I volunteered to help some friends load
their moving van. A neighbor of theirs was also helping. He
overheard a discussion I was having with a colleague about my
research. "You're doing your dissertation on your family reunion?"
he asked incredulously. "I changed my oil yesterday, too," he
continued, implying that a family reunion was as trivial (or as
impactful) an event. Need I note that without clean oil an engine
will destroy itself?

There is a curious paucity of information concerning this "oil
change" for American families. In 1966, Millicent Ayoub noted
that the family reunion, an event "so common to the American
Midwest," had not been studied or even noticed by anthropologists,
sociologists, psychologists, and historians. She undertook a
study to partially remedy that situation, but to date stands out
as the lone champion of family reunion research in academic
circles.[13] Ayoub did a ground-breaking typology intended to aid
studies concerning the American principle of descent (following
Firth, and Schneider and Homans). Based on fieldwork in Ohio, she
defined reunions as "an annual assemblage of approximately 50
persons, more or less, who gather one day each year on the basis
of sharing a cognitive image of descent..."[14] Ayoub described
very regular, structured reunions of relatively long duration.
From this description, she developed a typology of assemblies
which could be designated as family reunions.

Ayoub's description and typology, along with her discussion
comprise the scholarly consideration given family reunions per se
in America. Other investigators of the family have mentioned
family reunions as significant events in a family's identity.
Looking at reunions which circulate around a church gathering,
Karen Baldwin described the gathering of her family as "... the
single social occasion for the individual member's expression of
his or her large group identity."[15] Gwen K. Neville also gave
some brief consideration to family reunions in her study,
"Kinfolks and Covenants: Ethnic Community among Southern
Presbyterians,"[16] and studies such as Steven Stern's with
Sephardic Jews in Los Angeles also view family gatherings as
significant events in preserving identity.[17]

Our understanding of the American family today, however, is
not a legacy left by von Sydow or other folkloric studies, but one
left by social scientists studying what they saw as deviant family
structure. The impact they have made on our understanding of and
beliefs about the American family has not been limited to the
academic world. Through various media of transmission, the social
scientists' view of the American family has become one shared by
almost any American. We hear that the American family is falling
apart. We pass the word along. For the reasons behind this
belief, we must turn to the social sciences.

FAMILY SCHOLARSHIP IN THE UNITED STATES

Although folklorists and anthropologists have not tradition-
ally spent time studying the American family, sociologists and
psychologists have focused upon the family in its nuclear residential form (husband, wife, children) since particularly the Second
World War, although the family was studied well before that
time.[18] During World War II, patriotism and keeping the family
unit together were considered to be inseparable ideas. A "strong
America," was linked to family life even among scholars.

In 1942, Margaret Mead described the American character as one
which was always moving on, grasping at threads of shared experience (growing up in the same town, going to the same college,
vacationing at the same resort) as a means of establishing
intimate social relationships.[19] The family, she said, had to be
understood with this background. "To the family," she claimed,
"we must turn for an understanding of American character structure
... to understand the regularity of ... behavior we must investigate the family within which the child is reared."[20] Parents,
siblings, near relatives, and "nurses" are the mediators of
"American culture," according to Mead. So who are these people?
They are people on the move, Mead says to back up her character
sketch, geographically, economically, socially, occupationally on
the move--and they expect their children to be equally mobile,

unplanted as it were, prepared to adapt, to move, of course, upward.[21]

The lesson a child learns in this structure is to be individual, to outdistance his parents. He learns that "only his father and mother are really relevant to his life, ... that parents ... and a sibling of opposite sex ... are essential to make up a 'family.'"[22] Mead continues to contrast this "narrow platform"[23] with the "old societies" of extended family or clan where the child moves among many relatives, "with some one of whom he can almost certainly find a community of interest and even a common physique."[24] The American child is thus pictured as drifting with very tenuous anchors, threatened by such horrors as adoption and being orphaned. The family is seen as parallel to the nation. The child must outdistance its parents as the nation must progress. The family provides the necessary guidance into those waters of a mobile, progressing society, but it is an extremely limited "family."

Such a view of the American family has been carried throughout sociological inquiry. Talcott Parsons investigated the structure of the progressing American family in 1943. Fitting in with Mead's discussion of individuality and mobility, he described the "structural prominence of the conjugal family [in America] and its peculiar isolation," claiming that in "our" system, as contrasted to other kinship systems, persons did not have a stable status in

one or more kinship systems, focusing on the special importance of
the conjugal (nuclear) family.[25] In 1960, Parsons re-affirmed his
view that due to the "loss of function" of kinship units in
America (from mobility and individualism), there had been "a
further step in the reduction of the importance of our society of
kinship units other than the nuclear family."[26]

The primary importance of the nuclear family in American life
was reiterated by Lloyd Warner in the Family of God (1959). The
nuclear family's autonomy is "a central social experience that all
Americans share."[27] He claims that "The nuclear family, now
itself increasingly autonomous, trains the young and, more and
more, controls the deeper non-logical moral and symbolic life of
the mature."[28] Warner sees continuity with the fundamental basic
unit imaged in "god the Father, the Mother, Their Son, and through
Him, all of us."[29]

Mead, Parsons, Warner, and some of their students considered
the family to be functioning, albeit in a different way from those
of the "old societies." The nuclear family answered the needs of
the mobile, progressing nation. Other scholars more clearly
echoed the trace of panic found in the media articles about
improving family life in order to meet the current crises. At the
end of World War II, Carle Zimmerman determined that the American
family would completely break down. Based on studies done with
college students, and giving consideration to campus "anarchy"
among students, Zimmerman presented a theory of eventual

confrontation between tradition and anarchy.[30] Other sociologists
saw family disorganization and splintering in their crystal
ball.[31]

By the early 1970s, Vance Packard had extended the idea of the
breakdown of the family into an investigation of the resultant
American "rootlessness." The constant movement, recognized by
Mead and others, according to Packard had resulted in a nation of
"psychological nomads," due to the frequent migration and partially due to fragmentation of the family.[32] Packard did extensive
statistical research with such sources as telephone disconnect
rates and a comparison of two towns of 30,000 population: one in
New York State and one in California (leaving out the vast space
and population of most of the nation). Packard's message is one
of the urgent need to evolve ways "to slow down the accelerating
social fragmentation." It is an ominous message, one to be taken
seriously.

Other social scientists have pinpointed the industrial
revolution as the cause for family breakdown, particularly as it
effected the mass movement to cities and away from agrarian communities. In 1973, Ralph Keyes addressed this "loss of community
tied to proximity" in his work, We, the Lonely People.[33] We were
people on the move even as children, Keyes states, as he explores
the transient "communities" we create for ourselves: in an
audience, in shopping centers, in self-help groups like Weight
Watchers. Human contact has declined and continues to do so, he
claims.[34]

All these "doom" theories assume an American past when
extended families lived together and worked in cooperation. A past
which several sociologists and historians have recently questioned
as valid due to new research concerning such aspects of family
cycles as longevity, child labor laws, child apprenticeships,
childbirth deaths, and the like. This romanticized past family
unit seems to have rarely existed, at least in the northeastern
United States.[35] Because of this posited and contrasted past, the
studies also share a concentration on the family as a nuclear
unit. Mead's tenuous "narrow platform"; Parsons' "fewer and more
specific functions" of the reduced, nuclear family; and Packard's
"psychological nomads," are all given negative values by the
analysts. Fragmentation into "nuclear," "isolated" families is to
be regretted, if not abhorred. We are a "nation of strangers,"
Packard cries.

Studies of deviant behavior such as child abuse, wife
beating, and abandonment of the elderly are currently used to
support the idea that the American family is, indeed, breaking
down--a seemingly long process, not one of "confrontation" as
Zimmerman projected.

Further, the historical development of the American family,
beginning with the nuclear settlement of isolated areas after
splintering with the Old World family, has often been cited as a
negative impact, causing the emergence of "a conjugal family
system without much family tradition and without economic or

sentimental ties to a wide array of kin."[36] Variations on this
pattern, it has been claimed, were provided by large-scale
immigration at the turn of the century, as well as by the old evil
factor: urbanization and industrialization.[37] Despite these
variations, however, the basic pattern of the family was seen by
sociologists as nuclear and isolated. When they refer to the
American family, they refer to the unit of husband, wife, and
children. The family finds its origin in marriage, Levi-Strauss
has emphasized.[38]

Current studies done by some American social scientists and
humanists take a new look at the American family, veering away
from the doomsday approach. Researchers have begun to reassess
the statistics and field data. These current studies, however,
important as they may be, have not yet had an effect on general
beliefs. Efforts in the mass media--constant, daily noise in our
communication network--warn of the imminent demise of the American
family, and with it, of the nation itself.

MEDIA EFFORTS

Over the years, the foci alter in popular literature, but the
family as a major topic and concern does not. Previous to 1900[39]
and throughout this century, articles concerning family genealogy,
for instance, have abounded, primarily of the "how to" type. The

concern with American families and their gatherings is best
reflected in this mass media coverage.

Articles found in the Readers Guide to Periodic Literature
parallel the development of concern in academic work. Under a
section for "Family," articles concerning the woman's role and the
small size of the family appeared at the turn of the century--as
if adjustment to a small family was new and of concern. Family
and community interaction articles appear in the 1920s, and in the
30s we see a rash of articles about family life education.

As with scholarly prose, family life was linked to patriotism
in the media during World War II. Magazines such as The American
Family emphasized "home living" as "assurance for today's crisis,"
and featured stories with titles like: "As the Family Goes, So
Goes the Nation!"[40] The basic premise of this magazine
encapsulated what is yet today a continuing vision of the family
in America:

> The American family, heart of the American home, core of
> the American system, must be maintained at all costs. It
> must have the kind of guidance--moral, social, spiritual,
> educational and economic--that will see it emerge from the
> war a greater force for Americanism than ever.[41]

Also by the 1940s, the concern reflected in the periodic
literature is for holding the family together and dealing with
psychological problems of individual family members. "We have No
Roots!" one article complained in the 40s.[42] Apparently
responding to a public desire for advice, articles in the 1930s
and 1940s focus on social psychology, on "how to cope." From the

30s, then, throughout the 1970s, the articles heavily favor marriage counseling. The marriage bond becomes, for the "specialists," the center of attention. The nuclear family is it in America.

Current coverage ranges from political rhetoric and evangelism to television documentaries and commercial interests. Though several academic investigators have, as indicated, turned from an exclusive focus on the nuclear unit and begun to reconsider the message of doom for the family unit, this message is still prevalent in the media and, in many cases, has become a type of campaign slogan. The result is that we in American life are con-stantly bombarded by the noise of family crisis and the death of the nation as an inevitable result following the family's demise.

Service agencies such as Kiwanis International have actively campaigned for promoting patriotism through family life to reaffirm "the family's role as the basis of a strong community and nation ...," and politicians use family issues (abortion, divorce statistics, child care, care for the elderly) as campaign platforms. "Can America Survive?" read the advertisement for a three-night television evangelism crusade recently broadcast by James Robison. In such campaigns, "crises" somehow all become attached to the breakdown of the family:

> Face it--we're out of gas, strangled with inflation and teetering on the brink of recession. Nearly 10 million of us are drowning in alcoholism. God alone knows how many of our grade-schoolers are on drugs. <u>And social scientists say the American family may be a thing of the past in 20 years</u>! Can America survive?[43]

The same message comes from more established religion.
"Bishops study family crisis" bannered a recent article. The
article reports on preparations United States Catholic bishops
were making for an international Synod of Bishops. The U.S.
bishops were investigating the Vatican document which took a stand
against birth control on grounds that the family is in an
"identity crisis" in contemporary society. "A decline in the
strength of the extended family," is also cited in this document
as a present trend having an impact on the family (thus, Church)
crisis. The Vatican document warned that "families will become
the first victims of the evils that they will have watched idly
and with indifference."[44]

Presumably following trends of interest and concern, Edwin
Neuman hosted an NBC three-hour documentary in January of 1978
titled: "The American Family; an endangered species?" Three
hours. We are still looking for Carle Zimmerman's confrontation.
The special posed these questions: Is the American family truly
endangered?--or is it changing and surviving? Is it still the
keystone of American life? (No one asked whether or not it ever
was the keystone of American life. No one asked what was meant by
"American family.") Institutions--church, government, family,
political system--have weakened, Neuman commented as an opener to
the investigation. (No one asked how they had weakened.) The
journalists investigated various types of "families"--units of
residence--presenting statistics such as the divorce rate (an

appalling 38 percent of marriages now end in divorce) and the rate
of women working outside the home (supposedly an indication of
breakdown within the family unit).

Throughout the documentary, the term "family" always indicated
a sort of nuclear grouping. Residential units such as the
"single-parent family" or the "communal family" were modified as
types of "family." During the three hours, sketches of "family"
varieties, that is, varieties of residential units, were
presented. A panel of family specialists commented on each
category of "family" unit. They came to no conclusion. America
was left with the question: "Is the family an endangered
species?"

RECENT ACADEMIC WORK

Despite the cry and hue of press, politicians, and religious
leaders, some anthropologists and sociologists have recently begun
to investigate the American family as culturally operative and
involved with broader relationships than simply those of husband-
wife-children. The structural observations made by scholars such
as Mead, Parsons, and Lévi-Strauss have been questioned: the
nuclear family may not be the exclusive structurally functioning
unit for American kinship. In addition, the view of family as a
coherent unit only when also a neighborhood unit, that is, one of

high social interaction, espoused by Zimmerman, Packard, Warner, and others, is also being questioned.[45]

David Schneider's work with American kinship patterns forges a channel into the study of the American family as a distinctive social unit, not necessarily a degeneration from the unit of the Old Country or the romanticized past. Schneider's investigations of American kinship belie the idea that a lack of kinship terminology ("uncle" or "cousin" are imprecise terms, indicating a broad range of kin) implies a lack of kinship relationship and contact. He has found that, unlike other societies, kinship in modern, Western societies is highly differentiated from other kinds of social institutions and relationships.[46] Neuman's editorial view that all institutions have weakened may be a bit too sweeping in light of Schneider's studies. Schneider makes a case for the American "kinship system" (not just the conjugal unit) as the context in which socialization takes place. This is not a new view, but Schneider points out that as such, the kinship system must form the "essence of the dominant values of the whole culture."[47] This thought is terrifying if the social scientists are right and, as James Robison pointed out from his pulpit, the American family will no longer exist in twenty years. Can America Survive, indeed. If the American family is dying, what exactly is dying? The nuclear residential unit? Ties of affection? Social interaction? The span of the nuclear family as a residential unit is, in fact, fleeting, possibly one-third to one-half of any life

span. And, it must be kept in mind, the nuclear family in which
one spends childhood is likely only one of two or three nuclear
families to which membership is ascribed. With marriage, one
enters a nuclear family of affiliation, and upon parenthood, one
gains membership in a new unit, with an entirely differing role.
Studies focusing on the "nuclear family" have failed to take the
dynamics of membership into consideration, as if the role of child
and sibling is completely superseded by that of parent.

Initial studies concerning a broader kin network, such as that
done by Sheila Klatsky concerning the frequency with which married
males contact male relatives, give vague definitions of relationships. "There are no widely shared norms to prescribe the frequency of contact with any categories of kin," she concludes.[48]
But contact does frequently occur. What norms are we looking for?

Are we barking up the wrong tree with an overemphasis on
"marriage and the family"--the standard introduction to sociology
of the family offered in our universities? The focus on nuclear
relationships is assumed by public figures and the media, and this
belief is transmitted to the American public and by the American
public. High divorce rates, working mothers, free choice abortion, "hippie" communes, child abuse, and wife beating are given
for reasons that the American family is in distress. These are
affairs of a nuclear unit. If the family is in distress, the government is in distress, and the logic works both ways: surely if
the government allows free choice abortion, the family is falling
apart.

Boll and Bossard's study of family ritual as early as 1950 had
challenged the exclusivity of the nuclear family as a focus of
study. They found that, though the "American biological family
unit has often been related, by scholars, to lack of long-range
family responsibility," thirty-five of the eighty-six students
they studied described rituals whose definite purpose was to
secure the ties between generations.[49]

And recently Bernard Farber has told us that "Apparently the
stability of the kinship identity is more important in Western
American kinship than the unity of the nuclear family."[50] Faber
based his study on the comparison of state statutes on incestuous
marriage, a concern extending beyond the nuclear family. He was
able to distinguish two kinship systems: the Western American
System with stable bilateral affiliations before and after
marriage (such as sibling bonds)[51] and the Biblical Kinship
System[52] with "cumulative bilateral affiliation ... with
virilateral descent." In the Biblical System, covering roughly
the area of the United States east of the Mississippi River, an
individual gains membership in his spouse's father's network after
marriage, as well as retaining membership in his mother's and
father's networks (in this system, marriage with a spouse's
sibling would be incestuous). Though the systems vary somewhat,
they both indicate bonds previous to, adjacent to, and continuing
from any one nuclear unit.

In another recent study, following along with the assumptions
of family demise we are constantly reminded of, Mary Jo Bane
expected to discover that the American family was, in fact, an
"endangered species." She was jumping off from statistics such as
those offered by the NBC special. Bane found, quite to the contrary, that as she "delved further into the data that describe
what Americans do and how they live, I became less sure that the
family was in trouble. Surprising stabilities showed up, and
surprising evidence of the persistence of commitments to family
life."[53]

We are concerned here with such commitments. Bane and others
have just begun to point out that the loss of the extended family
in American life is, in fact, a "myth," that the coresidential
extended family situation rarely existed in some areas of
America.[54] Like Schneider, Boll and Bossard, and Farber, Bane
also found complex relationships existing among a broad range of
relatives. Yet Americans still by and large accept the idea that
the family is falling apart--how many of us, I wonder, consider
our family as the exception to this trend? How many Americans
travel hundreds of miles to participate in family gatherings, to
see a cousin married or share Christmas with adult brothers and
sisters and their offspring--or travel for no other reason than to
see them? How many exceptions are there to that rule?

Discussions during the planning of my own family's reunion led
more and more to such questions. Was the Swenson family one of

those few exceptions in a dismal world? I knew that not to be
true. More and more people I spoke with told me about people from
all walks of life who would regularly or occasionally spend their
vacation times and a good deal of money to go someplace for
nothing other than the purpose of seeing members of their own kin
group. The question grew in scope. Are the reunion families
making a last-ditch effort to regain lost contact, lost values?
Is it some new urge spurred on by Roots or the Bicentennial? We
really know very little about the American kinship networks.
Schneider's ground-breaking studies of terminology have told us
something about structure in American kinship. With family
reunions we turn to behavior, to feelings of identity that
directly affect the transmission of values and traditions.

CHAPTER 2

DEFINITION OF TERMS

Before discussing family reunions, it is necessary to clarify

terminology. As David Schneider has pointed out, the term "fam-

ily," to begin with, is one of imprecise meaning in the English

language, as are other kinship terms such as "cousin" or "uncle."[1]

As we have seen, sociologists and even some anthropologists have

usually used the term "family" to refer to a residential unit of

husband, wife, and children in American studies. This unit has

more precisely been designated as nuclear, immediate, or,

following Firth, elementary.[2]

Folklorists who have begun studies with family folklore in

America, including the Smithsonian Institution's Family Folklore

Program,[3] have been less narrow in their focus. "Family" for them

may range in depth and laterally across several generations and

residential units. A comparison of studies concerning the

American family is, in fact, nearly impossible due to the lack of

agreement and even lack of discussion concerning the definition of

family. Scholars assume that we all know what we are talking

about.

The same problem arises with the terms "nuclear" or "elemen-

tary." Is one's nuclear family that in which he resided as a

child or that for which he is responsible as a parent? Sociologists refined this terminology by designating those two varieties
as the "family of orientation" (status as a child) and that of
"procreation" (status as a parent).[4] I will use "family" in its
broader sense, designating family of procreation and family of
orientation when necessary.

Obviously, in looking at family reunions, my particular definition of the term has had to be adjusted to meet those of the
various family members with whom I've conversed. When I asked
questions concerning family, or when my informants spoke of the
family, we were dependent upon the context of the conversation for
the definition of the term. When asking one woman how her family
was doing, she immediately responded with news of her children.
Later in the conversation, while we were discussing the possible
distance people would have to come for the family reunion, I asked
if her family had all grown up around the same area, and she
answered with the histories of her brothers and sisters. After
speaking about a reunion on her husband's side of the family, I
asked if her family had any reunions--her response was "on my
mother's side of the family," using the term in its extended
form.[5] These responses are typical. To a question, has your
family spread out much? the answers would vary from immediate
children to immediate siblings. There seems, in fact, to be a
distinction here between "your" family and "the" family, "your"
designating the more immediate family--either sibling oriented or
children oriented.

When used as a designation for the organized family reunion,
however, all cases I encountered involved an extended family of
some sort. Those included in the reunion ranged from anyone with
the particular name to a closely defined group of three generations: parents (siblings and spouses), first cousins, and any
offspring. The "family," then, was defined as whomever was
included in the reunion. "Your" family, in conversations at the
reunions as well as with me, referred to ego and offspring (family
of procreation), or, especially if there were no offspring, siblings and parents, that is, the family of orientation.

A larger problem remains, however. The organized, planned
family reunions being investigated involve several families of
orientation and procreation, all linked with a blood bond. Family
reunions could not apply to a residential unit which has no need
to reunite, since it is yet a composite unit. To reunite, members
of a residential unit of necessity must have been separated. With
family reunions, as with most family folklore, we are considering
what anthropologists have called the "extended family," that is,
blood and affine relatives beyond the elementary family. The term
"extended family" however, is not applicable in many cases of
American family study. The anthropological extended family,
studied, for instance, in areas of Africa and Asia, is more than
an extended relationship; it is usually coresidential and an
economic unit as well. Based on studies conducted in various cultures, anthropologists over the years have refined a system of

kinship terminology used to deal with imprecise references. This
terminology does not apply to American kinship, and only in the
past ten to fifteen years have they turned their attention to the
American kinship structure, proposing new terminology.

As mentioned earlier, David Schneider has diverged from the
usual anthropological definitions and developed terminology for
the study of American kinship. He presented the terms "kinship
system" and "kinship network" as more precise definitions of the
relationships among American relatives, who often live hundreds of
miles from one another. Schneider points out that kinship in
modern Western societies is highly differentiated from other
social institutions and relationships.[6] The family no longer
occupies one village or attends one specific church. Neither do
American kin all vote in one state or for one party. We will
follow Schneider's terminology, using kinship network, a term
which implies communication and interaction, though not necessarily continuous or contiguous contact among relatives.

"Relatives" and "kin" will refer to both consanguine (by
marriage) and cognatic (of the same descent) kin. "Cousin," only
slightly less imprecise than "family," will be used to designate
only offspring of siblings, that is, first cousins by blood.
Other relationships will be designated by means of the more
precise kinship terminology available in English (i.e., father's
sister's daughter's husband, or cousin's husband).

THE ORGANIZED, PLANNED FAMILY REUNION

In this study, the family reunion is approached as what Gwen
Neville, in her study of Southern Presbyterians, has termed "a
significant gathered ceremonial." Such an event is considered as
a locus "within which cultural traditions and classic community-
cultural forms will reappear."[7] In terms of family identity
rather than ethnic or religious identity, the reunion is viewed
here as an infrequent visible manifestation of "enduring diffuse
solidarity," David Schneider's description of the American kinship
structure.[8] This is a feeling of identity which is transmitted
through the family over time.

The study is of organized, planned reunions, distinguished as
a specific type of family gathering, a distinction not made by
Ayoub in her typology. Kin groups throughout the world certainly
gather for a wide variety of reasons, most notably for rites of
passage (funerals, weddings) and festive occasions (Christmas,
Thanksgiving). Though without a doubt these gatherings are of
importance to family continuity and identity, gatherings of kin at
such events are secondary to another purpose (i.e., to celebrate
or mourn).

The planned, organized family reunion is an event developed
and attended solely for the purpose of spending some brief amount
of time in companionship with members of one's (or one's spouse's)
cognatic kin. As Joan Barthel noted in a Ladies' Home Journal

article, "all you need for a family reunion is to want to get together. . . ."[9] Ayoub developed the following typology for the reunions she investigated in Ohio during the 1960s:

(1) Sibling Reunion Type, characterized by a clustering of adults who shared residence during childhood, including consanguines and offspring

(2) Name Reunion Type, during which an indistinct group of people who happen to share the same name gather

(3) Cognate Reunion Type, intermediate between the first two involving a limited number of people.[10]

The reunions investigated here differ from Ayoub's typology in that they center around families from a different historical and cultural area of the United States, the north central area. Insofar as the reunions here are assemblages of persons who gather to share a cognitive image of descent, they do fit the pattern she has developed. In that the families concerned have not grown to the generational depth and length of duration, are farther scattered geographically, and their reunions do not share the typical features Ayoub describes (events of one-day, annual, out-of-doors, in summer) they do not fit the pattern she found in Ohio.

THE EYE OF THE BEHOLDER

   While I was writing this work, an acquaintance who had just
learned I was writing about family reunions asked me, "Are you pro
or con?"

   "Pro or con what?" I queried.

   "Family reunions," he persisted. "Are you for or against
them?"

   I'm not sure whether or not he was serious, but after pausing
for a minute, I seriously answered him, "I'm wholeheartedly for
them. Why else would I study them?"

   Why indeed. One of the well-known anecdotes passed about by
students of folklore and anthropology tells us that Bronislaw
Malinowski and others of the prominent early fieldworkers didn't
like the people with whom they worked. It is something we don't
quite understand. Certainly we assume that sociologists who study
child abuse, deviance, and crime don't approve of their subject
matter. We all have feelings about what is good and right about
family and what is degenerative. "Are you pro or con," a question
I at first assumed to be obvious and unnecessary is, in fact, a
question any researcher needs to ask and answer.

   I was and am all for families and for families getting
together for joyous occasions. The Swenson family reunion, the
planning for which presented me with an opportunity to study
reunions, was an event to which I looked forward and at which I

enjoyed myself. I wanted to see my family as much as I wanted to
study them. The accessibility of having everyone in one spot was
exciting both for research and for my own personal interaction and
feeling of identity.

Folklorists have often recognized the need to explain their
roles within the framework of their ethnographic research--both
affective and effecting influences.[11] For some reason, we feel
it even more obligatory to explain our subjective roles when dealing with our own intimate communicative groups. We have written
about the fieldworker as intrusive,[12] but rarely consider the
fieldworker as an insider. Participant-observation is a middle
ground on which we all stake a claim. When a fieldworker learns
as much as he can about the historical, social, political, economic, and cultural background of a group he is studying, he is
coming as close as he can to a sharing of common understandings
which will enable him to both understand what is going on around
him and to know what questions to ask, what "obvious" things need
interpretation. Fieldworkers working with their own groups of
orientation come armed with this knowledge of inner workings and
assumptions. What they must learn is to back away, to sort out
those assumptions in order to know what questions to ask and what
"obvious" things need interpretation. The processes are of a
different order--gaining and shedding assumptions--but they strive
towards the same middle ground, that paradoxical role of participant and observer.

Self-collecting is the point we ask our students to begin with when we teach introductory folklore classes, and self-collecting, whether we recognize it or not, is the point any fieldworker begins with in any research situation. We come with ideas and questions. We use them as part of the research. Karen Baldwin, when dealing with her family narratives in a recent dissertation, came to a point where "Personal cultural investigation subsumed and became a frame for extrapolated analysis about family folklore in general."[13]

I, too, began at a point of "personal cultural investigation," self-collecting. My position as a family member demanded this as part of my study. Only by looking at my own assumptions could I understand the assumptions of my informant, both Swensons and non-Swensons. This study is a look at reunions "Through Swenson Eyes." It is, perhaps, a study that could _only_ be done by a participant turned observer.

Family reunions offer a special problem to the fieldworker: they are closed events. Family gatherings at weddings, funerals, birthdays, and holidays include social friends beyond the blood kinship. Organized reunions which I investigated do not. One can only "observe" other family reunions on a surface level after becoming familiar with members of the family reuniting. In the case of the other Adams County reunions, I was "in" because I was of Adams County stock. Most of the people with whom I spoke knew someone in my own kinship; I could be located in the community,

and therefore was not a complete outsider. In addition, I was
also a reunion attender. Other reunionites were interested in
finding out what we did at ours in order to get new ideas for
their next one. In the case of the Swenson reunion, no one
outside of a specifically defined lineage was allowed to attend,
not even a cousin from the family of one of the affines, a professional photographer who volunteered to come with me and serve
as photographer for the event. I had to be a native informant.
Raymond Firth, in his seminal study of kinship patterns in London,
also noted the need for a native informant in such cases:
"Although in many cases we cannot observe the actual behavior of
our informants with their kin, we can nevertheless assess their
reports of their behavior in terms of our own experience and
knowledge of their cultural background. In a completely strange
society this is not possible."[14] Neither is it in a completely
strange family.

CHAPTER 3

FAMILY REUNIONS IN AMERICA

During the spring of 1979, "Roots, the Next Generation," was aired on national television. This sequel to the outstandingly successful "Roots" was equally well received according to the ratings. At the end of the series, Alex Haley, author of the "search-for-my-family" stories, had a small chat with the American public, during which he made an appeal for people to have family reunions.[1]

In June of 1978, the radio was airing a new McDonald's advertising ditty--the type you find yourself humming in the shower. "Whatever roots we have, they're growing side by side." The golden arch hamburger chain was launching a new advertising campaign, "McDonald's Salutes America's Families." Names drawn from entries at local McDonald's restaurants would receive "A Family Reunion Meal."

Also in 1978, Kraft Foods began an extensive advertising campaign with this jingle: "Kraft is having a family reunion. What we've been doing for all these years--bringing good food and families together." They were calling themselves "the family reunion people," and offering "family reunion recipes" for a label from Kraft products.

During the fall of 1979, on a segment of M.A.S.H., the popular
television series about a comical medical unit in the Korean War,
the regulars on the series decided to organize a "family reunion"
for their families back home. A segment in the fall of 1977 had
featured Radar showing movies of his family reunion in Iowa.

The June 1970 Better Homes and Gardens carried this feature
line: "Family Reunion: Help stamp out the generation gap." The
article told you how to "strive to get everybody into the act"
with step-by-step instructions, including a reminder to warn the
children about any relatives who might have infirmities so the
children won't embarrass them.[2] In the November 1977 issue,
Better Homes and Gardens again ran an article about reunions, "How
to Plan an Old-Fashioned Family Reunion," emphasizing the importance of planning ahead.[3]

The cover story of the Ladies Home Journal in August 1978 was:
"How America Lives: Family Reunions, 16 joyous pages of fun,
food, love, plus a Family Favorite Cookbook." This was ". . . a
journal report in words and pictures on the healthy state of
family togetherness. Whether your family is large or small, urban
or rural, from near or far, here is how you can share a special
time to reminisce and rejoice in that heritage closest to us
all."[4] These are just a sample of articles about family reunions
or how to do family reunions which have appeared now and then over
the years in family magazines.

Why? Magazines such as these listed, and others including
Colliers and Look, appeal to a broad segment of the population.
They are prominent on the newsstand. M.A.S.H. is a long-running,
popular comedy show, in fact a long-rerunning show as well.
McDonald's and Kraft Foods are major businesses which can nearly
be considered national institutions in America. And why didn't
Alex Haley appeal to people to do family genealogies, which was,
after all, the basic plot of "Roots": it was a genealogy fleshed
out. Is this some new urge? A stirring of patriotism similar to
the "family and country" urgings of World War II?

In 1968, Kiwanis International, in conjunction with the
Freedoms Foundation of Valley Forge (a patriotic organization
which has an awards program for efforts promoting patriotism),
developed a "Family Reunion Day" as part of its yearly program
suggestions for member clubs. The idea came from a Kiwanis member
involved with the Freedoms Foundation and was then expanded by the
two organizations. This is the only Kiwanis project which does
not involve clubs as such, but rather, encourages members to have
individual reunions. What Kiwanis does is to supply press
releases and suggestions for promoting the event, suggest activities, recipes, and other "how-tos" to club members. Their
supplies include copy for radio and television spots, as well as
press releases, photographs, and artwork.[5]

The organizations decided on the second Sunday in August as
the time to launch their campaign. This date is based on what the

Director of Public Relations for Kiwanis International termed "dog days"--those days when not much is going on. The media is willing to air information like this during those weeks, people aren't wrapped up with school or other activities, and motel and transportation accomodations are open. They took their campaign to all areas of public life, from the Congress to the churches to the hardware stores.

Through the efforts of the two organizations, legislation was passed in Congress during 1968 which led to a proclamation of August 11 as Family Reunion Day by then President Lyndon B. Johnson. The first informative and promotional flyer sent out to the various Kiwanis clubs included quotations from various members of Congress concerning the idea of family reunions, all similar to this one by John W. McCormack, Speaker of The House of Representatives:

> Family life is the very basis of society. Where we find a strong family life existing, there is a strong and stable government as well as society. On the other hand, where there is a weak family life, we find weak government and society. I congratulate Kiwanis International and Freedoms Foundation in their sponsorship of FAMILY REUNION DAY.[6]

Other commenters included: Gerald R. Ford, then the Minority Leader in the House of Representatives; J. Edgar Hoover, then the Director of the Federal Bureau of Investigation; George Meany, then President of the AFL-CIO; and Ramsey Clark, then Attorney General of the United States.

This same flyer introduced Family Reunion Day as

a time for old-fashioned get-togethers at home or around the
picnic table. It provides the opportunity for families to
become reacquainted, to relive shared experiences, to plan
together for the future. It is, in short, a simple yet
dramatic vehicle for reaffirming the basis of a strong
community and nation . . . the source of that high idealism
and morality without which the community of man cannot
exist. FAMILY REUNION DAY is an individual family matter
with no public or organizational program to backstop or to
highlight its observance.

The purpose of the program was to establish a "simple, easy-
to-do, human activity which could be a powerful weapon against
lawlessness, disorder, corruption and moral laxity." The flyer
also included a section on "What to do . . . ."

In addition to the Congressional effort, preparation of press
materials, and distribution of information to member clubs,
Kiwanis International suggested promotional campaigns to commercial interests. The food editor of the Chicago Sun-Times (the
wife of a Kiwanis member) developed recipe suggestions for them.
They encouraged Ace Hardware and Tru Value Hardware to put up ads
to "take home a grill for Family Reunion Day." They even
suggested promotional campaigns to the airlines and the telephone
company for traveling to see your family or calling them, though
they didn't have much success in those two areas. And there was a
real push to get famous people to help promote the day (Bob Hope,
Jimmy Durante, Jim Young, congressmen, and the like). In addition
to political and commercial interests, the national church
organizations cooperated by putting notices in their Sunday
bulletins.

During the years following 1968, various promotional kits
were sent out to the clubs suggesting programs and cooperative
emphasis. In 1971 the quarterly publication for the committees on
programs and music suggested that the clubs have a "minister or
sociologist speak on the importance of the family in the American-
Canadian way of life." In 1976 they changed the name of the program suggestion to "Family Day" to broaden the perspective. In
1977 they promoted Family Day in conjunction with a "Safeguard
Against Crime" program, encouraging that "Every device for
bringing the family together which has been recommended in the
past" be employed, additionally emphasizing joint church attendance, ethnic and national picnics, parades, and so on as
"Promoters of family solidarity." Attention was brought to the
popularity of the "recent" television series "Roots" as something
which should help spark interest in genealogical research by
families.

Patriotism, marketing, and human interest. Journalists know
that family reunions are a selling item. Companies like Ace
Hardware, Kraft Foods, and McDonald's know that they draw business. Politicians? They know, too.

While I was searching funding for my research during 1977, a
copy of my proposed project was forwarded to the Governor of North
Dakota. One of his assistants tracked me down and gave me a call.
She wished to let me know that the Governor was most interested in
my project and was wondering if there was anything he could do,

suggesting that he would be happy to send a letter of greeting to
the family. This he did, a letter composed by his assistant and
myself over the telephone.[7]

This interchange remains one of the more informative pieces of
my research. The idea of a constituency, of a group with (presumably) homogeneous political tendencies, was the attracting idea
for Governor Link's assistant, as it is for politicians throughout
the country.

A lengthy article concerning the Williams family reunion of
Florida explains that state politicians regularly show up at the
proceedings because "[the] awesome display of consanguinity lends
weight to the old Florida political axiom that any state-wide
election hinges on four decisive votes: Dade County (Miami),
Duval County (Jacksonville), Hillsborough County (Tampa)--and
the Williams family."[8] The article continues to tell us that
"Aspirants to state office ha're been known to drive 400 miles
in the face of a threatening hurricane just to hobnob with the
reunionites."[9]

At other reunions, politicians are guest speakers, or at least
guests. Reports about several reunions in the Ladies Home Journal
sported the picture of a young boy wearing a tee-shirt which pro-
claimed: "Vote for my dad."[10] In a CBS news report of 15 August
1978 a politician at a West Virginia family reunion commended the
family for maintaining a tradition and called them "the greatest
family in West Virginia, if not in the United States."

These current references to family reunions in American public
life point out the prevalence of such events today. Family
reunions, however, are not new or revived events in American life.
They are also not a thing of the past, something "old-fashioned."
Elveretta Meyer, who takes care of group arrangements at the State
Game Lodge in the Black Hills of South Dakota says that they have
been continuously housing several family reunions (as well as Army
buddy reunions and the like) for more than thirty years.[11] The
Solley reunion described by Lois Karen Baldwin in her work, "Down
on Bugger Run," though not strictly speaking an organized, planned
reunion, celebrated its twenty-fifth anniversary in 1976. Ayoub
presumes the origin of family reunions in the mid-1800s,[12] and
even some of the groups in Adams County, North Dakota, the location of this case study, go to reunions "back East" (Minnesota or
Wisconsin) which were taking place before the world wars. The
Williams 1951 reunion reported in Florida has been operating since
1903.[13] Others have not been continuous, like the Coffin family
reunion in Rhode Island, which is recorded as taking place
previous to 1881.[14]

There are journalistic accounts of reunions in the 1930s,[15]
1940s, and 1950s, reunions which are mentioned as regularized
events, not new events.[16] Even in more recently settled areas of
the United States, such as Kansas, newspapers report events such
as the "24th Annual Forsberg Reunion," or the "33rd Annual Keagle
Reunion,"[17] or the "45th Annual Bengtson-Nelson Reunion."[18] I

personally recorded interviews with persons who had been holding
reunions since the 1920s in Illinois;[19] in Kansas since the late
1800s;[20] and since the early 1900s in Minnesota.[21]

Reunions are also not events peculiar to isolated or rural
areas. During the course of my research, specific family reunions
have been documented in forty states and Canada through the media
or personal interviews. These reunions occur in all regions of
the United States, though fewer are evident in the yet young
northwest, and I have none recorded in Alaska or Hawaii (which by
no means means that they do not occur there). Reunions appear
frequently in the media during every decade since the mid-1800s,
except during the two world wars.

Family reunions are pervasive in American life. They are as
common as an oil change to some. What do they have in common?
People gather together--people related through a blood bond or a
conjugal bond; they share time in a common space; visit; plan; and
share food.

PLANNING IS THE KEY

Family reunions are never accidents, though they may be a
last-minute response to the visit of a relative. Normally the
event is planned well ahead of time by a committee or person who
volunteers or is elected. Some families continue a highly organized planning by electing officers at each meeting who are in

charge of organizing the next reunion. Others come to tacit
agreements concerning who is in charge or gladly allow the responsibility to rest with one or more volunteers. In some cases, the
"election" of family officers is part of the fun involved with the
event. A member of one New York Jewish family told me that "whoever can shout the loudest is the president."[22] Another interview
recorded by the Smithsonian Institution indicated that the family
had an "election" with only one candidate for the sake of joking
with one another.[23] The Schmidt family in Illinois, on the other
hand, has a serious election each year.[24]

    Not surprisingly, often a family member who is doing or inter-
ested in beginning a genealogy initiates or at least supports the
planning of a reunion. These, however, do not constitute a major
category of organizers, but are only one of the personality types
that may lead the planning. Men and women, young and elderly
adults, participate. In some cases, long-term affines with children in the blood line are the main organizers.[25]

    And the organization of a family reunion is no mean accom-
plishment. It involves coordinating communication to a, usually,
wide-spread group in order to find a compatible date; coordinating
transportation, housing, and food supply; procuring facilities for
various types of activities; preparing visual aids such as tee-
shirts, name tags, photographs, booklets; and making certain that
the sun shines.

The date for a reunion is set in various ways. Some families,
such as the Florida Williamses who have been reuniting since 1903,
determined the date for the first reunion by checking the Farmers'
Almanac for the most sunny day. They meet every year on the first
Thursday in October and have never been rained out.[26] Other
families take into consideration school vacations, harvest time,
and weather, so that dates and months vary throughout the United
States. A favorite reunion time is near the end of summer, just
before school, just before or just after harvest (depending on
where you are), and during the slackening tourist season.

As with the date, the place for some family reunions is set
and known by all from year to year. Families may meet at the
family farm, in a specific park in the hometown, at someone's home
or lake cottage, or at the family church. These spots are
reserved well in advance or have a standing reservation. A member
of the Hahner family, for instance, camps out in the Paola, Kansas
city park each year in order to claim the space for the weekend
family reunion.[27]

Such a location works out only if a substantial number of kin
yet live near what is considered as the family origin place.
Other families who are more widely dispersed will meet at resort
areas; church camps; rent facilities at small colleges, often the
family college; or rent other municipal or private facilities--
dining rooms, dance halls, restaurants.

Previous to the reunion--usually several months, and sometimes more than a year, in advance--committees are formed, persons are appointed, elected, volunteer, are volunteered, or assumed to be in charge of various aspects of the gathering. Duties vary depending on the reunion, but somebody is in charge of whatever happens.

WHO ATTENDS

As indicated by Ayoub's typology of reunions in Ohio, reunions, even within one geographic area, vary as to inclusion of members. Her typology of family descent is one categorization of family reunions necessary for a kinship analysis. In general, however, her types--Sibling Reunion, Name Reunion, Cognate Reunion--can be used in other parts of the country only with some modifications and a large category of exceptions.

Who is "family" to be included in a family reunion, of course, is something determined by each family and often by the person or persons organizing the reunion. Most often, in the north central United States cases documented, the "family" consisted of the descendants (with their affines) of the first immigrant and/or homesteading couple. Such a decision is not unique to that area, however. Two reunions documented in Florida, for instance, included the descendants of founding fathers, one a Confederate soldier who migrated to Florida and founded a cattle ranch.[28]

Similar cases have been recorded in other states. The Coffin
family of Rhode Island includes in its reunion the descendants of
the first American Coffin,[29] and the Gish Family International
includes descendants of the immigrant Gish.[30] Other more recently
American families also date the family of the reunion to the immi-
grants--or to the migrants to another part of the country, the
first homesteaders in Dakota, for instance. I have recorded no
case when the reunion included anything but an American branch of
the family.[31]

If not a couple, a strong figure is seen as the founder--male
or female--and the reunions often take the name of that person.
Any descendant of the perceived pinnacle couple or person is eligible to attend the reunion, with their affines. A family reunion
is not a social reunion, in that invitations have nothing to do
with social interaction or acceptance. Eligibility to participate
is not a matter of club membership or even friendship. It is
determined by blood.

The list of who actually attends any given reunion varies
considerably from that of who is eligible to attend. Some
families have a regular group who like to get together with a
variety of others in various years.[32] People attend from curiosity, for the food, as an obligation, to see family who are also
friends. All age groups, all occupations, all social and economic
groups attend. As one reunionite commented to a journalist:
". . . on the first Thursday in October we're all the same--just
plain Williamses."[33]

Again, there seems to be no rule. There does, however, seem
to be a feeling that families must be large in order to have a
reunion at all. Many informants who had only one or two siblings
and few cousins commented to me that "there would be no point" in
having a family reunion with so few people.[34] Part of the
rationale behind this feeling, of course, was that a small group
saw each other more easily at other times (not necessarily more
often). They could all gather around a table at Thanksgiving, for
instance, or see each other individually on a more frequent basis.

TYPES OF REUNIONS

One limitation of Ayoub's typology is that it relates exclu-
sively to kinship and principles of descent. The reunions she
describes do not vary in that they include descendants of some
chosen pinnacle, though they vary in depth of generations, as she
has pointed out. Though varying in attendance, the reunions she
investigated were of one type in organization and activity. Each
is an "annual assembly of approximately 50 persons, more or less,
who gather together one day each year on the basis of sharing a
cognitive image of descent from the same ancestor or ances-
tress."[35] The reunions upon which her typology was based were
annual, out of doors, and in summer, that is, they were annual
picnics.

Reunions as events do vary, however, in length and activities.
Some reunions, like those in Ohio where Ayoub did her work, are
one-day, annual picnics or potluck meals involving a set date and
place each year. Invitations are not needed for these reunions,
because everyone knows when they are, where they are, and, often,
just what to bring for the table. During the summer months, the
person or committee in charge each year will see that an announcement of the upcoming reunion is run in the local newspaper.
Obviously, such an annual, locally publicized event can continue
only in an area where a large number of the kin yet reside. Out-
of-town relatives attend annually, occasionally, or never. When
they come, they stay with closest relatives or old friends.
Carter Walker Craigie, in a recent dissertation concerning the
picnic as a folklife custom in Pennsylvania, has described this
type of family reunion for that area as consisting of an
"unwritten but mutually understood schedule."[36] Sharing of food
is essential. Playground equipment for the youngsters is
essential. Religion and patriotism are emphasized, and
"Sociability is a requirement. . . ."[37]

During the course of the day, family members talk, eat, play
together, sometimes conduct a worship service or other program,
and sometimes hold a family business meeting, usually to elect
officers for the next reunion. Often awards are given for categories such as oldest member, youngest member, or person who
traveled the farthest to attend. A typical newspaper report of a

one-day picnic reunion reads: "The afternoon was spent visiting,
looking at pictures, reading letters and reviewing family history."[38] Often at these events, families continue "traditional"
reunion activities. The Guerber family of Ohio, for instance,
kicks off its reunion with the "firing of grandpa's rifle" and
runs various races throughout the day.[39]

But one day is not enough for many families, particularly
those west of the older settled woodlands. The annual, one-day
pattern documented by Ayoub, Baldwin, and Craigie varies greatly
on both counts throughout areas of the United States, particularly
for families that are spread out over a larger space with a dimin-
ishing core of hometown residents. Families decide to meet every
two years or every five years, some even every ten, and they meet
at different places throughout the country for two to seven days.
Such variations demand an even higher degree of organization,
coordination, time, and money.

Typically, the person or persons in charge will contact family
members (a predetermined group by tacit understanding) asking for
ideas concerning a date and place to meet. Decisions are then
made about both previous to each reunion, keeping in mind school,
harvest, weather, vacation time, and cost. Members of the family
or committees of members take specific duties. These longer
reunions usually involve a formal banquet, sometimes a dance,
often a family church service, and, in some cases, a picnic as
well, and plenty of time for visiting. Entertainment at the

weekend to seven-day reunions includes slide shows and old picture
displays, playground games, sometimes a family talent show and/or
social hour in conjunction with the formal banquet. Often booklets of some sort--genealogies, family stories, cookbooks--are
prepared for the event. Any of these activities may take place at
a one-day reunion as well, but, with the limited time, not as many
will occur.

VISUAL AIDS

    Visual aids such as photographs, booklets, or cookbooks are
central to either type of reunion. No family reunion is complete
without the taking of photographs: the group, oldest and
youngest, candid shots, and so on. And, in many cases, conversations and activities circulate around old family photos, slides,
and home movies. One New York family shows movies of last year's
reunion at each new reunion.[40] Many families put up displays of
photographs, highlighting the family founders but also showing
current reunionites at younger ages or in a festive or humorous
situation. If photos are not displayed or shown as slide shows,
reunionites more than likely have a pack of snapshots along,
showing the latest grandchild or a favorite cousin at the age of
three.

    Other important visual aids have to do with family genealogy
and identification. Name tags are used frequently to identify

family members within the lineage. T-shirts are also used. The
family historian, volunteer or appointed, will often design a
large tree of lineage covering all participants for display during
the event. Booklets containing family history, anecdotes from
elders, grandfather's or grandmother's diary, family recipes, or a
family member's poetry are usually available for each reunionite.

FAMILY INTERACTION

"Everything from soup to nuts," one informant answered when
asked what his family talked about at the reunion.[41] American
families do not reunite for family history lessons. Babies are
the center of attention. Divorces, marriages (and the new affine
members), new and old recipes, school, new jobs--current events in
general--are the topics of conversation. The atmosphere is festive and the conversation is congenial, according to all reports
available. We "catch up" with what's been going on, most reunionites say, although first attenders are often there to discover
just what has been going on. Families share time, some in organized activities like cleaning up the family cemetery, but more
often simply in visiting with one another. Some family stories
and anecdotes come up regularly, others are created. I have
recorded no instances of feuding taking place at a reunion.

This overview of reunions in America has been gleaned from personal interviews, magazine and newspaper articles, and scholarly accounts of families. What emerges in the overview is that there are general patterns, but few rules that family reunions follow. In order to gain an in-depth understanding of what appens at family reunions and what place they take in the lives of family members, we will now turn to, first, a specific locale, Adams County, North Dakota, and then to a specific family and its reunion.

CHAPTER 4

ADAMS COUNTY, NORTH DAKOTA

SETTLEMENT OF THE HETTINGER AREA

Settlement on the northern plains was linked to the railroads.
Unlike the settlement distribution in the eastern sections of the
United States, the railroad did not plan its route to service
settlements in this area. Rather, the settlement followed the
track of the railroad which was being built to connect the eastern
cities with the west coast ports.[1] In the area of the northern
Great Plains, this movement of the railroads coincided with the
opening of land for homestead settlement after the Civil War, and
the granting of access land to the railroads by the United States
government.

In North Dakota particularly, the settlement of land was
actively promoted by the railroads who owned a great deal of such
access land. The wheat-rich eastern and central sections of the
state (east of the Missouri River) were settled during what is
termed "The Great Dakota Boom" (1879-86), due to the active promo-
tion of settlement by the Northern Pacific Railroad which began
laying track westward to Seattle. The section of North Dakota on
the west side of the Missouri River ("West River Country") was not

settled until the "Second Boom" between 1898 and 1915.[2] This
land, which includes the Badlands, has a more rocky and hilly
geographical configuration, and because of lower annual precipita-
tion is less rich as wheat country. The West River counties,
including Adams County in the southwestern corner of the state,
remained Indian territory until 1896. The land was then surveyed
and opened for homesteading in 1907.

The settlement of the West River area, although it occurred a
bit later than settlement of the rest of the state, followed the
same general pattern. Scandinavians (mostly Norwegian), Germans,
and Germans from Russia (Ukraine) came either directly to the
Dakota territory or, more often, came to Dakota for their own land
after having spent some time in Minnesota, Wisconsin, or Iowa. In
addition, several groups from Indiana and Kansas, after having
poor years in those areas, moved on to Dakota when the railroad
opened the land.

The very southwestern corner of the state was not serviced
directly by the Northern Pacific. Settlers took that line as far
as Dickinson to the north and headed overland to file claims. A
few years after initial settlement, the Chicago, Milwaukee, and
St. Paul Railroad serviced this area, going through what became
Hettinger, Adams County.[3] In 1907, however, during which year the
town was founded, the settlers came in from rail stations to the
north or south.

Similar family histories from this county are repeated over and over again in the local history which was prepared in 1977 for the town's 70th anniversary. It is a story of immigrating to North America from northern Europe or the Ukraine; settling in (usually) the northern central states; possibly being dried up or eaten out by grasshoppers; hearing of the rich, good land in the Dakotas; and immigrating yet again to the Dakota territory and breaking new sod after 1907.[4] The early years for these settlers were spent breaking sod and building homes, churches, and schools. The families worked together on the farms, their major opponent being the elements, not their neighbors.

The boom did not last. World War I halted the production of new rail lines, and an outward migration began after 1915. This migration away from the territory was due primarily to the fact that 160 acres of land allotted by the Homestead Act and, following, by the railroad, was not sufficient to support a family, or even a single farmer on the high plains.[5] In addition, 1911 in Adams County was a terribly dry year. During that year, vast prairie fires swept the grasslands. Settlers left after such catastrophes, leaving behind reclamation claims or selling out.

The 1920s were by and large good years for wheat production in the county, although during some of the dry years and grasshopper years, an out-migration continued. The 1930s, of course, were the worst years for massive out-migration. Sons and daughters left the state simply because there was nothing to do (no farm work)

and no way to maintain themselves. The majority of people moved
on to the northern west coast states, finding work in industry,
often logging.[6] During the 1930s, Adams County had a population
loss of 26.5%.[7] By 1940, the average size of a farm, rather than
160 acres, was 710 acres.[8]

Most natives feel that the out-migration was not from choice
but from necessity. When asked why people left, they answer: "To
find work," or "Because there was nothing I could do here." Part
of this problem was the impossibility of living on 160 acres.
Also, when the family included several children, as they usually
did, everyone could not stay. There is no pattern as to who
stayed; for instance, the oldest son did not necessarily stay on
the farm. This tradition seems to have had no power with the
homesteaders. Sons who were old enough left to find work.

The population of Adams County today is just a little over
half of what it was before the Depression. One man commented that
the people "were just driven out of here." Southwest North Dakota
was particularly hard hit during those years. "It seems as if the
whole world was against us," another man said. The area was
plagued with drought, grasshoppers, and dust. In 1936 even the
lake dried up, and there was no crop whatsoever that year, not
even Russian thistle (tumbleweed) to feed the cattle.

The families who settled the county seem to be close and in
contact, particularly those of immigrant stock rather than Indiana
or Kansas stock. One reason for this is that those of immigrant

stock stayed in the county during the Depression, and some members
of those families remain. Settlers from other areas of the United
States went "back," or further west after the periodic natural
catastrophes.

The third generation who grew up after the Depression has
further dispersed, although, again, not necessarily by choice.
The problem of too many people for the land, and a relatively
sparce population to be supported by services, has continued to
support an out-migration. Many of the third generation left the
area to attend institutions of higher education or technical
schools. They do not return except for visits and reunions
because they cannot find employment in the area. They also cannot
farm since there is not enough land or rainfall. Elwyn Robinson
has explained this phenomenon as the "Too-Much Mistake."[9] There
were too many people, and too little rain for the productiveness
of the land and climate during the early days of settlement. The
following generations have paid for the mistake by being forced to
leave.

REUNIONS IN ADAMS COUNTY

In this area with a short, intense, seventy-year history, we
find reunions of families who mark their beginnings with those of
the town. The children and grandchildren of the homesteaders,
when reuniting, do so with the descendants of those founding

homesteaders, not with further generations in the old country.
Some families reunite with extended kinship "back east" (Minnesota, Iowa, Wisconsin, eastern South Dakota, eastern North Dakota, some in Ohio and Indiana, some in Kansas), who are descendants, again, of the first immigrant couple, the first "Americans."
D. J. Shults, who has owned and run several newspapers in the West River County for more than fifty years says that reunions of various kinds have been taking place for years but have become much larger in recent years.[10] Why the recent expansion? Some of it is due to nostalgic visits from the first and second generations, joined with economic and transportation factors in historical development of the country.

    During the early years of the 1900s, the families in Adams County were primarily occupied with creating farms out of unplowed prairie. Some families during those years had small reunions or occasionally went "back east" to see kin who hadn't come out to Dakota. There were, during those early years, church and family picnics. The settlers from Indiana, for instance, had annual Hoosier picnics, and the Swedish settlers regularly got together to celebrate Midsummer and other festivals. During the Depression years, of course, the major concern was staying alive. There were reunions of people in the area, but no one had the money to travel or to feed any large group of people. In addition, those were the years during which families were dispersing, mostly to the west to find work.

The early 1940s were occupied with World War II, again
dispersing families, with sons going off to military service and
some of the women working in the war industries. Those who stayed
to farm "just worked," as one informant put it.[11] Due to one of
the great coincidences of history, the war years were wet years,
and there was a demand for anything any farmer could raise. Those
who had tenaciously hung onto their land by one means or another
during the 1930s prospered in the 1940s.[12]

During the 1950s, 1960s, and 1970s, the out-migration has
continued due to the lack of employment opportunities, though not
to the extent of the 1930s.[13] The first, second, and third generations who had left during the Depression, the wars, or later
for education or employment return to the area to visit, many of
them on an annual or more frequent basis. The reunions around
Hettinger last usually two to three days, but reunionites stay
around for a week or so visiting their old haunts. Shults thinks
that people in general love to go back to home areas, explaining
some of the nostalgia attached to the Hettinger reunions. A
surprising number of people return to the area to be buried in the
Hettinger cemetery.

There seems to be a great deal of nostalgia attached to the
idea of having built Adams County. "Children" in their 50s and
60s remember plowing virgin prairie and herding cattle on open
range. Natives in their 40s and 50s remember struggling through
the Depression and watching relatives and friends being forced to

leave. Shults, who turned down a teaching position at the
University of Montana to stay with his newspapers during the
Depression, believes that people visit this place where they
failed due to outside conditions because it was a special time:

> They had a brotherhood and a sisterhood out in this country
> in those years. We had, . . . we didn't have T.V. and radio
> wasn't too good. In fact, the radio was so bad that we
> couldn't even listen to Dickinson on the basketball
> tournaments . . . it didn't carry down this far [80 miles].
> There's something that brings people back because, people
> were such good friends then. Well, we had no money to
> spend. We couldn't put on shows or anything like that, or,
> in other words, we couldn't show off, we didn't have enough
> to show off on anything. And so, there's something there, a
> friendliness that developed in those years and it's
> remained--to quite an extent.[14]

Reunions formed by the second and third generations of
Hettinger families do not, according to Shults, "come back" to the
same extent. Partially because they are better off financially,
they go to a location where they can vacation: the mountains or
oceans. Obviously, this also has to do with the fact that the
second and third generations do not have this binding force to the
land--they did not struggle through the Depression and homesteading years together.

Organized family reunions around Hettinger started to be more
prevalent than before (though they did exist) about fifteen years
ago, during the mid-1960s, with increased activity in the last
five or six years.[15] The reunions occur mostly in the summer,
between harvest and haying. Shults estimates that Adams County,
with a population of less than 4,000 people, has thirty fairly
good-sized reunions per year, at least ten of these being family
reunions.

Given the history of the county, this would mean that members of the second generation following the homesteaders proliferate family reunions as they reach adulthood and begin rearing families, or that the first generation of homesteaders began having family reunions after their children had dispersed and had begun their own procreative families. In other words, families of orientation from the early days of the county are reuniting with each other's more recent families of procreation and their descendants.

We can consider these reunions illustrative of the developing history of the area. Pioneering years were busy with survival and the inner workings of the growing community; additionally, the transportation and economic systems did not favor any long-distance traveling. The Depression, of course, was also a time when people could not afford to travel or have large gatherings, except for traveling outward to look for employment. The war years of the 1940s were nearly impossible times for family gatherings, again for economic reasons as well as problems with transportation and the increased dispersal of families into the military. The 1950s were a time when families visited back to Adams County frequently; those who had dispersed were becoming established in the areas in which they lived and gaining economic capabilities. When the reunions increased in the late 1950s and 60s, transportation was not a problem, families were better off economically so were able to travel, communication systems were

established and easy to use, and the nostalgia for old times was
just reaching a maturation for the elder family members.

A contrast is provided in studies of other communities in the
United States. The hamlet of "Plainville, U.S.A." investigated
by James West in the early 1940s offers the picture of a community
settled in a "clan system." Not only were the families not dispersed, they settled into whole neighborhoods. The area West
investigated was settled in 1830, so reacted as well to differing
historical forces.[16] In this area, according to West, "Migration,
machinery, money, have all weakened the functioning of kinship."[17]
Such a view concerning family development has been widely held by
sociologists, as demonstrated in Chapter 1. As can be seen,
however, the unavoidable migration of family members, especially
during the Depression, in North Dakota, and the post-World War II
economic stability which allowed people to travel, brought those
kinship networks to a stronger affirmation of family, reflected in
the proliferation of visiting and reunions. The reunions around
Hettinger vary in several ways, but also have similarities. To
begin with, the individual family histories do not vary significantly and are tied in with the historical development of the
cultural area.

The reunions described on the following pages are some of the
most recent gatherings recorded around Hettinger. The families
and their reunions share general patterns; they are unique only in
terms of specific activities. My information concerning the

Hettinger reunions is gleaned from personal interviews, newspaper
accounts, and in two cases, personal observation at certain sections of the reunions which I, as a non-family member, was able to
attend.

THE SVIHOVEC REUNION

    John Svihovec came to the United States to avoid military
service in Czechoslovakia. He met his wife, also a Czech, while
working for a wealthy household in New York City, moved to
Wisconsin to homestead after they married, and then came on to
homestead in North Dakota when Adams County opened up in 1907.
His parents and eight brothers followed, six settling on adjoining
claims to form what they came to call "Svihovec Valley" in the
northeast section of the county. The brothers were all craftsmen
by trade but soon learned to farm, because "that's what there was
to do."
    After some time, one of the brothers went back to the east
(Minnesota). During the Depression, three sisters in that first
generation settled in the Chicago area and one settled near
Denver. The other brothers stayed in Adams County. They were all
Catholic and, as one granddaughter commented, "took the command to
'go forth and multiply' seriously."[18] The following generations
have scattered widely, largely for reasons of employment, so sections of the extended family have not grown up knowing each other.

During the summer of 1977, 250 of the Svihovec descendants
gathered for the first time, both for a family reunion and to take
part in Hettinger's seventieth anniversary celebration. In order
to do this, the Hettinger area cousins found kin from all over the
United States with whom they had lost contact. One branch of the
family had been completely lost during the seventy-year family
history until one of the oil companies started checking leases for
the homestead lands and tracked them down in New York. This
family visited North Dakota before the reunion, then came back for
the reunion.

The volunteer committee who began corresponding with family
members to see if they might be interested in the reunion managed
to find leads to each of the other major branches except that of
the brother who returned to Minnesota after proving up his claim;
they believe the name was changed. After searching for addresses,
a Hettinger member of the kin then took responsibility for contacting each branch. Response from the kin was enthusiastic.
Four generations assembled at the reunion, the youngest descendant
being born on the day of the reunion.

In the case of the Svihovecs, a volunteer committee planned
the reunion by asking themselves what they could do to entertain
the visiting family members when they came to Adams County. They
wanted to show them their specific type of hospitality. This
included arrangements for quantities of food, participation in the
city's celebration, and a special commemoration of their common

heritage: cousin Rudolph was building a monument to the founding
Svihovec brothers.

Rudolph decided to build the monument and encourage the family
reunion after the relatives from New York were located by the oil
company. He is one of the Svihovecs still farming in Svihovec
Valley. "I look around my farmstead," he told me, "and see that
the Svihovecs are disappearing. Twenty-five years from now no one
will know what happened here, so, I thought, 'I'll fix that.'"[14]
His feelings spurred on the rest of the family. The monument was
built on 48/100 acre of Rudolph's land. The land was donated to
the local historical society so that, if there are no Svihovecs on
the land at some point in the future, the monument cannot be
destroyed.

A rather massive endeavor, the monument consists of a concrete
column surrounded by nine sunken cannisters. These cannisters
were filled after the reunion as time capsules. Mementos of the
family and the seventieth anniversary reunion, in addition to some
newsworthy items from the year 1977 were included in each capsule.
Cannisters for the two brothers who did not homestead in Adams
County were arranged on one side of the monument, and cannisters
for the seven brothers who did homestead were on the other.
Relatives from the Hettinger area helped pour the concrete and
planted spruce, cedar, and pine around the structure, all in preparation for the big event.

Rudolph's monument became a central theme of the reunion. One
of the organizers of the event commented that after the idea of
the reunion came up, it wasn't really solidified until Rudolph
told them he was going to build the monument and donate the land
for it to stand on. "You can't give up a ship at that point," she
said.[20] And nobody wanted to. Once they started organizing the
event, they were surprised at the affirmative responses received
from their first letter to the kin, especially since they were
planning a one-day reunion and many of the family members were at
least 2,000 miles distant. But they came, 250 strong.

The first day of the reunion, the Hettinger volunteers set up
a registration booth to greet the family and record attendance.
Name tags were given to each reunionite. These were color-coded
for family branch and featured a sod house to celebrate the homesteading. One North Dakota branch of the family supplied a large
breakfast in the city park, leaving the morning for time to "try
to get acquainted." Each major branch then gathered together
separately to share the noon meal.

That afternoon, family members went out to Svihovec Valley to
dedicate the monument. In the evening, the family sat together
for a more formal banquet and dance. At the banquet, an area was
set aside for displaying pieces of information such as photographs, mementos, or histories which reunionites had brought along
to share. The family, being too large for the hall, ate in shifts
of eighty, leaving the others to pass the time in conversation.

During the banquet, a cousin from California who had begun to work out the family genealogy passed around a form for all members to fill in. Pictures were taken of the family in all its groupings, and the family passed a hat for donations to pay for the reunion.

During the weekend, people from outside the area stayed either with other families in the kinship or in motels in the area. According to all reports, everyone had a wonderful time, especially the children, who got acquainted very quickly. The group tentatively decided to hold another reunion in five years but to extend the time over a weekend rather than limiting it to one day. The decision to wait for five years was made from consideration for the expense involved for some of the family who travel long distances to return to Dakota. Who will organize the next reunion is uncertain, but likely it will be the same or a similar group in the Hettinger area, people like Rudolph who want to leave traces of the founding homesteaders and Betty Svihovec, a cousin who was curious to know about her relatives.

THE ZIMMERMAN REUNION

On June 17, 1978, 136 Zimmermans gathered in the city park of Hettinger, North Dakota, to begin a weekend-long reunion which included the descendants of the twenty-two children of Carl Zimmerman and his two wives. Cars in the parking lot, other than those from North Dakota, included South Dakota, Washington State,

Colorado, Montana, Idaho, and two from "back east":   Illinois and
Wisconsin.   One Volkswagen bus from Washington proudly displayed a
banner: "Zimmerman Reunion."

This family's history is similar to that of the Svihovecs.   A
German from Russia, Zimmerman came from the area of Odessa,
Russia, in 1910 to homestead in Bison, South Dakota, "seeking
something better."   He later moved to a ranch 18 miles north of
Hettinger to homestead on a reclamation claim, settling near his
oldest son who had homesteaded in Adams County.

Following Carl in migration to North America came the five
surviving children of his first marriage and his second wife who
was with child, along with her daughter by a previous marriage.
The second Mrs. Zimmerman eventually gave birth to sixteen
surviving children.   Of the first five children, three stayed in
the Hettinger area, one moved to Minnesota, and one married and
moved to California.   During the Depression, some of the children
from the second family had to leave North Dakota to find work.
They spread to the west, to Washington State and California, with
a few to Montana, Idaho, and South Dakota.   Though the family is
large and somewhat spread out, they seem to be in touch with one
another.   Those who left during the Depression return to the area
frequently to visit family and friends, so the cousins and
brothers and sisters have known each other as they were growing
up.   One reunion-attender of the second generation told me that
she comes back every three years, another that he makes an annual

trip to Hettinger. For those who remained in the Hettinger area
and raised their procreative families nearby one another, the kin
interacted more regularly in school and church. The family had a
reunion of sorts, though not on the fully organized scale, in
1950. Why this reunion twenty-eight years later?

It seems to have been Uncle Pete's idea. He is number one
child of the second sixteen children, and served as a motivator
for the rest of the family. Pete returns to Hettinger on a regular basis to visit both family and friends. Having been forced
to leave during the Depression, he is part of the nostalgic homesteading generation mentioned earlier.

Another organizer, of the generation following Pete's, was
Chris Zimmerman. He had another compelling reason to help organize this reunion. The family had been through a series of tragic
deaths in the 1950s and 1960s. They were a close family, Chris
said, but it "seemed like the only time they ever got together was
for funerals." They wanted to see each other "for a more joyous
reason." He was also concerned to pass on the heritage to his
children. An organizer of the third generation, Linda Shauer
volunteered as secretary for the reunion because she felt the Lord
wanted them to get together and give more love to one another.
Each volunteer had a similar motivation for the work they put into
the reunion organization--connection with other family members in
the vast network was important to them.[21]

Volunteers started planning in April 1978 by contacting
everyone by mail to see if there was any interest outside of the
group who had been discussing a reunion. Unlike the Svihovecs,
the Zimmermans had the advantage of knowing who and where everyone
was. The initial letter suggested a reunion in June as the best
time in order to work around harvest and vacations and asked for
suggestions and comments from other family members. During the
spring, the volunteer committee received answers from everyone.
The responses were enthusiastic, and family members began to plan
their vacation times around the reunion.

Activities were planned for Saturday and Sunday. Hettinger
area relatives were the hosts and divided the responsibilities for
the event, including correspondence, gathering information about
accommodations, preparation of food, preparation of entertainment
and audio-visual equipment, and making arrangements for facilities
in case of rain and for a social hour and banquet. Expenses were
covered with donations and a free-will offering collected during
the reunion.

Saturday, 17 June, proved to be the perfect day for a picnic,
though dominated by a strong Dakota wind. Mirror Lake Park was
crowded with the beginnings of a 160-person gathering early in the
morning. The children immediately appropriated the park's playground equipment, which they occupied for the entire afternoon and
part of the evening. Members of the family bustled about hooking
up a loudspeaker system, and several women were busy ladening a

very long table with enough food to feed the Zimmermans and half
the town of Hettinger. The mood was convivial and full of sur-
prises. Cousins who hadn't seen each other for several years
pounced upon each other. Cousins who had seen each other the week
before pounced upon each other. While the children squealed on
the swings and teeter-totters, the adults got reacquainted or
acquainted. One arriving child asked his mother, "Is this the
family reunion people? It's a lot of people!" A great fuss was
made over the oldest member attending as he arrived; with shutters
clicking, family members went up to give him their greetings.
Introductions abounded. "Where do you live now?" "What are you
doing these days?" "Is that your little girl?" "Look who's
coming late!" "You know the last time we saw each other?--
Probably twenty years ago!" and similar comments revealed a group
of people who were or felt themselves to be far from strangers.
They knew something about one another and were curious to know
more.[22]

Gospel music played over the loudspeaker. Uncle Pete interrupted it to give the blessing and welcome everyone who had come.
Then the family settled down to the business of eating and
"catching up" on one another. Groupings of people under the trees
did not seem to follow any pattern of gender or age, with the
exception of the children who remained with the playground equipment and chased each other around the park. Though it was a cool
day, picnickers lingered in the park until after dark; some

groupings dispersed earlier to visit old haunts in the area or to
visit non-Zimmerman friends and relatives.

The plans for Sunday included attending the church of choice.
During the afternoon, the family rented the Senior Citizens
Building for an afternoon of visiting and coffeeing. "We talked
about everything," one Zimmerman told me. The younger members
were getting acquainted, and the older ones were reminiscing.
During the afternoon, they took group pictures and sent them to
the local newspaper.

Sunday evening was a more formal gathering: a banquet.
During the banquet, family members staged a talent show, showed
slides and movies, and required the head of each family branch to
introduce the members present. People did not talk about family
history, but concerned themselves with current events, although
the volunteer family secretary began a family register during the
evening.

As do the Svihovecs, the Zimmermans plan another reunion in
three to five years, giving consideration to the expense and
distances which must be traveled. They also intend to extend the
reunion so that it will be longer than two days. Unlike the
Svihovecs, the Zimmermans will move their reunion--next time it
will be hosted by the branches of the family in Washington State.

THE STEDJE-HJELLE FAMILY REUNION

Evelyn Haag is an "elected" volunteer for the Stedje-Hjelle
Family reunions which are biannual events that began in 1974.
Around Hettinger, North Dakota, she's known as the "reunion lady."
As secretary, Evelyn writes to everyone in the kinship network
four times a year to keep them posted on the developments for the
coming reunion. She does this so that family members can plan
their vacations to fit into the reunion schedule. She also sends
birthday cards to every family member and has completed five
generations on the genealogy. Norwegian-Americans, her parents
left Minnesota to homestead in Adams County in 1907-08. She and
her siblings, as with the other families in the area, spread out
from North Dakota westward, with the second and third generations
dispersing yet further.

The Stedje-Hjelle reunion is a bit more businesslike and
organized than some of the others around Hettinger.[23] At its
inception in 1974, forty-five family members got together at a
planned session in Montana and elected a president. The job of
the president was then and is now to locate a facility, preferably
a church camp, where the family can meet, and to work out the
financial arrangements for obtaining the camp. At that first
meeting, a Montana member of the family was elected president
since the first reunion was to be in Montana.

Mrs. Haag was elected secretary. Through her influence, the
family decided to expand its reunion to include an ascendant
branch of the family rather than just the descendants of her parents. The reunion includes, then, the Stedjes, descendants of the
Adams County homesteading couple, and the Hjelles, Mrs. Haag's
mother's kinship, most of whom remained in Minnesota. Part of
this reunion constituency, then are related only through the
Stedje-Hjelle union of Mrs. Haag's parents. It is an unusual
reunion.

During that first plenary session, the forty-five family
members decided to hold all reunions during the second week in
July, between harvest and haying in that part of the country.
Each year, however, the reunion is held in a different location.
The family membership votes during each reunion to decide what
area they will meet in the following year, looking for a central
location (so far in Montana, Oregon, Minnesota).

To date, each reunion has been held at a church camp. The
family rents the entire area for a weekend, moving into this
ready-made community setting as a group. People begin arriving on
Thursday and continue to pull in Friday morning. Friday they have
supper together and share the pictures from the last reunion.
Since the family includes five ministers and two missionaries,
family members conduct Bible study on Saturday morning. The
morning is also used for "show and tell" time for those who bring
pictures, old-time objects, and handicrafts to share with the

others. Saturday afternoon is devoted to reacreational games and visiting over coffee.

Saturday night during the Stedje-Hjelle reunion is designated as "Fun Night." The family puts on a program for each other, with every family required to do a piece. These acts range from jokes and recitations to musical numbers. Some family history is presented. One year some of the younger kids practiced on a dramatization of "The Three Bears." At the latest reunion, a third-generation newborn was baptised.

Elections are held on Saturday night. A president, who will choose the facility for the next reunion, is elected based on his or her area of residence. In this way, the family also chooses the general location for the next reunion. Saturday evening is also used for choir practice in preparation for the next morning's service.

The family shares in a regular church service on Sunday morning and takes a free will offering. They also vote each year on where to send the offering as a donation. People wander off throughout the afternoon and evening on Sunday, some stopping "on their way" home to visit with relatives with whom they have just spent the weekend. Contact during the reunion is reinforced throughout the two-year interim by means of the birthday cards Mrs. Haag sends and with Christmas cards. Through this correspondence, more news is known more frequently about widely dispersed family members. This continuous contact has an effect on reunion attendance.

THE OLSON FAMILY REUNION

There were twelve children in the family of Nels and Anna Olson, Swedes who immigrated to the Hettinger area to homestead in the early 1900s.[24] These children also dispersed during the Depression, and their children have further fanned out throughout the United States. More than one hundred of them were back in Hettinger during the weekend of 1-2 July 1978 for the first Olson Family Reunion.

In contrast to the highly organized Stedje-Hjelle Reunion, the Olson Reunion was planned in an off-hand manner. The planning began when some relatives were visiting in Hettinger during the summer of 1977, and a second-generation Olson from Indiana mentioned at a picnic that it would be fun to have a full-sized reunion. Pauline Olson, who helped organize the event, said it got going because "last winter was cold and nasty, so I guess we just got funny ideas. . . ." A volunteer committee started planning in January of 1978 using ideas from such events as high school reunions.

The first step was to mail out a letter to the family asking if there was interest and soliciting ideas. A tremendous response from others spurred them on to continue with the plans.

The committee decided on the weekend before the Fourth of July as an ideal time for the event so that family members could come without having to take off too much time from work. Since so many

people were coming so far (all areas of the United States were
represented), they decided that the group would need at least two
days for the reunion.

As the reunion weekend approached, however, family members
started arriving as early as Wednesday, a full four days before
the planned events, usually to spend time with a more limited set
of kin before the full group gathered. Saturday morning became
the first recogndized gathering time for the full membership,
though it was not planned as such. One of the Hettinger Olsons
donated meat for a Sunday afternoon barbecue which had to be put
into a pit on Saturday morning. Family members wandered out to
the firing site during the morning and used the pit area as a
mixer and get-acquainted place.

Formal events began on Saturday evening with a social hour.
During that time, the family displayed old pictures various
members had brought with them. The Hettinger committee had constructed for the evening a six-foot tree which carried leaves for
each family, and opportunity was taken to get as much information
as possible from the "original children." Beginning with this
social hour, everyone wore name tags which displayed the names of
the wearer, his or her parents, and grandparents. The social hour
was followed by a banquet during which one of the sons of Nels and
Anna told the story of the immigration. As with other reunions,
however, the conversation did not concern family history, but
current events in the family and the world. The banquet was

followed by a dance which the Olsons opened to the community in
hopes of being able to see old friends as well as family.

On Sunday, the family gathered in the park for a picnic,
featuring the barbecued meat which had served as the excuse for
gathering on Saturday morning. During the picnic, group pictures
were taken, otherwise the day was informal.

In keeping with the informality of their event, the family
made no definite plans for the next reunion. Members expect that
they will reunite again--as soon as someone volunteers to organize
a reunion--and they do not expect that it will necessarily be in
Adams County.

As we see, some of the families in the Hettinger area who
dispersed during the Depression and continued dispersing for work
reunite with one or two major branches of the family. Some of
these alternate or plan to alternate the reunion site so that it
is central but not at any one family member's home. In addition
to the families who reunite with western branches of the family,
some of the families who homesteaded in Hettinger reunite with kin
who stayed "back east" in Minnesota, Wisconsin, or Iowa. These
reunions are older.

Harley Erickson's family, for instance, has a reunion every
two years, one year in Minnesota, the next in Hettinger.[25] The
Erickson reunions have been taking place for at least forty years.
As with the newer reunions, the reunion takes place in mid-July in

deference to the farmers and includes descendants of immigrants
who first settled in Minnesota, then moved out to Dakota in 1907.

Despite the variations in the Adams County reunions, general
patterns shared by all can be discerned. Though the events
themselves are organized to greater and lesser degrees, the preparation for the event, that is, contacting the family members and
setting dates, is a first step and is highly organized in all
cases. Consideration is always given for occupations, particularly the schedules of the farming members of the family, and for the
expense of long-distance traveling and loss of working days. The
families all scheduled both formal and informal time together, and
all prepared some form of visual aid (name tags, family tree, old
photographs) for the event. For these families, though the heritage of the homesteading was a shared, recognized force in their
gatherings, family history was not the main concern. Rather, the
concern was to get acquainted or reacquainted with the current
lives of other family members. In like manner, the location of
the event was not the focal point of organization, but the gathering of people was the object of plans, even in the case of the
Svihovec reunion. Though the Svihovec monument was central to the
activities of the reunion, the motivation was to gather together
all these lost relatives and share with them their heritage.

In general, actual reunion activities did not vary considerably from those of reunions documented in other parts of the
United States. Adams County reunions, however, tend to be longer

than those recorded in areas such as Ohio, Indiana, and the northeast. Families based in Hettinger partake of a one-day picnic
during their reunions, but extend the time together throughout a
weekend. These families are widely dispersed; they are also
families with a short history; because of this, many family
members consider the reunion as a time to reacquaint themselves
with brothers, sisters, and cousins with whom they grew up and
from whom they separated due to necessity.

In order to gain an understanding of how and why such families
go to such lengths to maintain contact with one another, we turn
now to an in-depth look at another Adams County family reunion,
considering first the family background and interrelationships.

CHAPTER 5

THE SWENSON FAMILY

THE FOUNDERS

Erik Swenson came from Tännäs, Härjedalen, Sweden to the
United States in 1896. As was normal for that time of immigration, he came directly to a location in the United States where
people who had also come from his home area had settled.[1]

Although the massive emigration of Scandinavians at the end of
the nineteenth century is often attributed to economic reasons,
such an explanation cannot be given for Erik's departure. He was
the eldest son in a line of eldest sons. As such, he would have
inherited a large portion of property in a sparsely populated
section of northern Sweden. This property now belongs to the
descendants of one of his half-brothers who returned to Härjedalen
after a short sojourn in the northwest section of the United
States. At least three other reasons are given by Erik's descendants for his emigration and consequent arrival in Minnesota.

First, Erik lost his mother at the age of seven in a diphthe-
ria epidemic. His father remarried when he was nine, and there
are indications that Erik did not get along with his step-mother,

78

or even with his father thereafter. Whatever the reasons, as a
young man he was unhappy with his situation at home.

At the age of nineteen, another personal loss deepened his
unhappiness at home. The procreative family of his father's
sister lived in one-half of the house on the family land. One of
Erik's first cousins from that family was a boy his age. These
two grew up as inseparable best friends and, when they were older,
hunted together in the mountains for ptarmigan. In the winter of
1895, these two cousins were trapped in an avalanche while out
checking their traps. Erik's cousin, it was found later, was
crushed against a tree and killed immediately. Erik himself
managed to dig out after approximately twenty hours and walked
several miles for aid. The experience affected Erik deeply and is
one of the few stories from Sweden known by his descendants.[2]
Some of Erik's children believe that the two cousins had been
planning to emigrate together, and apparently the loss of his
companion spurred Erik to leave.

In 1968, Erik's oldest son, Swen, recorded some of his memories of family history for his children and grandchildren. Swen
gives these reasons for Erik's departure from Sweden, reasons
echoed in the family histories I recorded from each of Swen's
siblings:

> His decision to emigrate was no doubt due to a number of
> reasons. His mother died in an epidemic of diphtheria when
> he was seven. This loss affected him deeply and caused him
> to resent his father's remarriage and the acceptance of his
> stepmother. He did not really appreciate what this woman
> tried to do for him until he himself was an old man. At the

age of nineteen he was buried for twenty-four hours by an
avalanche. Although not seriously injured physically by
this experience, it left permanent emotional scars. Together with others he also resented the compulsory military
training required of all able-bodied men who reached the age
of twenty-one. The cumulative effect of these stresses,
coupled with the adventuresome spirit of youth caused him to
leave Sweden without a passport. This was comparatively
easy. The United States of America welcomed the sturdy
Nordics with open arms. Travel agents crossed the palms of
ship captains, immigration officials, and others with cold
cash to make passage and reception favorable. Thousands and
tens of thousands of northern Europe's finest young men
reached America in just that way.[3]

The most concrete reason presented for Erik's emigration was

to avoid military conscription. No one knows why, however--none

of his children ever heard whether it was for philosophical, theo-

logical, or physical reasons, but it is the one reason on which

they all concur and about which they are certain. This uncertain-

ty about that period of Erik's life is not unusual. His life in

Sweden and the specifics of his emigration and immigration were

not, apparently, topics of conversation in his American home. It

is known that shortly after his cousin's death, at the age of

nineteen or twenty, Erik obtained help from his mother's brother

who was also his legal guardian. This uncle helped him to secure

the papers he needed for travel and the inheritance money from his

mother's estate. Erik left Sweden through Röros, Norway, without

his father's knowledge, leaving behind a full brother and sister

and several half-siblings, as well as his further extended family.

From Röros, Erik took the train to Kristiania (Oslo), where an

agent for the Cunard Line created a passport for him. He sailed

from Kristiania to a port in England, then on to New York. In New

York he boarded a train that took him via the Canadian route
directly to Hoffman, Minnesota.

Upon reaching Hoffman, Erik went to the farmstead of Magnus
Swenson, an acquaintance from Tännäs (no relation). It is not
clear whether or not arrangements had been made for him to work
for Magnus previous to his departure from Sweden, but, in any
case, Erik knew Magnus was in Hoffman and went directly to his
homestead. Other Swedes from Härjedalen had also settled near
Hoffman (see below).

During his first years in Hoffman, Erik hired out to Magnus
Swenson and other farmers. He also worked as a carpenter, logged
in northern Minnesota, and worked on threshing crews in Minnesota
and North Dakota. Shortly after he left Sweden, Erik's father
passed away. The inheritance from his father was then distributed, and Erik convinced his full brother and full sister to join
him in Hoffman.

Both his brother, Christian, and sister, Carrie (Karin), also
based themselves in the Hoffman area when they arrived. Carrie
spent several years in Minneapolis employed as a seamstress.
Christian hired out to other farmers as Erik had, worked on the
railroad, and later worked with Erik on two different homesteads.
At a later point, two of Erik's half-brothers also followed in
this chain migration to the Hoffman area. One of the half-
brothers remained in the United States and is buried in Hoffman.
The other returned to Sweden just before World War I and settled
on the home place near Tännäs.

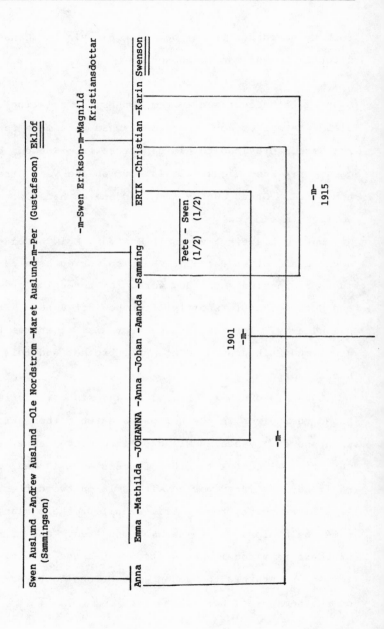

GENEALOGY OF THE SWENSON FAMILY, IMMIGRANT AND FIRST GENERATIONS

Swen Laurentius-Per Gustaf-Oscar Fredrik-Magnild Margareta Evelina-Christian Nathanael-Linnea Christina Sophia

Nov. 4, 1902   Nov. 15, 1905   Dec. 23, 1907   Oct. 16, 1910   Dec. 12, 1912   May 29, 1917

Hoffman,   Pine River,   Pine River,   Hoffman,   Hettinger,   Hettinger,
Minnesota   Minnesota   Minnesota   Minnesota   North Dakota   North Dakota

d. Sept., 1977   d. Jan., 1961
Seattle,   Worthington,
Washington   Minnesota

Johanna Maria Eklof was born of Swedish parents near Spencer, Iowa, in 1875. Her mother, Märet (Sämmingsdotter) Auslund, immigrated with two brothers to Fort Dodge, Iowa, from the province of Härjedalen, Sweden, in 1868. Another brother had emigrated earlier. In Iowa, Märet met and married Johanna's father, Per Gustaf (Gustafsson) Eklof, who came to Iowa in 1869 from the province of Östergötland, Sweden. Per and Märet homesteaded near Spencer, Iowa, from 1872 until the late 1870's when grasshoppers devastated the area.

While the Eklofs were homesteading in Iowa, Märet's three brothers moved up to Hoffman, Minnesota, where countrymen from Härjedalen had settled. These three convinced Märet and Per to join them in Hoffman in 1877. In Hoffman Per filed on a tree claim, beginning a new farm.[4]

Johanna was only two when her parents moved. Her sibling group at that time included two older sisters and one younger sister. Shortly after the move to Minnesota, Johanna's sibling group increased with two brothers and another sister. Her father, Per Gustaf, died at an early age in 1890, leaving the family to work the Hoffman farm, led by her mother, Märet. Obviously due to his early death, little is known about Per Gustaf, but Märet became a strong force in Johanna's life and in the lives of her other children and descendants.

Surrounded by kin and Swedish friends, Johanna grew up in Hoffman. Although she and her cousins were educated in English,

their daily lives transpired in Swedish, reinforcing an ethnic
nesting. During her growing years, Johanna worked on the farm
with the rest of her family of orientation. As a young woman, she
worked for some time in Minneapolis as a housekeeper for a dentist's family, but returned frequently to Hoffman.

    Erik and Johanna met in the circle of relatives and friends
around Hoffman. Johanna's sister Emma had married Magnus Swenson,
the man for whom Erik worked when he first arrived in Minnesota,
so Erik and Johanna saw each other frequently during Erik's early
years in America. Photographs from those years show each of them
with varying siblings and cousins in the Hoffman relationship, as
well as with friends who later became relatives through marriage.
Erik, apparently a favorite among several of Johanna's cousins and
one of her sisters, proposed to Johanna, and they were married on
6 June 1901.

    After their marriage, Erik and Johanna moved to northern
Minnesota to homestead in the cutover area of Cass County, near
Pine River.[5] The first winter after staking the homestead claim
was spent once again in Hoffman on the Eklof farm. There Johanna
gave birth to her first son, Swen Laurentius, in November of 1902.
Per Gustaf, the second son, was born on the homestead in November
of 1905, and a third son, Oscar Fredrik, was born in December of
1907. During the years Erik and Johanna spent proving up the

claim, Erik's full brother, Christian, spent time at the homestead
and helped him build a house, barn, and other farm buildings.

Though Erik and Johanna were happy with their neighbors at
Pine River and built sturdy buildings for a complete farmstead,
the land was not productive enough to support their growing
family. In addition to farming, Erik hired out to other farmers
and worked on the threshing crews in the Red River Valley. In
1907, they decided to leave Pine River. At this same time, Erik
and Christian heard about land in Cuba through an effort to establish a Swedish colony there. Christian went down to see the land
and returned with a good report. Later, in 1908 or 09, Erik went
to Cuba with Christian, and they purchased land for themselves and
some smaller acreage for their sister, Carrie, with the intention
to move the family down as soon as they could afford it.

Meanwhile, Erik moved his growing procreative family from the
Pine River homestead back to Johanna's mother's (Märet) farm in
Hoffman. This move was scheduled only as a "visit" on the way to
Cuba. However, an insurrection broke out in Cuba which extended
the visit into three years. Additionally, in 1907 when Erik and
Johanna moved back to the Hoffman farm, Johanna's youngest
brother, Sam (Sämming) Eklof, left to stake a claim on newly
opened land in western Dakota. Erik took over Sam's farming
duties on the Eklof place. He also did carpentry and worked on
threshing crews each year, as he had done since his arrival in
Minnesota. In 1909 or 1910, he went into partnership with

Johanna's other brother, John (Johan). They purchased a kerosene
tractor and separator in order to do commercial threshing in
western Minnesota and North Dakota. The intent at this point was
still to earn enough money to move the family to Cuba and develop
their acreage there.

In October of 1910, a fourth child, Magnild Margareta Evelina,
was born. Apparently the Eklof farm was a crowded place in those
days. In addition to Erik, Johanna, and the four children, Grandmother Märet Eklof, Johanna's two younger sisters, and her brother
John resided there. It was becoming evident that the troubles in
Cuba were not going to be resolved, and Erik felt that it was time
to establish a separate home for his family.

In 1911, Sam Eklof decided to return to Minnesota following a
drought year in western Dakota where he was homesteading (now
Adams County, North Dakota). Erik went out to Sam's homestead to
look over the situation. He and John then decided to take their
tractor and separator out to Dakota to break land and thresh
wheat. This was, again, a temporary plan, a stopping place on the
way to Cuba. The plan was to stay for five years, gather enough
money, then move to the land in Cuba. In the fall of 1911 Erik
and John moved out to take over the homestead claims of Sam and
those of some other Swedish bachelors from Hoffman who had homesteaded on claims adjoining Sam's. Just before Christmas of that
same year, Johanna and the children moved out by railroad. Erik
and Johanna's son Per Gustaf gives a version of these plans which

reveals historical events as the causes of Erik's change of goals

during those early years of marriage:

> . . .
> PG--They were not happy in Pine River. I think they were
> very happy when they first started there, then it was too
> hard to make a living there for some reason, or they felt
> kind of, I don't know, whether they felt kind of lonely
> there. It was hard to make a living there. So they decided
> to settle in . . . I don't know how he got the information
> about Cuba, but I think it was from some advertising in some
> Swedish paper, because it was a Swedish colony started in
> Bayate, Cuba, in the Oriente province. And he sent Uncle
> Christian down there to check on that, see how things were.
> And Uncle Christian came back with very favorable reports
> about Cuba. "It was just wonderful down there." And Dad
> decided to sell the farm in Pine River and move to Cuba.
> GS--Did you ever hear what your mom said about that?
> PG--Well, she was kind of undecided, I think, about going to
> Cuba. At first I think she approved of it. Then Dad went
> to Cuba after we had moved to Hoffman; Dad, and I think
> Uncle Christian too, there were several of them in the
> company that went down to Cuba, to see how they liked . . .
> this must have been about 1909, I believe, that Dad went to
> Cuba. And he approved of everything that Uncle Christian
> had told him, probably a little bit, probably he really
> hadn't told enough, because Dad was definitely enthused
> about Cuba. So he bought forty-five acres of land there.
> And Uncle Chris bought forty-five acres of land. And they
> bought five acres of land for Aunt Carrie, with the
> intention of all of them moving down there. But when he
> came back, he figured that he didn't have enough money to
> take the family down there and get started, so, well, he
> didn't know just what to do, I guess, we started living at
> Grandma's. For three years, he'd work out, he'd do some
> carpentry work, he'd go out threshing and so on and so
> forth, and he'd work, help Grandma, too. So in 19--- he
> decided then that he had to establish a home of his own for
> his family, you see, cause it was kind of crowded at
> Grandma's too, cause Uncle John was home, and Aunt Anna was
> home, and Grandma was home, so there were three grown-up
> people besides us, you see. So, then, the ones that had
> homesteaded here in Dakota, including Uncle Sam, decided to
> move away from Dakota, go back to Minnesota again. So he
> went out here to check. [pause] And I think, now whether
> that was 19--- whether he was up here twice, or once, that I
> don't know, but that was in 1911, I believe, spring of 1911.
> So then he decided to take his family up to North Dakota and
> live here for five years. At the end of five years, he'd

pack, he'd have enough money to go to Cuba. At the end of
five years, I don't know whether he had enough money to go
to Cuba or not, anyhow, the World War One was on. He didn't
want to leave the U.S. at that time, you know. So then, in
19--- let's see now, 19--- he decided to buy Uncle Sam's
homestead land, then, in 1915. Uncle Sam wanted to sell, so
Dad decided to buy that. And Mama was not very enthused
about going to Cuba, anyways, because we were getting up in,
well, 1915, Swen would have been thirteen, fifteen years old
and about ready to go to confirmation class. And there was
no church, no Lutheran church, anyway. So Mom was not very
enthused about going to Cuba. So they changed the plans
about that again. And, when I was seven years old I started
school down in Kansas City number one.[6]
. . .

In the winter of 1911-12, Erik, Johanna, the four children,

and John Eklof lived in a 12x14 homestead tar-paper shack. That

next year Erik and John worked the land and improved a second room

attached to the shack. A fourth son, Christian Nathanael, was

born at the homestead in the winter of 1912.

During that time period, John Eklof and his sister Anna filed

on homestead land approximately 100 miles south of where the

Swensons were located, near present-day Buffalo, South Dakota.

Back and forth interchange between the Dakota grouping and the

Hoffman kin continued throughout the homesteading period.

John and Erik continued in partnership until 1915, when John

decided to return to Hoffman. Anna stayed in Buffalo. Since

World War I was beginning, Erik apparently then decided that it

wouldn't be possible to go to Cuba for some time, so he would

settle down in Dakota. Another factor in that decision stemmed

from the reality of his growing family. By 1915, the older chil-

dren were at the age for church confirmation instruction, and

Johanna seems to have had some qualms about moving them to an
unsettled place such as Cuba (see Per's account, above). Also at
that time, the older boys were beginning to help with the farm
work. In 1915, Erik bought the land he had been renting from Sam
Eklof and began to develop the farmstead. In the spring of 1917,
a sixth child, Linnea Christina Sophia, was born, creating a
sibling span of fifteen years in the nuclear family.

SOCIAL AND KIN RELATIONS OF THE FOUNDERS

    Erik Swenson is characterized by his children as a hard-work-
ing, stubborn man; Johanna as a modest, pious woman. As founders
of the family, they have taken on legendary proportions, although
Erik's influence, at least on the surface, outweighs that of
Johanna. Though Johanna was American born, and Erik did not want
to return to Sweden, they both highly valued their Swedish culture
and insisted on using only the Swedish language in the home. This
may be due in part to the ethnic and familial nests in which both
had grown up. In Sweden, Erik had been part of an extended family
shared residence; his best friend was also his first cousin. The
same was true to a modified extent for Johanna in Iowa and, particularly, in Hoffman, Minnesota, where not only her own family of
orientation, but also all of her first cousins on her mother's
side were her playmates and schoolmates.

When Erik came to Hoffman community, he stepped into a world
of countrymen abroad, for other settlers, including Märet Eklof
and her brothers, had come from the same sparsely settled province
in northern Sweden. With his brothers and sister following him in
immigration, the nesting was increased.

During the early years, the young men from Hoffman went off to
hire out or work on threshing crews, and the young women went to
work as housekeepers or seamstresses in the Twin Cities, but
Hoffman remained the hub of social activity for them. It was also
the center for a loose system of mutual aid. When Märet Eklof was
widowed with a young family, her brothers and their families were
nearby to help. At some point in her education, Johanna's uncles
offered to send her on to school. Though she did not go, the help
was there. During the courting years, the families became
intertwined into what one kin member has called being "just too
related."[7]

When he first arrived in Hoffman, Erik worked for Johanna's
brother-in-law, thus meeting her through a family connection.
Johanna had rivals amongst her cousins and sisters when they were
courting. Through the social connections of Hoffman and Erik and
Johanna, Johanna's brother Sam met and married Erik's sister
Carrie, and Erik's brother Christian met and married Johanna's
first cousin, Anna Auslund. There is also reason to believe that
Erik and Johanna themselves were second cousins once removed, as
Johanna's mother, Märet Auslund (Sämmingsdotter) Eklof, was

apparently related to Erik's maternal great-aunt. Considering
that Härjedalen is yet today a sparsely populated part of Sweden,
this is not surprising.

The relatedness extended to social and economic relations. As
shown, the years of settling and homesteading for the various family members were spent in cooperation. Erik's brother, Christian;
half-brothers, Pete and Swen; and Johanna's brother John Eklof
were all at various times a part of the Swenson household as
partners or hired work. Erik worked the Eklof farm when Sam was
gone and bought Sam's claim in Dakota. The Cuba plan was also a
joint family venture, including Erik's brother and sister in the
company of other Swedish settlers.

THE FIRST GENERATION

By the time John Eklof and Erik split up their partnership in
1915, the older sons were already helping with the farm work and
herding cattle. Swen began working in the field when he was ten
years old, right after the move to Dakota. The younger boys
helped their mother around the house and kept the cattle out of
the unfenced fields. As the family grew older, the boys gradually
all rotated out into the fields, leaving the youngest to herd
cattle and help around the house; the girls helped Johanna with
the household chores, which included keeping the garden, chickens,
and other farmyard duties.

During the teens and early 1920s, the entire immediate family worked together to develop the farm and build up the land holdings. At Swen's urging, the Swensons planted and tended a large orchard obtained from the county extension program. The cattle herd was increased, and the wheat harvests were fairly good. Johanna produced butter, eggs, and vegetables, which she sold in town.

The 1920s were a time of relative prosperity on the Swenson farm, as they were in most of North Dakota.[8] Most land was added to the original one-half section and improvements were made. The 1920s also saw the first dispersal of the nuclear residential unit.

During the teens, Swen, Oscar, Per, and Margaret had been attending the township one-room school. As did most schools in rural areas, they started in the late fall and got out early in the spring, depending on harvest and haying. Working around the farm schedule, the children all gradually finished the eighth grade. The boys did not immediately continue on to high school (later the girls did), but in 1919 Swen went to Hettinger during the winter to attend school. Since his brothers were able to do the farm work by then, he was able to attend for the full year. During the next school year, he convinced his father that Per should go to high school as well, and Swen stayed out to do the farm work. Per stayed on the farm again in 1921-22, however, and Swen returned to high school in Hettinger. The following year,

Erik and Johanna agreed to let him travel to St. Peter, Minnesota, to attend Gustavus Adolphus Academy. He finished his high school diploma in one year, but stayed on in St. Peter to attend college at Gustavus, finishing with a B.A. in 1927. From there, Swen moved to Nebraska to teach for one year, then entered the Augustana Theological Seminary in Rock Island, from which he obtained his Bachelor of Divinity degree in 1931.

Swen, then, effectively left the farmstead as early as 1922, returning only for visits. The other children were not so fortunate in their educational endeavors. To begin with, the 1920s were financially productive years for the family farm, so Erik and Johanna were able to help Swen. In addition, Swen's brothers and sisters were at home and of an age to be helping with the farm work. Christian, Margaret, and Linnea, who did later go to high school, did not begin until the late 20s, and Oscar and Per did not take the time off from the farm except for a few months of technical training done in the late 20s. By the time the younger children were done with high school, they were in the midst of the Depression. Margaret began high school at the school where Swen taught in 1927-28; she finished in 1930. Christian began high school in 1930, and Linnea in 1931. By then, times were already looking bad.

Among the second generation, particularly in the life history narratives of Oscar, Per, and Christian, the days of their primary and secondary schooling have become markers of time as well as

topics of family conversation and amusement. Years are remembered
in their life histories by who their teachers were any specific
winter. Christian's life from first to fourth grade, for
instance, was recalled by him in reference to his grade in school.
He also used this structure to pinpoint visits to and from Hoffman
relatives.

> . . .
> CN--It was in the fall of '19 . . . And that's the year I
> started school. Margaret was going to school. I guess
> Oscar had to stay home and herd cows. Cause he was five
> years older than I was. I was going to be seven. And, they
> didn't let me start until they were ready to have Oscar go
> to school. They figured I was too ornery and Margaret
> couldn't take care of me. We walked two and one-half miles,
> or drove the buggy with Mary. I don't remember but I think
> we walked to start with in the fall. I guess somebody had
> to use the horse to herd cows. We got to school and Johnny
> Richardson was there ahead of me, and he saw me coming and
> came running. Cause Johnny and I were pals all the time . .
> . He was a little older than I was, but he was a little
> shrimp . . .⁹
> . . .
> GS--I talked to you in the December of 1975, can you
> imagine? We went through most of the immigration, and then
> we talked about things that you remembered up to age seven
> when you started herding every summer, and we talked about
> the Christmas cheese.
> CN--Well. We got through that. Well, what am I supposed to
> say from then on?
> GS--Didn't anything else happen in your life from then on?
> CN--Well, I'm not so sure. Let's see. Seven years old, it
> was second grade in the fall. I was seven, I guess. She
> was, oh, when she was going to be hired, for some reason or
> other we were together, the Treeby girls and Florence
> Richardson and . . . I think they were over at our house for
> some reason or other. They were talking about the new
> teacher, and Florence said that she was Norwegian, and Lois
> Treeby said, "She's not either, she's Lutheran." I think it
> was the other way around, Florence said she was Lutheran,
> and Lois said, "She's not either, she's Norwegian."
> . . . But anyway, she was our second-grade teacher. And I
> didn't like her too much.
> GS--Who was she?

CN--Who was she? Well, she became Mrs. Leslie Bird afterward and was a neighbor over east of us.
. . .
And. 1922-23 was, I was in the third grade. And Arrabella
Howard was our teacher. She was married to Milo Howard.
They lived one-half mile away from the school.
. . .
And third grade was only seven months long. So we got out
of school at the end of March. And I remember on the last
day of school there had been snow drifting so that our buggy
horse, Mary, went through a snow drift up to about her
knees. On the last day of school.
. . .
And that was the last year Oscar went to school. He went
and took his eighth-grade examinations that spring. You had
to take state examinations to get out of the eighth grade.
And then, the next year was fourth grade. That summer.
1923. In the summer of 1923 we had the tornado that went
four miles away from us that hit the Lewis place.
. . .
CN--Anyway, let's see. Fourth grade. When I was in the
fifth grade . . . See, summer of '2 . . . . that would come
up now summer of '24 coming up I guess, huh? Now I'm not
sure if it was '23 or '24. One of those years. 1922 it
must have been that . . . . That Olaf and Margaret from
Hoffman were out and visited too. 1924? Remember Margaret
Anderson that you were supposed to go see in Chicago?
That's who. And Olaf Swenson from up at Hoffman.
Emma's daughter, . . . brother and sister. He was my age,
and she was older. Anderson was her married name.
And, let's see, it was either '23 or '24. It must have been
'24 . . . in the summer, anyway, that PG and Oscar [his
brothers] went down to Hoffman to visit. And that's when I
started cultivating corn. I guess that was in '24.
. . .[10]

None of the children were allowed to begin primary school

until the age of seven, very likely a carry-over from Erik's

educational experience in Sweden, where children were allowed to

begin school only after their seventh birthday. This meant that

Oscar, for instance, suddenly appeared with his two older brothers

in the middle of the school term since his birthday was in

December. Harvest, planting, illnesses, and even trips to Hoffman
kept the children out of school for various periods of time.

It seems that Erik's attitude about education changed over the
years that his children were attending primary school. The older
boys remember that he thought school less necessary than knowledge
about farming during those early years of parenthood. There is
some indication that he felt the schools were not as worthwhile as
those he had attended in Sweden. What or who motivated Swen to
pursue higher education is unclear, though it is likely that
Johanna was some influence. Erik's attitudes, however, shaped the
early experiences of the children, particularly after the eighth
grade. Margaret and Linnea went on to high school as a matter of
course, but his sons were to be farmers and couldn't afford the
time or cost of high school.

While in primary school, the children walked, rode a horse, or
drove a buggy to the schoolhouse, keeping one another company.
Erik's ambivalent attitude about their schooling was demonstrated
by his concern over the school's physical operations. At one
point, he hauled an old shed down to the school yard to serve as a
shelter for the horse since the school board refused to build a
barn. In another incident, he charged the school district mileage
for his children and used the money to buy windows for the school
house. Later in life he served on the school board.

But high school was a different matter. In order to attend
high school in Hettinger, the Swenson children had to move into

town for the winter term. Since the school terms were longer
during high school, whoever was attending school in town was away
from the farm during some harvesting and planting times, and
Erik's main concern was the farm. As noted, Swen's motivation for
attending high school is unclear, though it is generally understood that he did not want to be a farmer. His influence on his
siblings is evident. He convinced Erik to let Per go to high
school in 1920-21 by staying on the farm. Per stayed with a farm
family near Hettinger working for his room and board, as did the
other children when going to high school.

At his father's urging, Per later attended agricultural school
in Fargo, North Dakota. He spent part of the winters of 1927 and
1928 living in Fargo. Oscar, who didn't attend high school, also
went to Fargo for technical training--automechanics--during
January of 1925. Except for those brief winter excursions, however, Per and Oscar were on the farm during the late 1920s. In
addition, Christian had finished the eighth grade in 1926 and was
not able to begin high school until 1930 (age 18). In those
years, the farm blossomed with the three sons being active on the
land on a full-time basis.

Margaret was also on the farm full-time until 1927. Swen's
influence is again seen with her, as she attended her first year
of high school at the Luther Academy in Wahoo, Nebraska, where
Swen was then teaching. When Swen entered the seminary in Rock
Island, Illinois, in 1928, Margaret returned to the farm, but

lived in Hettinger to complete high school during the winters of
the next two years. Linnea was yet attending the township primary
school during the three- or four-month winter term, so lived at
home, not starting high school until 1931.

With the exception of Swen, then, the Swenson family remained
a basic residential and economic unit throughout the teens and
20s. At this point, the only thing drawing the second generation
away from the homestead was to continue their educations, an endeavor at which they, in effect, took turns.

It is easy to speculate that Erik had plans to maintain the
homestead as a family farm not so different from that which he
left behind in Härjedalen, Sweden. Swen had become a minister,
but Per and Oscar were to be farmers and received the technical
training for that life. The plans were not so clear for Christian
and the girls, but both Margaret and Linnea were sent to high
school at earlier ages than were the boys. Education was presumably more necessary for daughters who would not be farmers. His
children and history were to change Erik's plan.

SOCIAL AND KIN RELATIONS OF THE FIRST GENERATION

The Swedish-Americans of the northern central territories in
particular, were noted for their conservative views on religion--
no dancing, drinking, or other uncouth behavior was allowed. They
were largely followers of the pietistic movement headed by Carl

Olof Rosenius. Erik and Johanna raised their family in this tradition, as well as in the tradition of hard work. Johanna, some
of her children report, seemed afraid of how the outside world
might corrupt her children.[11] This fear partly explains her
reluctance to move to Cuba when the older boys were at the age for
confirmation class, and also partly explains the years each child
waited out before grade school and high school.

Social life on the farm was restricted to church activities
(Luther League, Ladies' Aid) or visiting the neighbors. When the
family first arrived in Adams County, they joined with a Norwegian
Lutheran congregation there. Later, several Swedish families
gathered together to form their own congregation. Religious festivals and occasions such as Midsummer's Day were spent with the
other Swedes, who gathered from several miles distance. Sundays
were spent at home, in strict observance, as indicated by Linnea:

> . . .
> GS--What did you do for games and entertainment? [on
> Sunday]
> LF--I guess we used to sing. Margaret used to play the
> organ and we'd sing a lot Sunday afternoons. And, of
> course, we really weren't supposed to do a lot of things
> on Sundays. We were supposed to sit and be pretty much
> quiet. We weren't even supposed to look at catalogs or
> things like that on Sunday. We could play the organ and
> sing, but, no, we weren't supposed to look at the catalogs
> on Sunday. Nor read the newspaper, the Sunday newspaper
> and things like that, you know? We weren't supposed to do
> things like that, either.[12]
> . . .

For the children, particularly the older boys, school life and
home life were separate worlds. One important reason for this was
that Swedish was spoken in the home, and English was spoken at

school. This was not exclusive to the Swenson family; a large
number of the children with whom they attended grade school spoke
Swedish, Norwegian, or German at home (some do yet today in that
area). Another reason for the separateness was just plain boyish-
ness. Christian, the youngest son, relates that he had an agreement with his older brothers that whatever happened at school
wasn't recounted at home, but when he was left as the lone brother
going to school with his two sisters, the sisters told about everything at home.[13]

School, as mentioned, occupied only a short period of any one
year, so workmates and playmates for the Swenson children were
largely restricted to the sibling group. In addition to the
sibling group, schoolmates, fellow Swedes in the area, and church-
mates, the Swenson children knew their first and second cousins at
an early age, despite the great distance between Hettinger and
Hoffman. Several trips were taken visiting back and forth with
Hoffman and South Dakota (where Johanna's sister Anna had settled)
while the family was homesteading. Johanna particularly visited in
Hoffman now and then, bringing with her one or two of her children
in a rotation similar to their entrance into school. Occasions
such as weddings and funerals were also times to return to Hoffman.
In addition, Erik's and Johanna's siblings would visit Dakota
during some summers, bring with their offspring and sometimes bring
the Swenson children back and forth to Hoffman. Beginning with the
years that Swen, Per, and Oscar lived in Hoffman, and continuing

throughout the years on the farm, each of the Swensons remembers
specific times during their childhoods when cousins were playmates
and aunts and uncles were part of the household. These events, as
the school grades, also structure the life histories of each of the
first-generation siblings. Christian's earliest memories are of
visits from relatives:

> . . .
> GS--What things do you remember then?
> CN--Well, I suppose the first vague memories I have, when I
> was two years old, we were down in . . . Mother and Margaret
> and I went down to Hoffman for Christmas, or right after
> Christmas. And I remember some instances from that. Like,
> for instance, I kind of remember . . . I remember the train.
> I had a notion of the train. I had vague memories of one or
> two instances down at Hoffman. And those I remember. Now
> some things I was told about that trip, other people remem-
> bered, I don't. Like, for instance, coming home. And my
> mother used to ask me did I remember that I used to . . .
> that I . . . before we left there was a hole in the door
> between the two rooms that I used to stick my head through.
> I guess there was a hole in the tarpaper. And that had been
> fixed, and I came in the house and ran over to the door, and
> the hole had been closed, and . . . but, I don't remember
> that. But I have vague recollections . . . . Then, I know
> that I remember in the fall when I was two, almost three,
> that I remember that Uncle Sam and Aunt Carrie and Walter,
> cousin Walter, came, were out there in the fall of the year.
> And, I remember quite a bit about that. Walter and I were
> the same age; we played.
> . . .
> But, I remember when Walter and I were playing "horse."
> Aunt Carrie was sewing, and she had given us a long strip,
> edging of cloth, or something she had cut off, that we could
> play horse with. And we'd put that around one person, the
> other person was the driver. And this went for awhile, and
> after awhile both of us wanted to be the horse, so we were
> tugging at each, at one end of the line, this rope, and, I
> guess, we started screaming. And Aunt Carrie took the
> scissors and cut the thing in two. [laughs] And we started
> to bawl because she cut it apart. So she sewed it back
> together for us again.
> . . .
> And then, I remember we wanted to go outside. So they
> bundled us up, and we were going outside. We got outside,

and, of course, it was cold outside, so it wasn't long
before we were back at the door again. I remember them
scolding us: "You wanted to go outside, now why don't you
stay out." It wasn't that cold, I guess. It was cold enough
that we didn't want to stay out. And, I remember being
around the barn and Uncle Sam milking the cow, kicking cow.
Now, I don't know, he used some sort of a deal to keep it
from kicking, but I don't know what it was, I don't quite
remember. Uncle Sam didn't remember either.
. . .
Then when I was three years old, the summer when I was
three, then Uncle Chris got married. And Grandpa went down
for the wedding [his father]. But none of the rest of . . .
nobody else did that . . .
And I remember Grandma and Margaret and I went in the buggy
to meet the train when Grandpa came back. When he came off
the train, I remember seeing him when he came off the train.
Then . . . And, then Uncle Chris and Aunt Anna came out
afterward. And they were there that summer.[14]
. . .
Then, the other thing that happened the summer that I was
three was that Aunt Anna and Conrad Anderson were married.
They were married down in Hoffman, and they came through
Hettinger.
. . .
In 19 . . 16, in the spring of '17, when I was four years
old, then of course, Linnea was born. . . .
. . .
after Linnea was born, then Aunt Amanda and Aunt Ebba came
from, and Ebba my cousin, came from Hoffman. And Dad took
them down in the Ford--he bought the new Ford in 1916, fall
of 1916.
. . .
Anyway, it was an open touring car, and they went down to
Buffalo. It was a sunshiney day. It was hot, not boiling
hot, but . . . a stingy wind, I guess, and driving in . . .
and, I have never seen anybody as red as Aunt Amanda and
Ebba were when they came home. [laughs] They were just so
weather beaten, you know, their faces were just raw.
GS--Didn't they have bonnets on?
CN--Ya, but you couldn't have too big a bonnet, you know, it
would blow off. You'd drive out from under them. The wind
would stand still and take the hat with it. But they washed
their hands and faces with buttermilk. That was supposed to
be good for it. And I guess it was. I can still remember
that. But . . . and Ebba and I were the same age, and we
got into more mischief and orneriness than any two kids
could've ever thought of. And Ebba still remembers all of
those things [laughs].
. . .

. . . But . . . just about every time I see her, Ebba
remembers just how ornery we were that summer. And, then,
the next year, Grandma was, came [his mother's mother]. Was
it the next year? No, it wasn't the next year, because the
next year, then Aunt Anna came to our place, and she was
there. Conrad went back to Buffalo. No, he didn't either,
he stayed too. And I was with him fixing fence and stuff.
He told me all kinds of stories in Norwegian. I don't
remember all of them. As a matter of fact, I don't think I
remember any of them.
. . .
Then that was in May, Martha [his cousin, Anna and Conrad's
daughter] was born that spring. They came in the morning to
the bed, and there was Aunt Anna in the bed, and there was a
baby with her, and she said, "See, now I've got a baby,
too." And I said, "Ah, that's not your baby, that's
Linnea." [laughs]
. . .
It was in the fall of '19 when Grandma came, and Aunt Ebba
was with her then too. And they were down in Buffalo when
Carl [his cousin] was born. And that's the year I started
school.[15]

Oscar, Per, and Linnea all related such "antics" with their

cousins in their life history narratives. These are stories they

have told their own children, as is this one which Oscar's daugh-

ter Karen reminded him to include in his narrative:

Karen (from the living room)--How old were you when you and
Vangie got into your grandma's [Johanna's mother] bedroom?
OS--[laughs] I suppose I was three. . . . Oh, I suppose it
was in the fall before we were leaving there [Hoffman],
or it, we were over there some Sunday afternoon. Lindquists
were there. And Vangie and I were the same age, and so when
they were visiting, Vangie and I went into Grandma's bedroom
and, one of us became sick, I think Vangie was the one that
became sick, that is, imaginary sickness, you know? So she
had to go to bed, and I was the doctor, and I got hold of
some of Grandma's salve, and smeared it all over her and, I
guess [laughs] . . . Course, we probably did get kind of
sick, because she had some soap in there, and we took safety
pins and poked in the soap and ate soap.
GS--What happened?
OS--Well, what happened was that we caught Hail Columbia
when they caught us, that's what happened. And there was
another Sunday, I guess, and the Eriksons were over there,
and Orval and I were about the same age--well, he was a

little bit younger than I was--but when we were upstairs.
And back in those days, you know, they used to buy sugar in
fifty-pound sacks, you know, and 100-pound sacks, and this
was where the sugar sack was. And it had been opened, so we
got in the sugar sack, and we got our hands full of sugar
like this, you know, and then we'd turn them off and eat
sugar, and then we'd run back and forth across the floor,
so when they caught up with us there, why the floor was
[laughs] full of sugar. The Erikson boys used to dig pota-
toes out of the ground and eat them raw.[16]

As mentioned, Erik's brother, Christian, had lived with the

family for some time in Pine River, Minnesota, and Erik had been

in partnership with Johanna's brother John Eklof for several years

after taking over her brother Sam's homestead claim. In the ensu-

ing years, Erik's half-brother Pete Morin also worked with him in

Dakota. Johanna's sister Anna, who had stayed in Buffalo, South

Dakota, and married a Norwegian neighbor, spent time at the Swen-

son homestead with her husband as well. Anna's first child, in

fact, was born in the Swenson home.

Grandma Märet Eklof also visited in Dakota while the children

were young, as did some of Johanna's siblings and cousins. In

1926 a large gathering of the Hoffman kin took place on the home-

stead in Dakota to celebrate Erik and Johanna's Silver Wedding

Anniversary. This event is a time marker used in the life his-

tories of most of the first generation. It was a type of family

reunion, including nearly all of the American kin network.

Stories and arguments about who came out from Hoffman and up from

Buffalo or who and how many slept in which shed are topics which

arise at family gatherings.[17]

DISPERSAL OF THE FIRST GENERATION

As with most Adams County families, the 1930s saw a fragmentation of the residential unit of the Swenson family. Swen, who
had left as early as 1922 to complete his education, finished the
seminary in 1931. He was married that same year to Mildred
Gulbranson, a Swedish-Norwegian-American from Iowa who attended
college where Swen was in seminary. They took a parish in
Minnesota, not far from Hoffman, and began their family with a
son, Norman Erik, in 1932.

Meanwhile, during the later 1920s, the family members still
living on the homestead together planned and began building a
large house to replace the two-room frame structure in which they
had all grown up. When Swen married in 1931, the new house was
partially completed so that he and his bride were able to stay in
it during their visit to the home place on their wedding trip.
Pieces of the house were completed during the next couple of
years, and the entire family gradually moved in. The years of
prosperity, however, were coming to an end as the drought years
began. The house, which included plumbing facilities though no
sewer hook-up was available at the time, was never finished.

The second child to leave the farm permanently was Margaret.
In 1933 she began nurses' training in Bismarck, a course of study
which included the summer months. That same year, Oscar left the
farm to find work, traveling to Florida after working harvest in

Iowa corn fields. There was simply not enough work for four able-
bodied men on the farm during the years of drought, and as was the
case with other Adams County families, someone had to leave.[18]
Oscar chose to be the one in part from necessity, and in part
because he wanted to do some traveling, see the country, and meet
some people. He left Dakota with a friend who had grown up in the
Swedish colony in Cuba. They picked corn in Iowa for two cents a
bushel, then went down to Florida and managed to get work on the
construction of the Tampa Bay bridge. After his friend moved on
to California, Oscar worked for some time in the orange groves,
then planned to follow him to work in the California wheat fields.
His brother Swen, however, wrote him to tell him that he shouldn't
go to California since rain was beginning to fall again in the
northwest. Swen suggested that Oscar go home, so he worked his
way back up to North Dakota in 1935.

Though Swen left the farm at an early age, his influence upon
his parents and siblings is evident throughout their lives. When
his wife was pregnant with their third child, he asked his parents
if Linnea could spend a year with them while she finished high
school. This Linnea did, being absent from the farm during 1934-
35, her senior year in high school. Margaret, remember, had also
spent a year of high school where Swen was teaching.

The summer of 1935 brought a great change to the family and,
subsequently, to the family farm. In August of that year, Johanna
died of an unknown cause. Per, Oscar, Christian, and Linnea were

on the farm that summer, with Margaret close by in Bismarck.
Johanna was sent to Bismarck for an operation to remove a tumor.
The operation was successful, and the doctor expected full
recovery. Johanna, however, unexpectedly passed away during
recovery--possibly from post-operative shock. Several family
members feel that she just "gave up," being afraid, perhaps, of
the possibility of cancer. In the midst of the Depression, Erik
had to borrow the money for her funeral. Johanna was buried in
Hoffman, Minnesota, an event for which all of her children
returned to Hoffman.

It is impossible to ascertain the effects of her death upon
the dispersal of her offspring and changes in the farmstead, since
events during the 1930s were to a great extent products of the
Depression. Linnea, just finished with high school, was relegated
the household responsibilities. Though interested in further
education, several factors kept her on the farm until 1941. Economically, Erik had no means to help send her to school, and as a
female during that time in history, she was not able to wander off
as had Oscar. Her mother's influence was gone, and she was needed
on the farm.

During the fall of 1935, Oscar, who couldn't see any change on
the farm, returned to Iowa to pick corn, this time going to the
town where Swen's wife, Mildred, had grown up. He returned to the
homestead after harvest. The situation got worse in 1936. Southwest North Dakota was particularly hard hit during the Depression.

Some years the only crop in Adams County was Russian thistle (tumbleweed), which was fed to the cattle. In 1936 there wasn't even any Russian thistle to harvest. Some of the cattle were shipped by the government to the northeast part of the state where there was some grazing. And the grasshoppers came, black clouds filling the sky from the northeast. Oscar left again for Iowa. That winter he took a course in diesel engineering in Des Moines, Iowa, going to Illinois to look for work, then returning to Iowa to hire out on a farm. Influence from his brother Swen and his continued contact with his siblings is revealed in the story of these wanderings:

. . .
GS--Why did you leave Florida?
OS--Well, I didn't find anything more to do there, and I had intended in going to California, but I had no way to get to California except hopping a freight. This Olaf, he had left the spring before, and he'd landed out in California. He'd gotten work out there in some of the wheat fields around Sacramento. So I thought I'd go out there too. But I went and mentioned that to Swen, and he wrote back and said, no, don't you do that, he said, rains were falling in the northwest again, and he thought I should come home. So I came home. And I was home then that summer. And then in August, then, Mother died. This was in '35. I came home in the last part of May, I think it was. I could have stopped in Chicago . . . but I didn't exactly fancy that idea either. I stopped in Michigan. Some people that had been down in Florida and gone back to Michigan. And he had a filling station there that he said I could, if I wanted to work for him, well, he'd open it up again. But, then I kept on and went home instead. . . . Well, then, in the fall of '35 I went back to Iowa and picked corn. Different place. I went down to where Mildred [Swen's wife] came from, you know. That's the town we went to. I had Olaf Berge with me then too.
. . .
Let's see, '35, '36. What did I do in '36?. . . . '36, ya. That was the year there was nothing but grasshoppers. And dry, and hot. Temperatures went up to 90 and 100 in May.

And the grasshoppers were so thick, that when they'd fly
over, you know, you could stand there, and the first thing
that you'd notice that the sun kind of paled away; it wasn't
so bright. And you looked up and there's grasshoppers, a
cloud of grasshoppers so thick that it shaded the sun. So.
I said, "Well, there's no sense in hanging around here." So
I went back to Iowa. I wrote to the guy that I had picked
corn for and asked if there was any chance of getting a job
down there, and he said, "Come right down," he said, "Work
for me in threshing." So I went. And then the fall after
we got through threshing, he didn't need me. He said I
could come back and pick corn, but he found me a job with a
carpenter down there. So, I worked with the carpenter till
Christmastime. And then, I had saved up a few dollars, so I
went to Des Moines and took a short course in diesel engineering. And then I tried to find other work. I went to
Moline, Illinois, and tried to find work there, but I
couldn't find it, so I came back . . . .
I came back and stayed on the farm and worked for my board
and room for a month, and then when spring came along, why,
this carpenter wanted me back. So that I could have either
have gone there, or else work on the farm, so I stayed on
the farm. I had sciatica that was bothering me so bad for
climbing that I . . . otherwise, I liked carpenter work. So
I stayed till that fall, and then I get a letter from Gus,
could I come home. That was in '37. Could I come home and
help him. So I came home, and . . .[19]

Christian was the third Swenson child to leave the farm perma-

nently. Christian finished high school in the spring of 1933, at

the age of twenty, just before Oscar left for Florida and Margaret

started nurses' training in Bismarck. Linnea at the time was

still in high school and only home during the summers, so for two

years the farm was occupied by Per, Christian, and their parents.

Crops were not good, so at the end of the summer of 1934, Chris-

tian decided to look for work in Hettinger. Erik suggested that

he ask a neighbor for work in his coal mine as well. Christian

spent that winter and the winter after his mother's death working

in that local mine. He wanted to go to college as had Swen, but the funeral expenses and the Depression would not allow Erik to

help him along.

When everything dried out in 1936, Christian hitched a ride

with a cattle trucker to the Red River Valley (border between

North Dakota and Minnesota) where there was need for harvest help.

Through a connection from Hettinger, he got work on a threshing

crew and then hired out to another fellow, first for threshing,

and then for other farm and carpentry work. Christian's story

echoes the forced dispersal of others from Adams County:

> . . .
> CN--But then, 1936, of course, there was nothing. Every-
> thing dried out. So then, I had heard that there was some
> need for harvest help up in the Red River Valley. And Oscar
> had gone back to Iowa to work for the people that he worked
> for in Iowa. Gus and I were the only ones home--well,
> Linnea was home. And, so, we found out . . Laurence Gustin,
> a neighbor, was going to take a load of cattle to Fargo. I
> asked for a ride with him. And so, he stopped outside, and
> I went and got in the truck. And, we didn't know that there
> were two others were going to ride with him, too, we didn't
> know that. And started out. So there were four of us in
> the cab of that truck going to Fargo. And when I got to
> Fargo, I'd contacted--there's a, a secretary up in the
> courthouse in Hettinger who had an uncle who lived up in
> Thompson, North Dakota. And that was, so she referred me to
> him. So I got a ride with someone from Thompson out into
> the country. I had a little suitcase that I carried a few
> clothes in. Then I walked for about two miles over to where
> this uncle of Ingeborg Johnson lived. Johnson was her
> married name. And the name of her uncle, I guess, was
> Jalmsted.
> When I got there, they didn't have any, they said that they
> had hired all the help they needed for their run, but this
> Jalmsted said that Henry Raider was looking for a man. So
> they called on the telephone and, yes, Henry Raider needed a
> man. So I was over to Henry Raider's, and I got on the
> threshing crew. That lasted a couple weeks. This was in
> July.
> And then, I got in with some other boys there from down,
> Fessenden, I think, is where they were from, or Gwinner, or
> someplace like that. One of them had a car. When we got

through with that run--it didn't take more than about a week
and a half. Then we got paid off, and they took me with
them and we went up to Adams, North Dakota. And I got,
well, there I went to the home of this Ingeborg, and that
was Jalmsted's too. Well, they didn't need any men on their
crew, but they'd heard that the Pices needed another man or
two. So I went over to Pic's. They were Bohemians. And I
got a job with them. A couple of us got jobs over there.
And that was the first and only time I've been with a
threshing crew that had the whole crew hired. They had a
cookwagon and everything with the threshing machine. And a
very interesting part of there, one of those Pic brothers,
P-i-c [spells name], made an offer to me that I, it was a
little strange, I thought--then. I still think it was a
little strange. He said he was going to start a hardware
store in Adams, and he wanted me to go in with him.
GS--Why didn't you?
CN--Well, I had my head set on going to college.
GS--When you left the farm then, what did your father think
of it then?
CN--Oh, it was agreement that one of us go, and PG [Per]
couldn't go, I mean, I was, . . . he couldn't have made it.
But, there wasn't anything for us to do there, so we should
go and find work.
. . .[20]

As noted in his story, despite economic problems and an offer

to go into business with a man in northeast North Dakota,

Christian was set on going to college. He had applied to Gustavus

Adolphus College, where Swen had attended, and asked for work. At

the end of the summer of 1936 he got a letter from the college and

took a bus south to St. Peter, Minnesota, with enough money in

savings for one-half of the year. That Christmas was spent with

Swen's procreative family and in Hoffman.

During that winter of 1936, Margaret finished her nurses'

training in Bismarck and moved to southwest Minnesota to take a

job at Worthington hospital. Thus another of the first generation

relocated not far from Hoffman. For the next several years, Swen,

Margaret, and Christian centered their activities in Minnesota, while Per, Oscar, and Linnea were yet attached to the homestead.

In 1937, Per wrote to Oscar in Iowa asking that he return to the farm. This he did. During that same fall, Per's siblings urged him to leave the farm for some time, and Swen obtained a job for him at a dairy near his home in Evansville, Minnesota. Up to that point, Per had only left the farm for three winters of agricultural training in Fargo, and his brothers and sisters felt that he would benefit from working elsewhere for awhile. The difficulty of keeping two men, Oscar and Per, busy on the farm during the still dry years was also a factor in his move to Minnesota. Here we find the first inklings of a strong disagreement between Erik and his children, one which continued for some years.

Erik apparently envisioned himself as the patriarch on a family land holding, much as his father and his grandfather had been in Sweden. His children didn't necessarily see the world in the same manner and pursued their own ends. Oscar did not always agree with Erik on how the farm work should be managed, so it seems that Erik preferred to have Per with him on the farmstead if there was to be a choice. Per's siblings thought he needed the opportunity to see some more of the world and put his agricultural training to use, thus convinced him to take a job in the dairy.

After Per had been at the dairy for awhile, however, a case of undulant fever was traced to its cows, and the dairy shut down. Per then moved down to Hoffman to work for a man who was married

to one of Johanna's first cousins. He planned to work into an
area of northeast North Dakota because a girl with whom he was
corresponding lived there, but in the spring of 1938, Oscar developed peritonitis from a ruptured appendix. Erik called Per and
asked him to come home for the spring work, so Per left Hoffman
and returned to the farm. That summer, Oscar again made the
decision that one or the other of the two brothers needed to leave
the farm. He began to work for the Agriculture Adjustment Administration in Hettinger. It was there that Oscar met his future
wife, Norma de Butler, a Norwegian-American also from Adams
County. For the next three years, Oscar worked in the offices of
the Agriculture Adjustment Administration in a couple of towns
nearby.

      Meanwhile, Christian stayed in Minnesota during the late
1930s, working and attending college. In the summer of 1937,
after Margaret had moved to Worthington, he sold books and worked
on threshing crews, basing himself out of Worthington. While
there he roomed with a local boy he met at Luther League. During
the course of the summer's socializing, Christian eventually introduced his sister Margaret to his roommate's brother and her
future husband, Arthur Mahlberg, a Swedish-American. During the
summer of 1938, just after Per had left Hoffman, Christian took
his place working at the farm of his mother's cousin. During that
next school year, he returned to Gustavus and roomed with one of
his first cousins from Hoffman. The next summer, he returned to

the same job in Hoffman, and then went back to finish his third
and last year of college. During that year, 1939-40, he met his
future wife, Anna Marie Sandahl, a Swedish-American from Minnesota. She managed the cafeteria at the college. While Christian
worked his way through college, Margaret aided him with a loan,
and Per and Swen helped him get to Hettinger for one Christmas.
The year after he graduated, Christian taught in southern
Minnesota.

Just previous to World War II, then, the Swenson siblings were
still distributed in the two areas of southwestern North Dakota
and western Minnesota. Dispersal from the homestead was to a
certain extent "back" to familiar areas. As they left the homestead for varying periods of time, the first generation continued
a type of chain migration, going to places first lived in by
sisters and brothers, and aiding one another socially and, when
possible, economically. They maintained contact through frequent
correspondence, telephoning, and, when possible, visiting. The
dispersal of the first-generation siblings was primarily undertaken for employment and education, a pattern that is evident
among most Adams County families. With dispersal, the social life
for the siblings was as a matter of course expanded well beyond
the sibling and kin grouping: their spouses, though all Scandina-
vian-American, were from different areas of the United States.

The continuing contact, influence, and exchange of aid for the
siblings, as well as the family's intricate associations with

Hoffman relatives is illustrated in this section of Per's life

history:

        . . .
        GS--Where was Margaret in '37?
        PG--Worthington.
        GS--She went there because she knew a girl in training with
        her, Linnea said. Dad was at Gustavus, did he come back in
        the summer?
        PG--No, he worked out. He came back for his Christmas vaca-
        tion in '38, no [pause] ya, it must have been '38.
        GS--And Oscar had taken the job in Hettinger . . .
        PG--Ya.
        GS--And Swen was in Clearbrook still?
        PG--Swen was in Clearbrook.
        GS--So, you and your dad and Linnea were on the farm after
        '36.
        PG--In '36 and '37, but in '38 [pause]. In '37 I left. I
        went to Evansville [Minnesota] to work. I worked for some
        people by the name of Person. Swen located the job for me.
        Oscar figured there were too many of us here at home, so
        Swen located a job for me in Evansville, at the dairy there.
        GS--Didn't you want to go?
        PG--Well, yes, in a way I did. . . . Well, I worked there
        until Swen took sick with undulant fever. Then the authori-
        ties started, and find where that undulant fever had come
        from.
        . . .
        and they decided it had come from Person's dairy, the place
        where I worked. [pause] So, they closed down the dairy; they
        weren't allowed to sell anything anymore . . . They were
        selling raw milk from untested cows. So, of course, I lost
        my job. So then I went to Hoffman and worked for a farmer
        by the name of Peter Johnson, married to Mama's cousin Ester
        Auslund. At the wage of $10 a month. But at Person's I had
        good wages, I had $25 or $30 a month there, you see. In
        fact, I paid for your dad's fare home, then, when he was
        going to go home for his Christmas vacation. No, I think
        Swen chipped in half and I chipped in half. That was in,
        that must have been the Christmas of 1937. Ya, I was really
        doing quite well.
        I didn't do very much at Johnson's, but I helped with
        the milking and the chores, and so on and so forth. So,
        anyhow, he liked to have somebody around so he could go to
        town [laughs]. Kind of looked after the dairy herd. He had
        Holstein cows, and I kind of enjoyed that. It was a nice
        place to work.
        GS--Did you spend a lot of time with your cousins, then?
        PG--Oh, not too much, but I'd run down to Eklofs, it was a

hop and a skip, you know, down to the Eklof place. But
then, he said, when spring work comes, we're going to raise
your wages to $35 a month. So, I was real happy. I was
going to work my way back into North Dakota again; those
were my plans. I mean, to the Bottineau country. I really
liked that Bottineau country. I wanted to look things over
and see if I liked it up there, and furthermore, I was
writing a girl up there [laughs].
GS--How did you meet her?
PG--They took care of our cows during the Depression, during
the winter of 1936, you know. But then, Oscar took sick.
That's when he had appendicitis. So they called up Swen and
wanted me to come home [Erik called Swen]. So Peter Johnson
said I could go. He was real nice about it.
. . .21

FIRST GENERATION AS FOUNDERS

    Linnea, the youngest child, remained on the Swenson homestead

throughout the Depression, taking care of the household duties for

her father and whomever of her brothers were in residence. During

those years, her social life remained much the same, being mostly

dependent on church activities. Through community and church

events, she had met and started dating a local Hettinger boy,

Frederick Forthun, Norwegian by descent. In 1941, Linnea began

what have been referred to as the "snowball marriages" for the

remaining siblings. By this time, Swen had a well-established

family of four children, and her other siblings were in their late

twenties and early thirties; Linnea herself was twenty-four.

After marrying, Linnea and Fred moved into Hettinger where he

worked in the grocery business.

In June of 1941, Christian and Anna Marie were married in
Minnesota. That month, Erik's brother Christian and his wife Anna
also celebrated their twenty-fifth Wedding Anniversary, so the
North Dakota branch of the family traveled to Hoffman, then on to
Christian's wedding. After their wedding, Christian and Anna
Marie traveled first to Swen's home, then spent the summer in
North Dakota before returning to the town where Christian was
teaching.

That winter, January of 1942, Oscar married Norma de Butler,
whom he had met during his years with the Agriculture Adjustment
Administration. With Per and Norma's cousin, they drove to Minnesota to get married by Swen. The Hoffman relatives all came over
to wish them well:

> . . .
> OS--We just went and got married. We didn't have a wedding.
> We just got married. They [their parents] knew that we were
> going to go get married, but . . . we picked up Gus and
> Norma's cousin, took along as witnesses, then we drove to
> Swen's in Evansville [Minnesota].
> Norma--Your folks were there too [Christian and Anna Marie].
> OS--Well, they kind of wanted to set up the wedding for us,
> and we told them it would be pretty one-sided, there'd be
> nobody from her side of the family there. But then when we
> came there . . . We just told them we wanted to come there
> and get married, they said they expected us for supper that
> night before. And when we came there, then they had all the
> uncles and aunts from Hoffman there for supper. So . . .
> Norma--Yes, we had a shivaree before we were married . . .
> OS--And then later, why, the next thing we knew here, they
> were all on the front porch there just a banging away. And,
> here were all the cousins were there--and there was quite a
> few of them. The house, it was just absolutely reeking with
> people. This was before we got married, but they sure
> greeted us before we got married. We hadn't expected to see
> any of them.[22]
> . . .

The original plan for their wedding trip was to drive to Florida,
but historical events prevented the trip. Pearl Harbor was bombed
in December of 1941, and gas had been rationed. They returned to
Stanton, North Dakota, where Oscar was working for the AAA.

Margaret married in Evansville, Minnesota, in October of 1942.
By that time, the lives of her siblings were interrupted by World
War II. In March of 1942, Christian was activated by the Navy.
In April, Oscar was inducted into the Army, and that fall Linnea's
husband, Fred, also entered the Army. During the war years, Swen,
in his late thirties and a minister, was not called upon to serve
in the military; Per stayed to farm with his father; and
Margaret's husband, Art, was also not inducted. Oscar's wife,
Norma, stayed in Hettinger while he was away, and Christian's
wife, Anna Marie, moved back to her parents' home in Minnesota.
Linnea moved to Minnesota where she obtained a job through the
help of Anna Marie's father, then developed a case of mumps, so
went down to stay with Margaret until her first child was born,
then returned to Hettinger to work until the end of the war.

It was during the war years that further dispersal took place
among the first-generation sibling group. In 1942, Swen received
a call from a parish in Washington State. He accepted this call
in part because his wife suffered from asthma; other reasons are
unclear. He moved his growing procreative family of four out to
Washington State. In the ensuing years, both this geographic
separation and the difference in ages between his children and

those of his siblings created a distinct branch of the family.
Swen's offspring did not grow up with first cousins to visit, play
with, or go to college with, because his brothers and sisters did
not start their families until after World War II, ten years later
than he had.

While other members of the family were scattered throughout
the world during the war, Per stayed on the farm with Erik. The
1940s were rich, wet years for those who had held on during the
Depression, and there was a market for anything they could raise.
Per worked at the farming while Erik spent time with civic duties,
serving on the school board, hospital board, and the like. In the
spring of 1943, the two of them applied to have Oscar relieved of
military duty so that he could return to help farm. He was re-
leased at the end of that summer and spent the rest of the war
years helping on the farm.

Both Christian and Fred were sent to the South Pacific. In
the middle of the war, Christian spent one year back in the States
in officers training, but was again shipped out to the Pacific.
At the end of the war, more changes occurred in resettling the
families. Christian and Anna Marie had their first child in the
winter of 1945. When Christian returned from the war in 1946,
they spent the summer farming in Dakota, then returned to Minnesota where Christian began teaching at a private high school.

In the fall of 1946, Fred and Linnea relocated for some time
to Worthington, Minnesota (where Margaret lived) while Fred

trained at a greenhouse. When his training was done, they returned to Hettinger and set up a florist business.

Meanwhile, Oscar and Norma had moved off the Swenson homestead
in March of 1945, renting land in Adams County from Norma's
father. They stayed on this farmstead, expanding the acreage
through purchases, renting, and inheritance. In July of 1945,
their first child was born, the third offspring of the snowball
marriages. Margaret had given birth to a boy in 1943, and in the
winter of 1945, Christian and Anna Marie had a girl. From the end
of the war until the late 1950s, this second batch of cousins grew
to number seventeen.

The Swensons maintained the post-war geographic configuration
until 1960: Swen's family in Seattle, Washington; Per with Erik
on the homestead; Oscar's family on another farm in Adams County;
Margaret's family in Worthington, Minnesota; Christian's family in
Minneapolis, Minnesota; and Linnea's family in Hettinger.

Erik passed away on the homestead in 1956. He was buried with
his wife in Hoffman, at a funeral attended by all of his children
and half of his grandchildren, as well as the entire Hoffman kin
network. Four years later, Christian moved from Minneapolis to
Kansas, beginning a "Kansas branch" of the family. He took a
position at a Swedish-Lutheran college in Lindsborg. In January
of 1961, Margaret passed away, the first of the siblings to die.

DESCENDANTS OF ERIK AND JOHANNA SWENSON

                                                              Erik—m—Johanna

Swen—m—Mildred Gulbranson — Per Gustaf — Oscar—m—Norma De Buttler
    1931   1942

├─Norman Eric   ├─Karen Margaret
  Mar. 20, 1932   July 14, 1945
  Bemidji, Minn.   Hettinger, N.D.

├─Norris Carl   ├─Orven Fredrick
  July 15, 1933   July 2, 1948
  Bemidji, Minn.   Lemmon, S.D.

├─Joanne Marie   ├─Carol Ardis
  Feb. 23, 1935   June 28, 1950
  Bemidji, Minn.   Lemmon, S.D.

├─Gordon John   ├─Orval Randolph
  Feb. 7, 1939   April 4, 1952
  Evansville, Minn.   Lemmon, S.D.

└─Lawrence Dean   └─Twila Elizabeth
  June 27, 1949   April 18, 1954
  Seattle, Wash.   Lemmon, S.D.

Margareta–m–Arthur Mahlberg–Christian–m–Anna Marie Sandahl–Linnea–m–Frederick
     1942   1941   1941   Forthun

–Paul Arthur	–Anita Hilda	–Ardelle
Aug. 5, 1943	Feb. 15, 1945	Nov. 23, 1946
Worthington, Minn.	Red Wing, Minn.	Worthington, Minn.
–Mavis Naomi	–Johanna Marie	–Avis Ingeborg
Jan. 10, 1946	Feb. 3, 1948	Sept. 29, 1948
Worthington, Minn.	Minneapolis, Minn.	Lemmon, S.D.
–Arden Franklin	–Kristine Louise	–Arlyce Darleen
May 6, 1948	July 15, 1949	May 2, 1956
Worthington, Minn.	Minneapolis, Minn.	Hettinger, N.D.
	–Greta Esther	–Ardmore Randall
	Jan. 16, 1951	April 22, 1957
	Minneapolis, Minn.	Hettinger, N.D.

THE SECOND GENERATION

   When Swen moved to Washington State in 1942, a new configuration of the Swenson kin network began. With the return of his
brothers following the war, three realms of activity were defined
for the next fifteen years: Swen's family in Washington; Oscar's
and Linnea's families with Per and Erik near Hettinger; and
Christian's and Margaret's families in Minnesota. It is within
the context of these distant areas that we must consider the early
years of the second-generation Swensons.

Swen's Branch

   Swen, as noted, began his procreative family a full ten years
before any of his siblings married and began theirs. When he
moved his family to Washington State, Norman, his eldest son, was
already ten years old. Norris was nine, Joanne seven, and Gordon
three. Though these four had early experience in Minnesota, they
were at young ages when they moved, so grew up as Washingtonians.
They also grew up without cousins with whom to visit and play.
The first offspring of the snowball marriages was not born until
1943, so the Washington cousins were distant both in miles and
ages. During the 1950s, when the other cousins were primary and
adolescent ages, the Washington Swensons were dispersing from
Washington State to attend college and serve in the military. A

new brother, Lawrence, was born into this sibling group in 1949.
That same year, Norman returned to the central section of the
United States to attend high school at Luther College and Academy
in Wahoo, Nebraska, the college where Swen had held his first
teaching job and Margaret had attended high school.

After completing his high school diploma, Norman moved to the
Swenson homestead near Hettinger where he worked on the farm with
Erik and Per. He lived in North Dakota two years, and was then
inducted into the Army. During Norman's time in the Army, he
traveled throughout the United States and was stationed in
Germany. While in Europe, Norman took the opportunity to visit
Swenson relatives in Härjedalen, Sweden. This was the first trip
to the Old Country undertaken by any of the American Swensons.
Norman, in fact, throughout his youth made a point of visiting
with his aunts and uncles whenever possible. Following his trip
to Härjedalen, for instance, Norman visited with Christian's family in Minneapolis, bringing souvenirs from Tännäs for his younger
cousins. He displayed an interest in family unity learned in part
from Swen, who had continued to play an important role in the
lives of the first-generation siblings.

Norman's sojourn on the homestead in Dakota was due to an
interest in farming on the home place. By that time, it seems
that Erik's attitude about education had changed, for he urged
Norman to go to college rather than farm.[23] After serving in the
Army for two years, Norman returned to Seattle, Washington, where

Swen and Mildred lived, to attend the University of Washington.
He also married that year to Phyllis Carlson, a Swedish-American
whom he had met while attending the academy in Wahoo, Nebraska.
Norman had returned to Washington by choice, and began his career
in Seattle after graduating with a B.A. in business administration.

Norman and Phyllis began their procreative family in December
of 1955. Their first son, Douglas Eric, was born one and a half
years before the youngest of Norman's first cousins, emphasizing
the age difference in the second generation with the generational
overlap. Their remaining children, Ruth Marie, Kathryn Louise,
Lois Jean, and Beth Elaine, were born in Seattle during the next
twelve years. In addition to concern over his own growing procreative family, throughout those years (mid-1950s to late 1960s)
Norman made a point of keeping track of his growing first cousins
--a group grown to number twenty-one by 1957. He managed to send
greetings and sometimes gifts on occasions such as high school and
college graduations and spent summer vacations traveling to North
Dakota to visit the Swensons on the way to visit Phyllis' family
in Nebraska, sometimes swinging through Minnesota as well.

With the exception of summer visits to the north central
United States, Norman's children have grown up totally as Washingtonians. At the time of the reunion in 1978, his eldest three
children were attending college in Washington State, and his
youngest two were yet in public school. In this section of the

third generation, at least, the chain migration to "family"
schools has ended.

As had the first generaton, the siblings of Swen's branch
followed one another in a type of chain migration out of Washington. This group of siblings, however, also migrated back to their
common ground in Washington State at later points in their lives.
Norris, Swen's second child, joined Norman at the Academy in
Wahoo, Nebraska in 1950. He then went south to Lindsborg, Kansas,
to attend Bethany College, a Swedish Lutheran college so far un-
attended by any of the Swenson kin. Following in his father's
footsteps, Norris attended the Augustana Theological Seminary in
Rock Island, Illinois between 1954 and 1958. In 1955, he married
Grayce Anderson, another Swedish-American. Norris, as had Norman,
met his wife while in school in Nebraska.

From 1958 until 1962, Norris served a parish in Des Moines,
Iowa, then moved to two parishes in Minnesota until 1975. Two of
his children, Krista Lynn and Karla Marie, were born in Iowa; the
third, Laurie Ann, was born just after the move to Minnesota.
These girls spent their earliest years in Minnesota, then attended
high school in Postville, Iowa, after Norris took a parish there
in 1975.

Before the reunion in 1978, Krista married a German-American
from Postville, and Karla married a boy of German and generations-
deep American background. Karla gave birth to the first fourth-
generation Swenson the winter before the reunion.

These two third-generation marriages right out of high school
are an obvious deviance from a family pattern of marrying at an
age in the mid- or late twenties. Whether or not further changes
in the marrying patterns of the kin group will develop is, of
course, not yet clear. We see in this instance the influence of
cultural environment and changes in historical events. Postville
is a German farming community in northeast Iowa where families
have rich land holdings. They tend to marry early and often stay
on the family land. Karla's husband is farming family land rather
than going to college, an opportunity the other Swensons have not
had. Krista and her husband are attending college together. At
the time of the reunion, Laurie was yet in high school.

Joanne Marie followed her brothers to Wahoo in 1952, where she
also completed her high school diploma, and then attended junior
college. In 1956 she married Clarence (Jim) Garrison, a man of
French, German, English, and Scotch-Irish descent whom she also
met at Luther College. At the time of their marriage, Jim was
stationed with the Army in El Paso, Texas. From there they moved
in 1956 to Lincoln, Nebraska, where he attended graduate school
for the next six years. Their two children, Bradford James and
Carolyn Anne, were born in 1957 and 1959, while they were yet in
Lincoln.

During the time that Joanne and her procreative family lived
in Lincoln, Nebraska, her Uncle Christian moved with his family

from Minneapolis to Lindsborg, Kansas, to take a faculty position
at Bethany College, where Norris had completed his degree in 1954.
In the summer of 1961, she had frequent contact with Christian
while he did summer course-work and research in Lincoln. After
completing a Master's degree at the University of Nebraska, Jim
and Joanne chose to move back to Washington State. Jim completed
a Ph.D. at the University of Washington in 1968, and they moved to
College Station, Texas, for a job. In 1970, the family returned
to the west coast, settling in northern California.

Bradford and Carolyn have attended high school in Washington
State. At the time of the reunion, Bradford was attending college
in Provo, Utah, and Carolyn was at San Diego University. As with
Norman's children, this branch of the third generation is not
following the pattern of chain migration to colleges or jobs in
places where other family members have been.

Gordon was the fourth of Swen's children to travel to Nebraska
in order to attend his last year of high school at Luther Academy.
He was also the fourth to meet his future spouse at that institution: Edith Anderson, another Swedish-American born and raised in
Nebraska. Gordon stayed at Luther for one year of college, then
returned to Seattle to attend the University of Washington. In
1961, after Gordon completed his Bachelor's degree in Washington,
and Edith completed a nursing degree in Nebraska, they married in
Funk, Nebraska. This event was the first time the entire group of

twenty-one first cousins in the second generation were gathered in
one place. By that year, Christian was living with his procreative family in Kansas, so came north for the weekend. Though the
rest of Swen's family was in school or back in Washington State,
they were at the wedding in full force. The North Dakota branches
attended, and Margaret's family came south from Minnesota. The
only member of the expanded kin group not present for the event
was Norris' wife, Grayce, who could not attend due to illness.

The Swenson kin took advantage of this opportunity and expanded the weekend into a type of reunion, centering around the
motel where most of the families stayed. Gordon's older brothers
and sister spent time with their spouses' families during the time
in Nebraska, and Phyllis' parents hosted an afternoon picnic at
their farmstead for the entire group.

The fall after this large family send-off, Gordon entered the
U.S. Air Force. During his time in the Air Force, Gordon and
Edith lived in Mississippi, Minnesota, the Philippine Islands, and
then returned to Washington State. In 1962 and 1963 they started
their family with Karin Mae and Jeanette Marie. When Gordon left
the Air Force in 1966 they chose to remain in Washington, settling
in Seattle where Norman's family lived at the time. Swen,
Mildred, and their fifth child, Larry, were nearby in Linden,
Washington, and Joanne and her procreative family were also nearby
in Bellevue. Norris was in Minnesota.

When Gordon and Edith moved to Washington, their girls were
one and three, so have grown up as Washingtonians. At the time of
the reunion in 1978, both were still in high school.

These first four of Swen's children are, as we have noted,
distant from their first cousins in age as well as geographic
orientation. They had all left their familial home to attend
academy and college by the time their last first cousin was born
in 1957. At that time Norman had already established his own
family and was beginning his career; Norris was completing seminary and had married; Joanne had married and started her family;
and Gordon was attending college in Nebraska. Larry, the fifth of
Swen's children, did not have this disadvantage in terms of
contact with his first cousins.

Born in 1949, Larry was a full ten years younger than Gordon.
As mentioned, he was born just a few months before his eldest
brother, Norman, left Seattle to attend the Academy in Wahoo,
Nebraska. As a child, his closest age-mate relative in terms of
geography was Norman's son, Douglas, who was born in 1956. Larry
grew up as a Washingtonian, but unlike his siblings, has not yet,
at least returned to the state. By the time he was ready for his
final year of high school, the Luther Academy had closed. Larry
attended in its stead the Augustana Academy in Canton, South
Dakota, then returned to Washington to attend Pacific Lutheran

University in Tacoma. In 1971 he followed the pattern of his
siblings, going to Omaha, Nebraska, to attend dental school. In
Nebraska, true to the Washington branch pattern, he met his wife,
Susann Doster, an Iowan of German and French descent. After completing his dental degree, Larry and Susann moved to Iowa, where
they have settled near her family. Their two children, Christie
Marie and Erik Dean, were born in 1973 and 1977, so at the time of
the reunion in 1978 were in the group of very young third-generation Swensons.

     Throughout the years that Swen's children were growing up and
leaving Washington State for school and the military, Swen and
Mildred continued to live in various homes in Washington. The
move west in 1942 proved to be a permanent one for themselves and
for most of their offspring. Swen was active in the regional and
national organization of the Augustana Lutheran Church (Swedish
Lutheran) as an administrator, parish minister, and mission devel-
oper. While he was raising his own procreative family, he continued to be an influence upon his siblings as they started and
raised their own families and began their careers. His leadership
in the family at large was undisputed.
     After Swen's retirement in 1968, he served as an interim
pastor and later an assistant pastor in Washington State. In 1973
he suffered a severe stroke and moved with Mildred to a retirement
home in Seattle. The next four years were difficult ones for his

family and himself, as his condition slowly deteriorated. During
those years, each of his living siblings made an effort to travel
to Seattle in order to visit with him. He died in September of
1977, the second of the first generation to die. Swen's funeral
in Seattle was attended by all of his siblings, all of his descendants, and several of his first cousins (Hoffman relation). The
majority of his nieces and nephews were at that time pursuing
college educations in the central U.S., so were unable to afford a
trip to Seattle.

As demonstrated during the years of first-generation dispersal, Swen's advice was given and sought by his siblings at times
of decisions. After World War II, he would visit his siblings and
nieces and nephews when possible. In Minneapolis as a very young
child, I remember looking forward with joy to visits from Uncle
Swen, who came to that city for meetings of the Augustana Lutheran
Church (Swedish Lutheran) regional presidents during his years as
President of the Pacific Synod of that Church. My sister Anita
reports overhearing a conversation my father (Christian) had with
him concerning the possible move to Kansas, at which time Swen
offered his advice to his younger brother. One spouse told me
that Swen fulfilled fathering functions that Erik did not ful-
fill,[24] and his siblings all credit him with influencing the early
development of the farm, particularly for getting the family to
plant a large orchard.

Reference to Swen's leadership was still evident in 1978, when
I was recording family and life history narratives from his
siblings. When I approached my aunts and uncles about recording
Swenson history, they all made some comment to the effect that it
was too bad that I hadn't or couldn't record Uncle Swen, since he
knew "better than anyone" about Grandpa and Grandma. They all
referred me to the "Family Tree" Swen had mimeographed in 1968.

Per Gustaf

Per Gustaf is the only unmarried sibling of the first generation. He remained on the Swenson homestead near Hettinger, North
Dakota, farming with Erik until his father's death in 1956, and
farmed by himself or rented out the land following Erik's death.
Except for the winters of 1958 and 1960 when he lived in Seattle
and attended the Lutheran Bible Institute, Per has spent his life
on the farm. In 1974 he semi-retired by renting out most of his
farmland to Linnea's youngest child, Ardmore.

Oscar's Branch

In the spring of 1945, Oscar and Norma moved to the homestead
of Norma's father because they felt that farming with both Erik
and Per Gustaf would not work out. They settled on this land,

twenty or so miles away in the same county, where they have remained for more than thirty years. Until his retirement in 1977,
Oscar's traveling days were over when they began farming and raising a family.

Their eldest child, Karen, was born in 1945, the same year as
was Christian's eldest. She attended the township one-room school
and later moved into Lemmon, South Dakota, near the family farm,
for high school. When she completed high school in 1963, she
decided to enroll at Bethany College in Lindsborg, Kansas, where
her Uncle Christian was then teaching. At that time, one of
Christian's daughters was already attending the college, and two
of their first cousins, Ardelle of Linnea's branch and Mavis of
Margaret's, followed the year after. Another chain migration was
in action.

Karen stayed in Lindsborg for two years, then moved to Kansas
City to complete the Bethany College nursing program, which she
finished in 1968. She then took a job in Kansas City for a year,
during which time she met and married Gary Gabrielson, coincidentally a native of Lindsborg, Kansas, and a second cousin to Jack
Berg, who had married Christian's daughter Anita two years
earlier.

In 1969, Karen and Gary took a teaching position with the
Lutheran mission in Tanzania. Between 1971 and 1974 they returned
to live and teach in Hutchinson, Kansas. In 1974, they again went

overseas to Jeddah, Saudi Arabia, where Gary teaches and Karen nurses at a clinic. During the summer of 1978, Karen returned to stay with her parents in North Dakota while she gave birth to their first child, Signe Liv, and then to attend the family reunion. Gary flew back for the reunion as well.

Orven was born in 1948, the same year as three of his first cousins. He attended high school in Lemmon, South Dakota as did Karen. Following high school, Orven did not enroll in a private Lutheran college as did many of the second generation, but went to North Dakota State University, where he completed both a Bachelor of Science and a Master of Science degree. In 1971 he entered the U.S. Air Force, being stationed first in Rapid City, South Dakota, then in Ohio. He began a Ph.D. program with the Air Force Institute of Technology in 1977 and was continuing that program at the time of the reunion.

At his brother's wedding in 1975, Orven met Deborah Lighthizer, a native North Dakotan of German-Russian stock. Deborah had been best friends with Orven's new sister-in-law during grade school and high school and so was maid of honor at the wedding; Orven was best man. They married in 1977 and moved to Xenia, Ohio, where Deborah is also enrolled in a graduate program.

Carol, Oscar's third child, has begun to raise a family earlier than her siblings and many of her first cousins. She was born in 1950, a year she holds to herself among the second generation. After completing high school in 1968, she moved to Grand Forks, North Dakota, to begin the nursing program at the University of North Dakota. In 1970 she married Wayne Hintz, a fellow student at the University, also a native North Dakotan of German-Russian descent.

When Wayne completed his Bachelor of Science degree in 1969, he moved with the U.S. Army to El Paso, Texas. During 1970-71, Carol and Wayne lived in Okinawa while Wayne finished his time with the Army. When they returned to North Dakota in 1971, Wayne completed a Master of Science degree in accounting, and Carol completed a B.S. in nursing. After a brief residence in Bismarck, North Dakota, they moved to Helena, Montana in 1975, where they yet resided at the time of the reunion of 1978. Carol and Wayne began their family in 1974 with the birth of a girl, Tanya Elizabeth. Just before the reunion in the summer of 1978, they had a second daughter, Tara Michelle.

Born in 1952, Orval is one of the younger of the second generation cousins. He followed his brother to Fargo, North Dakota to attend North Dakota State University in 1970. Following graduation, with a Bachelor of Science degree in agriculture, he returned to farm with Oscar on the home place near Lemmon, South

Dakota. In 1975 he married Renee Monzelowsky, North Dakotan of
German and Polish descent. In 1978 they were still farming with
Oscar and had given birth to a son, Nathan Andrew, the third new-
born in Oscar's branch to arrive just before the Swenson reunion.

Twila, Oscar and Norma's fifth child, was born in 1954. Like
her brothers and sisters, Twila attended a state university in
North Dakota, where she met her husband, Mark Zidon, another North
Dakotan, of English and Czechoslovakian descent. Mark completed
work at North Dakota State University in 1976, and they were
married that year. Twila completed her degree in 1975 and worked
for one year as a home economics teacher in Wolf Point, Montana
before her marriage. In 1978 both Twila and Mark were teaching
high school in Fessenden, North Dakota.

It is too early in the lives of Oscar's children to see a
clustering pattern such as that evidenced in Swen's branch of the
family with their Washington orientation. There is, however, a
distinctive pattern to this sibling group's dispersal. With the
exception of Karen, they all pursued higher education within North
Dakota and, perhaps because of this, married fellow native North
Dakotans--all of whom, again with the exception of Karen's
husband, Gary Gabrielson, are non-Scandinavian. This mixture, as
we shall discuss later, is a unique product of North Dakota's
history.

Margaret's Branch

Margaret's move to Worthington, Minnesota in 1936 remained a
permanent one. She and her husband, Arthur Mahlberg, a native of
Worthington, settled there and built a family business and family
in the city. Though she held an R.N., Margaret was concerned
about pursuing further higher education, so when her children were
old enough for her to be away from the home, she enrolled in the
Worthington Community College in 1959. This new endeavor in her
life was tragically cut short when she suffered a massive brain
hemorrhage in January of 1961. She was the first of her siblings
to die. Her funeral in Worthington, Minnesota, was attended by
all of her siblings, her children, some nephews and nieces, and
the Hoffman cousins. Most of her nephews and nieces were in
school at the time and could not attend.

When Margaret died in 1961, her son Paul, born during the war
in 1943, was finishing high school and making plans to attend
college in the fall. He attended the Norwegian Lutheran Concordia
College in Moorhead, Minnesota, from 1961 to 1965. As was the
case with most of his cousins, Paul met his wife, Judith
Simundson, while a student at this small Lutheran college. When
Paul finished studying at Concordia, he enrolled in the Harvard
Divinity School, where he completed a Master of Divinity degree in
1968. Judith, meanwhile, completed a Master's degree at Southern

Illinois University, and they were married in 1966. Judith is a
native North Dakotan of Norwegian and Swedish background.

From Cambridge, Massachusetts, Paul and Judy moved to Palo
Alto, California, where Paul pursued a graduate degree in philo-
sophy until 1974, when he entered medical school in New Orleans.
At the time of the family reunion in 1978, they were living in New
Orleans and had just given birth to their first child, Erik
Arthur.

Mavis, another of the cousins born in the late 1940s (1946)
left Worthington, Minnesota to attend college in Lindsborg,
Kansas, where Christian was teaching. She was in college at
Bethany when two of the Swenson cousins from North Dakota were
there as well as overlapping with two of Christian's daughters.
Except for an internship year with music therapy in Minnesota
during one school year, Mavis has remained in Kansas to pursue her
career, first working for six years in Larned, Kansas, then moving
to Kansas City. While working full time as a music therapist, she
has been pursuing a Master's degree at the University of Kansas.
Mavis is unmarried.

Arden was one of the four second-generation cousins born in
1948. He also chose to attend a Lutheran liberal arts college,
choosing, however, one of Norwegian affiliation as had Paul. He
completed a Bachelor of Arts degree at St. Olaf College, North-
field, Minnesota, in 1970 and moved to Minneapolis to work with

social change programs as a conscientious objector doing alternate service. Arden remained in Minneapolis until 1976. In September of that year, he married Linda Sura, a Minnesotan of Swedish and Polish descent whom he had met at work. In 1976, Arden and Linda moved to San Francisco, where he is enrolled in a Ph.D. program, and she is pursuing her nursing career.

It is impossible to assess the effect of Margaret's early death upon her children. Certainly they were affected by her concern for pursuing a higher education, something we see especially with Paul, although the high value placed upon education is seen throughout the Swenson kin network. In Worthington, they attended school and church with numerous cousins on their Mahlberg side, so were always with a broader kin network on festive occasions and even on a daily basis. For several years, Paul buried himself in his academic pursuits; beginning with college, Mavis quickly adopted Christian's household in Kansas as a second home; Arden did not leave Minnesota except for vacation trips until his late twenties. Outwardly they follow no patterns as some of the other family branches do, at least in terms of migrations and dispersal. In 1978, Paul and Arden were yet unsettled since they were still completing their educations. Mavis was relatively settled in Kansas City, but not necessarily for life. Margaret's husband, Art Mahlberg, is a lifelong resident of Worthington, Minnesota, the area to which his parents and grandparents

immigrated from Sweden. He was the oldest member at the Swenson
reunion in 1978, having turned seventy-five that spring.

Christian's Branch

A fourth area of activity developed for the Swenson kin in
1960 when Christian moved his procreative family to Lindsborg,
Kansas, to take a faculty position at Bethany College. During the
1960s, Oscar's daughter Karen; Linnea's daughter Ardelle; and
Margaret's daughter, Mavis all attended college at Bethany.
Having their children in college in Lindsborg was an added
incentive for Christian's siblings to visit his home in Kansas,
particularly during the end of the school year when one of the
cousins was graduating or moving for the summer. A favorite time
for visiting was also Christmastime, and sometimes Easter. As
with the second-generation members of Swen's and Oscar's branches,
the location of familial home influenced the educational and residential choices of Christian's daughters.

Anita, born in 1945, was a junior in high school when the
family moved to Kansas. She finished high school in Lindsborg and
entered Bethany College in 1962. After completing her degree in
1966, Anita moved to teach in Pensacola, Florida, where her
fiance, Jack Berg, was stationed in Navy pilot's training. Jack
and Anita had attended both high school and college together in
Lindsborg, a Swedish settlement to which Jack's great-grandparents

had immigrated. They married in 1967 when Jack completed his
training, and then moved to San Diego, California.

In San Diego, Anita worked as a case worker with the Welfare
Department until she had her first child, Eric Lano, in 1970.
Jack completed his Navy duty in 1969, and at that time they chose
to remain in San Diego. He obtained a job with the telephone
company largely because the man who interviewed him was also a
graduate of Bethany College. In 1973, Jack began work for the
police department. Their second child, Kjersti Ann, was born in
San Diego in 1972.

After eight years in San Diego, Anita and Jack decided to
return to familiar people and places. At that time, their eldest
child was nearing school age, and they felt he would get a better
education in Kansas that was available in the California school
system.[26] For these reasons, they moved their household back to
Lindsborg. Shortly after this move, their third child, Christian
James, was born.

While in Lindsborg, Jack completed his Bachelor's degree at
Bethany and began working in a nearby town. Anita taught again
from 1977-78, at which time her procreative family moved to Kansas
City, where Jack was scheduled to begin medical school during the
fall following the Swenson family reunion.

Johanna, another of the four cousins born in 1948, also
attended Bethany College in her home town. She began at Bethany

in 1966, so attended college with two of her first cousins, Mavis
(Margaret's) and Ardelle (Linnea's). Upon completing her B.A. in
1970, she moved to Wichita, Kansas, where she taught for four
years and worked as a medical aid for an additional two. In
August of 1976 she moved to Dallas, Texas, to begin training with
the Wycliffe Bible Translators, a missionary endeavor. At the
time of the family reunion in the summer of 1978, Johanna was
completing a Master's degree in linguistics with the Wycliffe
program. Johanna is unmarried.

Kristine, born in 1949, has remained in Kansas since her
family of orientation moved there in 1960. When she completed
Lindsborg High School in 1967, she entered a technical school of
hair design in a nearby town and obtained her beautician's license
in 1968. That same year she married her high school sweetheart,
R. Dale Whetstone, and moved for one year to Colorado Springs,
Colorado, where he was serving in the Army. Dale is of Dutch,
Irish, German, and Cherokee descent.

When Dale was assigned to Vietnam, Kristine moved back to
Lindsborg for one year. Between 1970 and 1977, Kristine and Dale
lived in three towns within forty miles of Lindsborg. During
those years, they began their family with two girls, Alisa Rene
and Rachel Ann, born in 1973 and 1975. In 1977, the Whetstones
chose to move back to Lindsborg, where both Kristine's and Dale's
parents live. At the time of the family reunion in 1978, Dale was

commuting to a nearby town for work, and Kristine was operating an
independent beautician's business in their home.

I am one of the younger of the second-generation American
Swensons, having been born in 1951, at the end of the late 1940s
cluster of cousins. My primary and high school days were spent in
Lindsborg, Kansas, but I returned to Minnesota for college in
1969. At that time I enrolled in Gustavus Adolphus College, the
first and last of the second-generation Swensons to follow family
footsteps back to that institution. During my college years, I
lived and studied in Yugoslavia and lived and worked in San Diego.
After working for one and a half years at Gustavus, I began a
graduate program in folklore at Indiana University. At the time
of the family reunion in 1978, I was involved with my dissertation
research and located in no particular residence. I am unmarried.
With the exception of myself, the siblings of Christian's
branch centered their lives in Kansas, where they had spent their
adolescent years, rather than in Minnesota where they had lived as
younger children. Obviously, the emotional influence wrought upon
Anita and Kristine from marrying men who had grown up in Lindsborg
is evident in their decisions to locate in Kansas. This factor
did not enter into the decisions of Swen's children to return to
Washington State, so is a varying pattern. Because of the fact
that Anita, Johanna, and I were all yet completing training and
education at the time of the reunion, we are yet among the

transients of the second generation. Though Karen (Oscar's) with
her husband spent one year in the mission field, Johanna is the
first of the Swensons to pursue a career as a missionary.

The move to Lindsborg became a permanent one for Christian and
Anna Marie. In 1978, Christian was still teaching at Bethany
College, though past retirement age. At that time they had no
plans to leave Lindsborg, and were enjoying the luxury of having
all of their grandchildren in the same town with them.

Linnea's Branch

Linnea and Fred have operated an independent florist business
in Hettinger, North Dakota, since 1948. Their children have grown
up attached to the community which was settled by their grandparents.

Ardelle, born in 1946 as was Mavis (Margaret's), also entered
Bethany College in Lindsborg, Kansas, when Mavis did in 1964. She
remained in Lindsborg for two years, following Karen (Oscar's) to
Kansas City to complete a nursing program. Ardelle returned to
North Dakota to work in hospitals in Hettinger and Minot after
finishing her degree, then began and completed a Master's program
in midwifery in Utah. During 1977-78, Ardelle taught in the nursing program at Luther College in Decorah, Iowa, not far from where
Norris (Swen's) had his parish. Ardelle was in the process of

moving to Bismarck, North Dakota, to teach in a small Catholic
college at the time of the reunion in 1978. She is unmarried.

Avis is the fourth of the second-generation cousins born in
1948. She did not leave North Dakota for her higher education,
opting to attend a school of practical nursing and, later, the
state university in Dickinson, eighty miles from Hettinger. Avis
also met her husband during her college years; he was an import
from Rhode Island, of "American" descent, mostly Irish with some
Scottish, English, German, and French blood. Unlike the other
second-generation spouses, Alfred Scott was not actively aware of
his ethnic background until Avis attempted to fill out the questionnaire I sent to each family member before the reunion.

Avis and Al married in 1971 when Al completed his Bachelor of
Science degree in Dickinson. They then moved to Al's home city,
Woonsocket, Rhode Island, where they were still living at the time
of the reunion in 1978. In Woonsocket, Al completed a Master of
Education degree and began teaching in the local high school; Avis
works in one of the hospitals. They began their family in 1975
with a daughter, Tanya Lynn. Their second child was on the way at
the time of the reunion in the summer of 1978.

Linnea and Fred began a "second" family with the birth of
Arlyce in 1956. Just previous to the family reunion in 1978,

Arlyce completed a Bachelor's degree in education at Minot State
College in Minot, North Dakota. She was scheduled to begin teaching in a one-room schoolhouse forty miles south of Hettinger in
the fall of 1978. Arlyce is unmarried.

Ardmore is the baby of the second generation. Born in 1957,
he is, as mentioned earlier, younger than his oldest cousin's
first child. Ardmore finished high school in 1975 and began
renting land on the Swenson homestead from Per. At the time of
the reunion, he was still farming with Per and working for his
parents at the greenhouse. To date, Ardmore is the only second-
generation Swenson who has not pursued a higher education or
technical training. He is unmarried.

Linnea's children have remained centered in the Hettinger
area and, from all indications, plan to stay there. Avis' move to
Rhode Island was due entirely to the origins of her husband.
Though the Scotts have made no plans for a move, Avis would like
to return to North Dakota at some time. Ardelle chose to return
to North Dakota and actively sought employment in the state.
Arlyce has also chosen to look for teaching jobs in or near
Hettinger, and Ardmore plans to continue farming in the county.
At the time of the family reunion in 1978, Linnea and Fred were
still in business in Hettinger, but were making plans for retirement. Those plans did not include a move from Hettinger.

SOCIAL AND KIN RELATIONS OF THE SECOND GENERATION

The picture of the second-generation Swensons as developing
adults is one of seemingly unconnected and geographically distant
branches. This is not, however, the case. Throughout the late
1940s, 1950s, and 1960s, particularly until 1956 when Erik died
and the older cousins of the second generation were becoming old
enough to work during the summers, there were family gatherings
during vacation times in North Dakota each year.

As a child growing up in Minneapolis, Minnesota, I remember
visiting Hettinger every spring or summer and seeing members of
the family at other times when they would visit Minneapolis or we
would meet somewhere in Minnesota for a picnic. We also took
family trips to Hoffman to visit the great-aunts and uncles and to
see some of my father's cousins and second cousins. Dakota visits
more often than not included a "half-way" picnic in the Slim
Buttes (South Dakota) with the second cousins from the Buffalo,
South Dakota area (descendants of Johanna's sister Anna) and whomever of the Swensons were visiting with the Hettinger cousins at
the time.

Despite the disparity in ages and the fact that I am one of
the younger children in the second generation, I have distinct
childhood memories of each and every one of my first cousins,
including the Washington branch. Some of these memories are asso-
ciated with gatherings at the Swenson homestead, where my cousins

and I would expropriate abandoned farm machinery to be used as
playground equipment. Other memories are from visits to the homes
of my aunts and uncles and from their visits to our home. Memories of my cousins' children also stem from such visits.

This childhood interaction between the second-generation
cousins, infrequent though it may have been, is significant to the
family reunion which took place in 1978 because none of these
cousins were strangers to one another at that time, nor had they
been during their lifetimes. For each of them as they were growing up, day-to-day social interaction did not include relatives,
even for Oscar's and Linnea's children in North Dakota who lived
near one another, but did not attend the same schools. Because of
the proximity of the North Dakota branches to one another and to
Erik, they were able to spend festivals and holidays together, but
for the other branches, distances, occupations, and the northern
winters did not encourage gatherings at such times as Christmas,
the most significant holiday for Scandinavian-Americans. Summer
visits to North Dakota and visits to one another's homes counter-
acted such separation. As could be expected with the geographical
distribution of the family, the cousins who grew up together in
and near Hettinger interacted with each other more frequently, and
Christian's and Margaret's families in Minnesota saw each other
more often than they did the other branches.

A continuation of the interaction between Christian and
Margaret, including a shared group of social friends, during the

years that Christian attended college and spent time visiting in
Worthington can be seen with their families of procreation. While
we were growing up in Minneapolis, picnics would be frequently
staged in the summers with Margaret's branch in a town half-way
between Minneapolis and Worthington. This landmark was, coincidentally, near St. Peter, the home of Gustavus Adolphus College,
and the town where Anna Marie's (Christian's wife) grandparents
had settled, and where they and her parents (my non-Swenson grandparents) were buried. Visits to the other cousins were made when
possible. One outstanding memory of my childhood is a camping
trip taken to Seattle (via North Dakota) to visit the Washington
cousins.

Communication between the cousins took forms other than
visiting. Each year for Christmas, for instance, the cousins who
had not yet entered high school exchanged names in a drawing for
an exchange of gifts. Events such as graduations, confirmations,
baptisms, and birthdays were acknowledged through the mail or by
telephone, particularly during the younger years of the second
generation. There was also a continuous traffic of correspondence
among the immediate families. When letters came from an aunt or
uncle (sometimes once a month), they would be passed around for
all to read--and each letter always told you what every one of the
cousins in that family was currently doing, or if someone was
sick, or going someplace, or had received some award, or needed
help, or whatever. My first cousins have assured me that an-

nouncements that a letter had come from Uncle or Aunt so-and-so,
and they should read it before it was put away, happened while
they were growing up too.[27] Occasionally--and always at
Christmas--these letters were from more distant relatives from the
Hoffman connections.

Somehow, an attitude towards one's cousins as special was
developed within us as youngsters. In a recent conversation with
one of my first cousins--who came out of his way with his wife to
visit for a few hours in Indiana on their way between Ohio and
Colorado--he mentioned that this attitude was conveyed to us by
our parents. "You have friends, but cousins are different--more
important. They had those feelings with the Hoffman cousins," he
commented.[28] It bothers him that his nephews and nieces don't
call him "Uncle"--their parents (his siblings) have not emphasized
the special relationship as our parents did.

As noted in the family history, there was a tradition of back-
and-forth occasional visiting in the Swenson-Eklof family group
while the root generation was growing up. This tradition was
maintained while the second generation was growing up, but in a
similar grouping, not the fully expanded grouping which would have
included the Hoffman branches. That is, the visiting was among
the children of Erik and Johanna and their offspring, although
there was some social contact maintained with the Hoffman
branches, particularly while the sisters and brothers of Erik and
Johanna were still living.

We have a visiting pattern, then, primarily with the adult
family of orientation, including the families of procreation (past
and present nuclear families of residence), plus some residual
visiting with a broader extension, for instance, the "half-way"
picnics with the Buffalo, South Dakota branch during visits back
to the North Dakota homestead and visiting with Hoffman relatives
while in Minnesota. Linnea's husband, Fred, explained the Swenson
visits this way:

> You get this group, now, just for the fun of it . . .
> Your dad [Christian], a teacher, had summers, theoretically,
> to waste. They were his. Swen, a minister, and taking for
> granted he had thirty days of leave. And, all right, those
> were the two that were farthest apart plainly.
> Then, when, in any family, you'll find in your own now
> [referring to the interviewer's family of orientation], when
> all of a sudden somebody goes away from, we'll say,
> Lindsborg, and two of your immediate family [siblings], you
> know, are going to spend two weeks in Lindsborg, you're
> going to bust your butt to get there. And it was the same
> way, Margaret would schedule, or get some way to try to get
> there. At the same time. . . .
>   And someone else has mentioned about our family here,
> our little group [his family of procreation], that we are
> very closely knit. Which we are. Basically we know where
> everyone is all the time. And, there are a lot of people
> that don't bother.[29]

It would not be an overstatement to say that keeping track of
other family members in the Swenson family is typical of each
branch and, in fact, is true among the branches as well, despite
the very broad geographical and occupational distances between the
family members.

Somehow the tradition of "too-relatedness" witnessed in the
root generation has been transferred to an evolving segment made
up of adult siblings and their offspring. This grouping seems to

be gradually breaking away from the earlier configuration with
Erik and Johanna's siblings and the complex relationships circu-
lating around Hoffman, but has regrouped in a following segment
which had its beginning focal point on the homestead in North
Dakota. With Swen's move to Washington State in the 1940s, Erik's
death in 1956, and Christian's move to Kansas in 1960, the role of
the homestead as a gathering point has greatly diminished over the
years.

As the second-generation cousins moved into their college and
military service years during the late 1950s and 1960s, gatherings
of large segments of the Swensons became fewer and farther apart.
With the exception of Gordon's wedding in 1961, in fact, the
twenty-one cousins had not been together in one place until the
reunion in 1978. For some of the cousins, however, the college
years have been times of increased interaction with one another.

Specifically for the second-generation members of Swen's,
Margaret's, Christian's, and Linnea's branches, their choices of
Scandinavian Lutheran academies and colleges fostered a social
continuity amongst themselves and their spouses. One could easily
make a case for the existence of a sub-culture which circulates
about the Lutheran colleges and churches, particularly encompass-
ing the North Central areas of the United States. Though there
is, of course, some interaction, this sub-culture would not extend
to the same extent into the more eastern and the southern and
southwestern Swedish settlements due to the varying times and

patterns of settlement. The interconnectedness engendered by attendance at these institutions is general in terms of ethnic, religious, and regional background, and also specific. As mentioned, Karen, Ardelle, and Mavis all attended college in Lindsborg, Kansas at the same time as did two of Christian's daughters; they all share social experiences and friends. Norris had earlier attended Bethany College in Lindsborg as well. A sister to Gordon's wife, Edith, married one of Christian's major students from Bethany. Greta and Arden also shared friends and social interaction at their small colleges in Minnesota.

More examples of interaction due to churches and colleges would be easy to find. While teaching at Decorah, Iowa, for instance, Ardelle occasionally visited Norris and his procreative family; while Jim Garrison was in graduate school in Nebraska, Joanne saw my family of orientation, and as a child I knew her children (my first cousins once removed). Some connections have to do with the cross-generational continuity with places such as Luther Academy and Gustavus Adolphus College. The exceptions to this college-age social interaction are seen with the North Dakota cousins who attended state universities. The break in shared social experience is emphasized for them by the facts of their marriages to people of varying ethnic and religious backgrounds who, however, share the same regional identity.

THE SWENSON FAMILY IN 1978

```
Swen-m-Mildred                    Per Gustaf        Oscar-m-Norma
 -Norman-m-Phyllis Carlson                           -Karen-m-Gary Gabrielson
        1955                                                1969
 -Douglas Eric                                         -Signe Liv
  Dec. 7, 1955                                           May 7, 1978
  Seattle, Wash.                                         Hettinger, N.D.

 -Ruth Marie                                         -Orven-m-Deborah Lighthizer
  April 10, 1957                                        1977
  Seattle, Wash.
                                                     -Carol-m-Wayne Hintz
 -Kathryn Louise                                          1970
  Feb. 13, 1959                                        -Tanya Elizabeth
  Seattle, Wash.                                         Nov. 15, 1974
                                                        Bismarck, N.D.
 -Lois Jean
  July 10, 1963                                        -Tara Michelle
  Seattle, Wash.                                         May 6, 1978
                                                        Helena, Montana
 -Beth Elaine
  July 18, 1967                                      -Orval-m-Renee Monzelowsky
  Seattle, Wash.                                          1975
                                                       -Nathan Andrew
 -Norris-m-Grayce Anderson                              April 26, 1978
        1955                                            Hettinger, N.D.
 -Krista Lynn-m-Cory Dru Cook
  Aug. 24, 1960                                      -Twila-m-Mark Zidon
  Des Moines, Iowa                                      1976
            1978

 -Karla Marie-m-Billy Jo Schlee
  Oct. 7, 1961
  Des Moines, Iowa
            1977
   -Jeremy William
    Oct. 10, 1977

 -Laurie Ann
  Sept. 21, 1963
  Brainerd, Minn.

 -Joanne-m-Clarence J. Garrison
        1956
 -Bradford James
  Feb. 2, 1957
  Lincoln, Nebr.

 -Carolyn Anne
  Oct. 20, 1959
  Lincoln, Nebr.

 -Gordon-m-Edith Anderson
        1961
 -Karin Mae
  May 25, 1962
  Seattle, Wash.

 -Jeannette Marie
  Dec. 19, 1963
  Duluth, Minn.

 -Lawrence-m-Susann Doster
        1972
 -Christie Marie
  Oct. 1, 1973
  Omaha, Nebr.

 -Erik Dean
  Feb. 16, 1977
  Manson, Iowa
```

```
Margaret-m-Arthur Mahlberg  Christian-m-Anna Marie  Linnea-m-Frederick Forthun

-Paul-m-Judith Simundson    -Anita-m-Jack Berg       -Ardelle
   ⌐1966                        ⌐1967
   └Erik Arthur               -Eric Lano             -Avis-m-Alfred Scott
    Oct. 13, 1977              July 18, 1970            ⌐1971
    New Orleans, La.           San Diego, Cal.          └Tanya Lynn
                                                         Sept. 27, 1975
-Mavis                        -Kjersti Ann              Providence, R.I.
                               Aug. 9, 1972
└Arden-m-Linda Sura            San Diego, Cal.        -Arlyce
      1976
                              └Christian James       └Ardmore
                               Dec. 5, 1975
                               Lindsborg, Kans.

                             -Johanna

                             -Kristine-m-R. Dale Whetstone
                                  ⌐1968
                                 -Alisa Rene
                                  April 4, 1973
                                  Lindsborg, Kans.

                                 └Rachel Ann
                                  Feb. 5, 1975
                                  Lindsborg, Kans.

                             └Greta
```

THE SWENSON FAMILY IN 1978

   The descendants of Erik and Johanna Swenson with their spouses
comprised a group of seventy-three persons in 1978. This group
included four of the first generation, five first-generation
spouses, twenty-one second-generation cousins with fifteen second-
generation spouses, twenty-five third-generation cousins with two
third-generation spouses, and one newborn member of the fourth
generation. The questionnaire I distributed to each of the
Swenson family members prior to the 1978 reunion revealed a family
of people with varying educations and occupations who live
throughout the United States. The results reveal as well, however, a group of people who know about one another and share a
common heritage and feeling of solidarity.

Knowledge of Kin

   A purposely ambiguous question asked each of the Swensons was:
"Can you name all your Swenson relatives?" My interest here was
in what a person thought about his relatedness. The family is
such that I did not have to wonder whether or not they knew the
names of their grandparents, parents' siblings, and first cousins.
The question, therefore, would cover the "extended" family, the
first-generation extensions which were not lineal to the

respondent. Questionnaires designed for the spouses did not
include this question.

By far the majority of the adult family members from the first
three generations felt that they could name all or almost all of
their Swenson relatives. The ambiguity of the question does not
allow a specific interpretation of these responses, since those
who responded that they could not name all of their Swenson relatives were envisioning a broader kin network stemming from the
Hoffman, Minnesota, connections. A further question asking
whether or not the family member had been to the Swenson homestead
in North Dakota, however, supplemented the question concerning
knowledge of kin.

Though a reasonably large percentage of the family did not
know the names of all of their Swenson relatives, very few of them
had never visited the homestead. Those who had never been to the
homestead near Hettinger, North Dakota, included five newborns
(four third-generation and the one fourth-generation members);
five third-generation children under the age of ten; and six
spouses, three of those newly-wed. All of the second generation
with most of their spouses and 65 percent of the third generation
offspring had been at the homestead at some time. Visits were
made to visit relatives, due to nostalgia, and to show the farm to
children and grandchildren.

No one indicated any feeling that such a visit entailed some
form of pilgrimage to the place the family started but, rather,

all indicated that it was an effort to maintain face-to-face contact with relatives by visiting them with their children. Most,
if not all, of the visits took place during family vacation
time.[25]

Family Solidarity

     The Swensons refer to a "family feeling" which has continued
over the years and generations. It is one of those "feelings"
that is not satisfactorily explicable in a family so widely dispersed. The concern for visiting one another in order to maintain
contact and knowledge of each other over the generations and years
highlights a care to maintain an identity with the family as a
whole. Norman, the eldest of the second-generation Swensons, has
this to say about the family's continuing closeness:

>   I think spouses don't necessarily understand the family
> feeling--just, primarily, because they haven't had that type
> of exposure to it in their own families. And I think that's
> probably more true of the younger ones who don't remember
> when people lived closer together [North Dakota and
> Minnesota], and we did get together more often.
>   And then there are a lot of people who aren't necessarily so
> young either, who haven't done a lot of visiting with family
> members--other than their own brothers and sisters
> [reference to the second generation].
>   I think, generally, the Swensons have always felt fairly
> close together. I don't know how you describe it. It's a
> family feeling that . . . common ancestors or whatever. . .
> .[30]

     The family history of recently pioneering together and the
deep religious upbringing for the first two generations are

certainly relevant connectives for the family feeling, though many
of the spouses who "don't necessarily understand" come from
similar backgrounds. Other impacts on the family's solidarity
stem from the complex inter-relatedness and traveling back and
forth among first Erik's and Johanna's siblings, then among their
children with their procreative families. An attitude about
cousins as a special relationship passed on from parent to child
discussed earlier is also a factor.

An aspect of the elusive solidarity is reflected in the zero
divorce rate found within the entire extended family, including
the more distant cousins of the Hoffman branches. In this particular aspect, the Swenson family is unlike other farmstead-rooted
families I have interviewed, including those in Adams County, as
most of them have at least one divorce within their ranks. No
doubt part of the "family tradition" of working together to build
a farmstead out of untouched prairie was an influence in this
statistic, although the following generations have not all stayed
on the land.

A more sociologically compelling reason for the lack of
divorce within the family has to do with the relative ethnic,
regional, and religious homogeneity of the first and second generations, including their spouses. All five of the first generation
spouses grew up in Scandinavian immigrant families: two Swedish;
two Norwegian; one half-Swedish, half-Norwegian. Of the second-
generation spouses, six are of Scandinavian descent, one is part

Scandinavian, seven are of German or part-German descent, and
three are of mixed descent. The two third-generation spouses are
mostly of German descent. Only three of the second-generation
spouses are of non-Scandinavian or German descent, being part
Slavic. All of the spouses except two of the second generation,
however, come from families which settled in the north central
United States during homesteading years.

In terms of religion, we again find a homogeneity throughout
the Swenson family. All members are Lutheran, with these exceptions: four second-generation spouses, one second-generation
member, and one third-generation member are Catholic; one second-
generation member is nondenominational Christian; one third-
generation member is Mormon; three second-generation members and
one second-generation spouse are nonaffiliated; and three second-
generation members, two second-generation spouses, and four third-
generation members are Methodist. The church affiliated second-
generation members who are no longer affiliated with a Lutheran
church joined the churches of their spouses. With the exception
of the one third-generation Catholic, however, all blood members
of the Swenson kinship were baptised as infants and confirmed as
adolescents in one of the Lutheran churches. All of the spouses
were confirmed in some church, Lutheran, Methodist, Catholic, or
Congregational.

In The Family in Social Context, Gerald Leslie has presented
statistics for the "Rank order of marital survival rates, by

religious affiliation types," in the United States.[31] The ratings
are as follows: Homogamous Catholic, 96.2 percent; Mixed
Presbyterian, 94.6 percent; Homogamous Lutheran, 94.1 percent;
Residual Specified Protestant, 94.0 percent; Mixed Lutheran, 93.0
percent; Mixed Methodist, 92.9 percent; Homogamous Methodist, 91.4
percent; Homogamous Presbyterian, 91.0 percent; Catholic-Lutheran,
90.5 percent. Eleven categories follow, but these listed cover
the Swenson family as it was in 1978.

Though the older Swedes and Norwegians might not consider
themselves a homogamous group, if Scandinavian Lutherans would be
considered in the Homogamous Lutheran listing, the survival rate
for marriages is 94.1 percent. Even if the Scandinavian groups
were considered separately (Mixed Lutheran), the rate would be 93
percent. Mixtures with the other religions represented by the
Swenson spouses all carry at least a 90 percent survival according
to Leslie statistics. Such homogeneity must have an influence
upon family solidarity, if for no other reason, due to a broadly
shared heritage and values system.

Another indication of family solidarity is revealed in the
relationship of godparents to godchildren. Within the Lutheran
church, the role of baptismal sponsor is to care for the child and
bring him or her up in the church should anything happen to the
parents; this is the obligation also assumed in the Swenson kinship network. Though social ties within the Swenson family are
more frequent with nonrelated friends, the choice for godparents

stays mostly within the blood bonds, usually resting with sib

lings. Of the blood relatives, only three of the first-generation,

three second-generation, and three third-generation members had

family friends only as baptismal sponsors. In all other cases, an

aunt and/or uncle were asked to be baptismal sponsors. This is

true for all generations, including the current ones. The first-

generation members of the family were, of course, baptised in a

time when travel was not frequent or easy, and relatives were left

in Sweden, possibly explaining the choice of family friends as

sponsors for 50 percent of that generation.

Leslie has this to comment about the backgrounds of kin

consanguine relationships. His evidence comes from a sampling of

families in New Haven, Connecticut, that is, families of quite

different ethnic, social, and historical backgrounds than is the

Swenson kin network. However, they do not vary significantly from

the indications of relationships found among the Swensons:

> When the young people married persons with ethnic, reli-
> gious, social class, and educational backgrounds similar to
> their own, the vast majority had harmonious relationships
> with their in-laws and almost none had relationships marked
> by mutual rejection. Sociocultural background was more
> highly related to intergenerational continuity than any of
> the other factors tested and seems to indicate that the
> price attached to marrying someone of radically different
> background often includes some alienation from one or both
> sets of parents.[32]

This tendency to marry people of similar backgrounds undoubt-

edly has had bearing upon the continuation of family solidarity

among the Swensons, though cannot explain the feeling of family

closeness purported to be not understandable by the very spouses

who are of that similar background. As the following generations
grow up and marry to persons of more diverse backgrounds, we will
be able to gauge the influence of this factor against the control
group of the first three generations.

A contributing element to the overpowering family feeling of
the Swensons is probably due to some extent to the fact that most
of the second- and third-generation spouses have extended families
much smaller than that of the Swensons. No doubt this lack of
kinship also contributes to the enthusiasm of the in-laws concerning family matters, which was evident before and during the
Swenson family reunion. Several of the spouses told me before the
reunion in the spring of 1978 that they were looking forward to
the reunion more than were their Swenson husbands or wives.

Education and Occupation

Although nearly homogamous in background and religion, the
educations, occupations, and places of residence of family members
have varied widely over the years. Of the first generation, Per,
Oscar, and Margaret's husband, Art, did not receive high school
educations, though all three of these received some technical
training. Of others in the first generation, all finished high
school and most of them completed some college work. The adverse
influence of the Depression years must be taken into consideration
for the members of this generation. During those years, there was

no money for school at the Swenson farmstead. In addition, as
mentioned earlier, Erik seemed to have had some ideas concerning
who did and who did not need an education. Farmers, for instance,
needed only technical training, thus Per and Oscar were not sent
to high school.

In the second generation, all Swensons except Ardmore, who is
farming, have undertaken post-high school education, including the
second-generation spouses. Four of the second-generation spouses
are nurses, and four of the second-generation blood kin are also
nurses. One of these, Ardelle, completed an M.S., and five hold
B.S. degrees along with their nursing degrees.

Six second-generation Swensons and five second-generation
spouses have completed Bachelor's degrees. Eight second-generation Swensons have done graduate work beyond their Bachelor's
degrees, and six hold Master's degrees. Four second-generation
spouses also hold Master's degrees. Three second-generation
Swensons and one second-generation spouse are currently completing
Ph.D.'s, and one second-generation spouse is a medical student.
In the second generation, there is one Medical Doctor, one dentist, and one completed Ph.D. Seven of the third-generation
Swensons are now in college and four are in high school. The
remaining members of the third generation are yet in primary
school.

These statistics reveal a concern throughout the family for
obtaining higher education. The Swenson kin network is an

educated group and, from all indications in the next generation,
will continue to be. In this respect, their levels of education
are yet another homogamous aspect of the whole family. The
occupations and major fields of academic inquiry vary throughout
the family, however.

All of the adult Swensons, both blood relatives and spouses,
have at some point worked outside the home. Current occupations
vary within generations and from generation to generation,
including: farm-ranching, teaching (including the college level),
medical fields (nurses, therapists, medical doctor, dentist,
dietician, midwife), accounting, engineering, small business ownership, administrative fields, the ministry, the military, and one
folklorist.

Over the years, other occupations pursued by family members
have included teaching, construction work, coal mining, office
work, missionary work, social work, working with the food industry, police work, sales, work with government agencies, and
farming. Though the occupations vary, none of the Swenson kin,
with the exception of Christian, who worked in the Dakota coal
mines during the Depression, have worked in the classic "blue
collar" areas of coal mining or factory work. The main reason for
this may be that none of the family has lived for any length of
time in areas of the United States, or in cities, wherein the main
employment depended upon those industries. The Swensons have also
not stayed on the land, a fact influenced by forced migration

during the Depression. As noted, only Per and Oscar of the first
generation, and Orval and Ardmore of the second pursued careers as
farm-ranchers.

Residences have primarily rotated among Washington State,
Minnesota, North and South Dakota, Kansas, Nebraska, Iowa, and
Illinois. Time spent in other areas of the United States by
family members was primarily due to school, the military, and
marriage. Those areas include: Florida, California, Massachusetts, Colorado, Indiana, New York, Texas, Mississippi, Missouri,
Montana, Wisconsin. Some of the second-generation family members
have lived for short periods in foreign countries. Family members
of an age to make such decisions who have completed their educations and military obligations are currently living in an area of
their preference.

A Modified Extended Family

The Swenson family as outlined above fits the description of
"a modified extended family" described by Leslie, following a
hypothesis presented by Eugene Litwak in 1960.[33] Litwak describes
the American family as "a network of visiting, mutual aid, and
emotional support." It may, he says, be easier to maintain inter-
generational continuity today than it was in the past due to a
variety of reasons, including the availability of transportation
and communication networks. In addition, he points out that

"Contemporary norms favoring equal status for all adults in the
family may make it easier for young people to continue relationships with parents, and yet to retain their independence."[34] With
the Swenson family, we see all of these factors at work.

The Swensons, as demonstrated, have maintained contact with
kin through occasional and long-term face-to-face interaction
(visiting, attending college together or near one another, attending funerals and weddings); telephoning at holidays and birthdays;
and correspondence, particularly at Christmas. Leslie's concept
of the modified extended family "assumes that cohesion of the
extended family in the United States is prohibited neither by
occupational nor by geographical mobility."[35] This concept deals
mainly with middle-class families, a change in norms governing aid
to married children (nondependency financially, continuing emotional support), and continued interaction with parents and kin
despite upward mobility.[36]

As a modified extended family, the Swenson family is far from
unique in the north central United States, but, in fact, illustrates a general pattern. This pattern is repeated in any number
of variations with the families who settled in Adams County, North
Dakota.[37] Their connectedness is illustrated with the extensively
organized family reunions planned and attended by a broad network
of kin. With this background and understanding of the Swenson kin
network, we will now take a close look at the organization of and
attendance at their 1978 Swenson Family Reunion.

CHAPTER 6

THE SWENSON FAMILY REUNION, 1978

PLANNING FOR THE REUNION

During the summer of 1976, Norman and Phyllis with three of
their daughters drove to Nebraska on their summer vacation to
visit with Phyllis' parents. They also visited in North Dakota,
and drove from Nebraska down to Lindsborg, Kansas, in order to
spend a few days with Christian and some of his procreative
family. Coincidentally, both my sister Johanna and I were also
visiting our parents in Lindsborg at the time, and our cousin
Mavis Mahlberg came from Kansas City to spend the weekend. My
sisters Anita Berg and Kristine Whetstone were both living with
their procreative families in Lindsborg, so the weekend became a
small family gathering. After dinner on Sunday, this group of
Swensons sat in the living room drinking coffee and catching up on
one another's lives. In the course of this conversation, we also
discussed many of our other Swenson relatives and noted that the
entire group had not been together since Gordon's wedding in 1961.
Thus began the planning for an event that would once again bring
the twenty-one cousins together on one spot.

A tacit agreement to "do" a reunion soon became apparent in
the course of the conversation, and the discussion became one
about a concrete event. Several tentative decisions were made
during that conversation. First, it was decided that if everyone
had two years to plan, they'd have time to rearrange their vacations or whatever else needed arranging in order to attend a
reunion. The reunion would be in 1978. Second, alternative locations were discussed. It was agreed that gathering at the family
homestead in North Dakota would create difficulties for Uncle Per
Gustaf, so that was not an alternative. In addition, everyone
present agreed that it would not be fair to have the reunion too
near any one of the family homes, for instance, in Hettinger,
North Dakota, because certain family members would then feel obligated to serve as hosts and hostesses. With these considerations
in mind, the discussion turned to locations with which family
members were familiar and at which they could combine the reunion
with vacation time. Places considered were the Black Hills, the
Badlands, Colorado, and Minnesota. The decision to have a family
reunion was, as I said, a tacit assumption. The Swensons had not
organized a reunion before, so members present at the Lindsborg
discussion were, presumably, drawing upon common knowledge of such
events in American culture.

Since the conversation had begun with memories of the gathering in 1961, discussion of the "family" to be included in the
reunion was tacitly limited to the immediate descendants of Erik

and Johanna, i.e., the parents and children of the twenty-one
cousins who were together at Gordon's wedding. During the conversation, Norman pointed out that an expansion of the reunion to
include the relatives of Hoffman, Minnesota and Buffalo, South
Dakota would defeat the purpose of getting everybody together by
creating confusion due to the mere numbers of people present and
the more distant relationships. Later on in the preparation for
the reunion, the Hoffman and South Dakota relatives were invited
to attend the last day of the reunion.

The fourth "decision" made during afternoon coffee in
Lindsborg was to appoint Norman to organize the event. When asked
how he got appointed, Norman responded, "I guess someone said,
'Why don't you do it?' and I said yes . . . I figured I was probably the logical person, also . . . I was interested in it, . . .
I've always had an interest in family. . . . My dad [Swen] did,
too."[1]

Because of the numbers of people involved (approximately
seventy at that time) and the distance they would all have to
travel, a fifth decision made that afternoon in Lindsborg was to
plan a weekend-long reunion, rather than a one-day affair. It was
felt that one day would not be enough for seeing everyone in the
family and that people would want to combine the reunion with
their vacations and be able to spend more time together.

Throughout the planning stages of the reunion, and during the
event itself, most decisions were arrived at in a similar manner

to these first five. No votes were taken, although Norman discussed the reunion and aspects of it with all of the Swensons at
some point during the preparations. Norman took the appointment
seriously. He had, in fact, discussed the possibility of a
reunion with Linnea previous to his Kansas visit, so was already
interested in the idea. This discussion with Linnea had taken
place when Norman went to North Dakota for Orval's wedding the
year before; he knew that some of the other Swensons were interested in a reunion as well.[2]

By August of 1976, Norman had sent a letter to his father's
siblings and the members of the second generation for whom he had
acquired addresses, "to determine the extent of interest in a
reunion and to obtain suggestions on time and location." The
letter included his suggestions (as discussed during the Lindsborg
visit) concerning location, length of the event, and date. He
started receiving answers by the end of August.[3]

Meanwhile, in September Norman visited again in North Dakota
to attend Twila's wedding and discussed the reunion with the
various Swensons who lived there and/or were present at the
wedding. Everyone was in favor of the reunion and interested in
having it in the Black Hills. This was a spot most of the kin had
visited before or after summer trips to visit on the family farm
in North Dakota. Norman also discussed the reunion with his
family of orientation, the Washington State branch, during the
early fall and continued to receive enthusiastic letters from

other kin. "Please count us in . . ," ". . . a great idea,"
"Keeping that summer in mind . . ," "We are looking forward to
attending . . ," ". . . almost any arrangement will be fine," "I'm
anxious to hear the plans . . . let me know if I can assist," "We
are in favor . . ," were the common reactions to his suggestions.[4]

During November, 1976, after checking with the American Auto-
mobile Association and the South Dakota Tourist Bureau, Norman
sent letters of inquiry to various resorts and camps in the Hills,
outlining the needs of the group. A Christmas letter from Norman
to the rest of the family gave an update on what was going on and
requested suggestions for the reunion itself. "Think SFR-78"
became the motto somewhere along the line in the correspondence.
Though, as noted in Chapter 5, the family always corresponded at
Christmas, that Christmas (and the next one) brought more Christmas cards than Norman, or anyone else in the family, had ever
received from relatives. The whole network was, indeed, "thinking
SFR-78," looking forward to an event that was two years in the
future. Oscar's wife, Norma, commented that on the cards that
year everyone said something about the reunion. If only to say,
"see you in '78," the entire kin network was demonstrating an
unquestionable enthusiasm for getting together.[5]

Information from the various possible locations for the event
came back to Norman during the spring of 1977. He then contacted
the relatives in North Dakota to see if some of them would be able
to go down to the Black Hills to investigate the accommodations.

During the late spring of 1977, Norman, Phyllis, and some of their
children vacationed in the Black Hills on their way to yet another
wedding in North Dakota (Orven's). After checking with the
various locations he had been corresponding with, Norman decided
on a location that would house many people with both cooking facilities and a restaurant which would be able to serve a banquet.

Why a banquet? "It was discussed at some point." For Norman,
it seemed a logical way to do it, to have at least one planned
get-together each evening. The idea perhaps came up at the
earlier wedding gathering in North Dakota, from a letter, or over
the telephone. Such was the nature of all decisions made during
the planning of the weekend: they "just came up" at some point
over the two years. Carol, for instance, suggested an evening
show of slides (especially old ones) based on her experience at
her husband's family reunion where they had shown old family
movies one evening.[6] Facilitation of any suggestion depended
largely upon an accompanying volunteer to take care of the
arrangements. The gathering in North Dakota during Orven's
wedding in 1977 included discussions of the reunion, and it was
there that several of the planned events were suggested.

In a letter sent out during the fall of 1977, the "final"
plans were outlined, indicating "who has the responsibility for
planning and supervising each activity." The letter included
information about the location and reservation of cabins at the
lodge in the Hills and for the banquet; plans for a Sunday morning

family worship service; a request for each member to bring ten
slides for a Friday night slide show; an appointment of me as
historian; a request for three recipes to be included in a family
cookbook volunteers in Washington were preparing; information
about T-shirts which would be color coded for each branch of the
family, a project cousins in North Dakota had taken charge of; an
announcement about a dance to take place after the banquet on
Saturday night; and a list of "key words [that] may be used to
start an ~~argument~~ discussion [sic] with almost anyone with Swenson
blood." This list was for the benefit of "those not born into the
relationship," and included allusions to such things as the
mountain where Grandpa Erik Swenson was trapped in the avalanche
before leaving Sweden, specific years, numbers, places, horses,
people, and Norwegians. They were, in short, cryptic references
to family history and legend, humor, and "disagreement,"
indirectly referring to aspects of the "family characteristics"--
food for laughter. When I queried Norman about some of the
"controversial subjects" he included in that letter, his responses
referred to assumed family traits and stories:

> . . .
> Norman--Some of the controversy involves people in Hoffman,
> too. Everyone has the true story, because nobody talks
> about anything other than fact.
> GS--the horses?
> Norman--They [our fathers and uncles and aunts] always
> talked about their horses. The horses all had names. Your
> dad [Christian] spent a lot of time when he was young herd-
> ing cattle.
> GS--the dates?

Norman--I don't have any specific reference for those, I
just kind of threw them in. As soon as you throw a date in,
why, some Swenson somewhere would have a story. That's a
family trait. It may be that it's that way with all people
as they get older, but I've never seen a Swenson of the
generation, well, of any generation older than our generation [second], who couldn't remember specifically a date
fifty years ago. And, you know, I take some of those dates
with a grain of salt, but, as I say, they never give anything but fact.
GS--25th wedding celebration in '37?
Norman--There's discussion about who all came and how many
slept in what shed.
GS--Buffalo?
Norman--There are any number of stories told specifically
for the benefit of people who haven't been there. People
who have married into the family. And they normally are
embellished slightly or greatly, depending upon how the
story seems to be going at the time.
GS--Norwegians?
Norman--And, Norwegians. I think--Grandpa was Swedish, and
Norwegians weren't Swedes, so they weren't necessarily at
the same level as the Swedes. I think it probably bothered
him that some of his children married Norwegians. No doubt
about it, Grandpa was Swede--certainly not Norwegian.
Grandma was probably more American. It's funny about the
Swedes. They wanted to be in America, but they still wanted
to be Swedish. When I was growing up in the 30s, it probably was the opposite. Then you were doing everything
possible not to be considered as a Swede. Particularly with
respect to languages. Now it's going the other way.
. . .

Sending in recipes and commenting upon the plans as outlined

in letter number three occupied the space in Christmas cards

during the 1977 season. Also during the winter of 1977-78, the

first controversy about reunion arrangements arose. The contro-

versy concerned the dance which was being organized by some of the

second-generation members of the family who had grown up in North

Dakota.

Certain other members of the second generation felt that the

grandparents (Erik and Johanna) wouldn't have approved of the

family dancing, as they had not allowed it in their home. In
addition, most of the first- and second-generation family members
did not know how to dance. Others also objected to a dance on the
basis of finances, feeling that it was expensive enough to travel
to and rent a cabin in a resort spot, and that a dance was an
unnecessary mixer.

Those objecting to the dance also felt that the dance was
initiated by "outlaws" (in-laws) who didn't know about the
"family" in any case, and that the first-generation elders should
have objected before it was too late. Art Mahlberg, an "outlaw"
himself, commented that those organizing the dance "weren't even
Swensons."[8] Of course, the spouses interested in the dance were
not alone in their interest. Their husbands and wives, mostly
Oscar's sons and daughters, were also enthusiastic about the dance
as a type of "mixer . . . something to do." The Washington branch
of second-generation cousins with older children also felt that a
dance would be fun and give their children something to look forward to--most of them took dancing lessons prior to the reunion.[9]

Swensons who objected to the dance contacted Norman with their
objections, but then left the decision to him. Someone did
suggest that Norman take a vote, although the family had never
done such a thing. Since Norman kept in contact with nearly all
members of the kin group, however, he made a general "tally" that
indicated the vote would be a rather even one, and probably come
out in favor of the dance.

This issue of the dance illustrates an interesting point in
the development of the extended family. Contrary to what might be
expected, the second-generation Swensons who grew up near the
homestead did not maintain the most homogeneity in their marriages, but, rather, the most heterogeneity. Cousins who grew up
in Kansas, Minnesota, and Washington married within a similar, if
not the same, cultural-religious group (see Chapter 5). Several
of the North Dakota cousins, however, married non-Scandinavians
and non-Lutherans, three marrying Catholics of German or Slavic
descent. This is not an unusual situation for the state of North
Dakota, where the population is largely either Lutheran or
Catholic as determined by the settling populations.[10] And, as
pointed out in Chapter 5, the North Dakota cousins stayed in North
Dakota to attend state universities, so met their spouses at
regional, rather than ethnic or religious institutions.

The dance issue served to bring into focus a pattern of cultural adaptation and generational differences within the Swenson
kin. Dancing is a normal activity at any celebration for German
and Slavic cultures, and the cousins who volunteered to organize a
dance were married to German and Slavic Catholics. Again, this is
not to say that they were the only ones interested in a dance.
The cousins with children in high school (mostly the Washington
branch) also were interested in a dance and even took dancing
lessons in preparation. Norman's response to the dance controversy took the generational differences into consideration:

I looked upon this reunion as something that's here and now,
and it's more for the benefit of getting acquainted and
dealing with people where they're at now and not getting it
too enmeshed in tradition. Because, I think it's more
important for people to relate to where they are now,
because they're different. This generation is entirely
different—my kids and some of my younger cousins, too.
Their frame of reference is entirely different than, say,
what mine would be. And, what they do every day is not the
same thing I did at that age. For that reason, when that
[the dance] was suggested by that generation, I felt it was
worthwhile going through with it. Because it was something
they wanted. There was no way, like my kids, want to sit
around and drink coffee and talk all day.[11]

The "controversy" over the dance mainly amounted to a situa-

tion where the family members who were opposed "stated their

minds," and then abided by the decision which was made by Norman.

This form of decision-making proved to be typical for the whole

event. Open conflict was always avoided, and no one ever felt

compelled to hold an election.

During the winter of 1978, final arrangements were made with

the Black Hills Lodge for the weekend of June 23-25, with the

dance band, and for the T-shirts. The T-shirts proved to be a

favorite idea among the Swensons. The idea for T-shirts had

apparently arisen during one of the North Dakota wedding discus-

sions in the previous years. They were designed by Twila and

Orval's wife, Renee. Each shirt pictured a "Viking" male and

female on the front and each individual's name on the back. The

shirts were color coded so that the descendants of, for instance,

Swen, would be wearing yellow, those of Margaret would wear light

blue, and so on.

The Washington branch of the family, meanwhile, was working on
the cookbook: typing recipes, making multiple copies, and binding
the completed work. As well as recipes both humorous and serious,
the cookbook also contained some family jokes, such as an entire
section on mush (gröt, milk and flour porridge), a staple food on
the homestead as the first generation was growing up.

Another issue which arose during the 1978 winter was that some
of the Hoffman, Minnesota, relatives wanted to attend the reunion
and see the Swensons. They expressed this desire when they
attended the funerals of Swen in Seattle and one of Johanna's
brothers in Hoffman previous to the reunion. Again, after phone
conversations with a few of his aunts and uncles, Norman decided
to suggest that the extended relationship attend the reunion on
Sunday (the last day), but that no general invitation would be
issued. As mentioned earlier, this decision was based upon the
confusion that would be caused by large numbers of people and a
consideration for the value of getting to know the closer family
better.

The last letter from Norman before the reunion indicated that
"everything seems to be on schedule." People were reminded to
bring with slides and photos "or whatever you wish for reminiscing
over coffee during the weekend," and it included news about each
of the "organized" events for the weekend. The events of the
weekend itself were, in fact, relatively unplanned. Structured
activities included a slide show Friday night, a banquet and dance

on Saturday night, and a family worship service on Sunday morning.
The cookbook was the only effort to prepare a reunion written
pamphlet; the T-shirts were an unique idea to serve as nametags.
As will be seen, the T-shirts also served as a point of cohesive-
ness during the reunion.

THE SWENSON FAMILY REUNION

The Setting

The reunion took place at the Black Hills State Game Lodge, a
state-run resort near Custer, South Dakota. The Lodge area consisted of the main lodge motel building, a campgrounds to the west
side, cabin area to the east side, and a gift shop with snack bar
beyond the cabin area. Though the area was quite broad, everything was within walking distance. Between the cabins and the
main lodge building was an open field in which stood an old
schoolhouse and a chapel. The Swenson family was spread out over
this entire area: some rented housekeeping cabins, some were in
sleeping cabins, and others set up housekeeping at the campgrounds.

The large housekeeping cabins were situated in such a manner
that a natural gathering place developed near the cabin occupied
by the second-generation procreative families of Oscar's branch.
Since other cabins were further spread out, some along a road, and

other smaller ones, across a creek with only a round-about access,
a grove of trees with picnic tables nearby was an obvious point of
contact. Over the weekend, the area under the trees by the cabin
of Karen, Orven, Carol, Orval, and Twila (with their families)
became a place to stop in order to find out what was going on,
being planned, or just in order to talk.

Another major area of activity developed on the other side of
the Lodge at the campgrounds. There Christian and Anna Marie had
come early and staked claim to an area with their camper. They
were joined by their daughter Kristine Whetstone, with her procreative family; Art Mahlberg, and Arden and Linda Mahlberg--these
all set up a cluster of trailers and tents.

In between the campgrounds and cabins, but off to the cabin
side of the Lodge, Norman and his procreative family resided in
the "schoolhouse," a building stranded out in the middle of a
field. This building was used during the weekend for the slide
show and dance, as well as for coffee gatherings. Plans had been
that this building would serve as a central meeting place throughout the weekend, but it was not used as such except for the formal
gatherings and for some gatherings within Swen's branch of the
family. Any number of reasons may be found for the lack of
interest in gathering at the schoolhouse. For one thing, going to
the schoolhouse meant walking out of the shade in the heat of the
open sun. More importantly, the two clusterings near the cabins
and at the campgrounds were in the midst of a group of weekend

"homes," whether campers or cabins. Coffee was close at hand on
each stove and more people were nearby. In addition, the cluster
around the housekeeping cabins was located next to the cabin where
three newborns (Karen's, Carol's, Orval's) were staying, and near
the cabins where other very young children were housed with their
parents. Gathering here was perhaps a point in deference to the
mothers of very young children who were not as free to roam about
as were others of the family.

The "coffee-ing" and visiting, though undertaken at every
opportunity in any and every location where Swensons were located,
mostly rotated between these two main areas. Various groupings of
individuals would occasionally go over to the "other side" to see
what was happening and stay for coffee or meals or else segment
off with new groupings for excursions. Family members on their
way to go sightseeing checked "at the cabins" and "at the campgrounds" before heading off to Mt. Rushmore or other tourist
attractions in case anyone at those locations cared to join them.

Meals were eaten at the campsite, in the large housekeeping
cabins, and at the Lodge snack bar. During the daytime, groups
who were out sightseeing in the Hills would, of course, eat wher-
ever they happened to be at mealtime. In general, meals were
spent within individual branches. Often, however, branches or
pieces of branches combined to eat together. Christian's and
Margaret's branches, for instance, who were centered at the campgrounds, placed themselves and their food out together on one

large picnic table. Branches at the cabins and schoolhouse also combined meals during the weekend, and various people were urged to share meals with others, particularly lone members such as Per or those who did not accompany their immediate families on excursions. If wandering Swensons met at the snack bar or restaurant, they would join one another as a matter of course. There was no particular pattern or specific gathering for meals beyond a tendency to gather within the branches.

The Friday night banquet took place at the Lodge snack bar (west of the cabins), and the dance in the schoolhouse basement. Little activity was directly related to the main Lodge building, though some of the reunionites went there for a drink or an occasional meal.

In all, the arrangement was casual, with no predetermined realms. Since everyone was in charge of securing his or her own lodging, the determination of who would be neighbors was in the hands of the unbiased Lodge reservation desk, except for the campground arrangement. Sibling units often made living arrangements together, sharing cabins or sharing cooking facilities in one cabin.

This arrangement allowed for a nonforced mixture of branches and a comfortable set of reunions within the larger reunion. There were several types of reunions taking place over the weekend, reunions which were as important to many of the family members as was the larger reunion. The various second-generation

members reunited with their families of orientation (adult siblings) as did the first generation in the broader group. The
Swenson Family Reunion 1978, was, for instance, the first gathering of three new third-generation first cousins in Oscar's branch.
The Washington State branch (Swen's) which is spread out between
Washington, California, and Iowa, also united with a new fourth-
generation offspring, two new spouses, and a relatively new third-
generation cousin. Margaret's branch also gathered for the
enjoyment of a first third-generation member and a new in-law.
First cousins within the third generation (Norman's and Norris'
children, for instance) were getting reacquainted as were the
first cousins of the second generation (Norman's and Norris' first
cousins).

I, for instance, personally welcomed the opportunity to see my
family of orientation and arranged to meet my parents a day early.
Though I had a separate sleeping cabin, I ate several of my meals
with "my" family down at the campgrounds and used the time to gain
fresh contact with my rapidly growing nieces and nephews, in addition to doing the same with my first cousins and their children.
I also took the opportunity to spend time with Arden, a cousin
with whom I had developed a close relationship during our college
years, and with Karen, Ardelle, and Mavis, cousins who had gone to
college in Lindsborg, Kansas, while I was growing up there.

Others did the same. Cousins who had spent time together
during college had little reunions of their own, catching up on

people and events related to their shared experiences. The first-
generation Swensons took advantage of the weekend to have a breakfast together without the "children"--something they had done over
the years whenever all or pieces of the kin group gathered, often
as a celebration for the several wedding anniversaries of the 1941
and 1942 marriages.

The multilocal and nonregimented physical arrangement for the
reunion events was important in facilitating a proliferation of
reunions and creating a sense of "neighboring" which prevailed
throughout the planned and unplanned time. The fact of being
somewhat spread out did, perhaps, lessen the accessibility of
family members to one another, but the visiting back and forth
compensated for this to a great extent. Interestingly, the
arrangement of Christian's and Margaret's branches together at the
campgrounds and the North Dakota branches at the cabins provided
an unplanned simulation of the geographical arrangement of the kin
network during the years when Christian's and Margaret's families
were centered in Minnesota, Swen's was in Washington State, and
the others were in North Dakota. Twila commented in notes after
the reunion that it seemed that people who already knew each other
the best seemed to spend the most time together.[12]

Without being planned, these reunions within the reunion were
partially aided by the living arrangements. Mavis Mahlberg noted
that it was difficult to plan events during the day since everything happened spontaneously--every time she started to get a

group together, other people would drop by and new conversations
and excursions would begin.[13] As the weekend progressed, she
decided that there was no point in trying to organize things, and
that the relaxed interchanges were actually more enjoyable. The
situation Mavis fought was, again, partially due to the living
arrangements—there was no central meeting place, but relaxed
wandering. The family members who seemed to be the least comfortable with this nonplanned arrangement were some of the in-laws who
were used to more organized family gatherings. Wayne Hintz, who
had organized his own family's reunion, felt this was the distinguishing feature of the Swenson gathering, something he had to
adjust to.[14]

The Beginnings

Armed with a giant shot of penicillin intended to ward off a
recently diagnosed case of strep throat, I headed south from
Hettinger across the "gumbo flats" sheep country of South Dakota
on the morning of Wednesday, 21 June 1978. While I waited for a
herd of sheep to cross the highway, McDonald's was saluting
America's families on the radio. "Whatever roots we have, they're
growing side by side," they assured me, offering the opportunity
to "Win a Family Reunion meal" in a drawing (see Chapter 1). An
auspicious omen for the weekend, I thought.

The Swenson Family Reunion was scheduled to begin on Friday; I was going to the reunion site on Wednesday in order to familiarize myself with the Lodge area and talk to some of the Lodge employees. I also scheduled a rendezvous with my parents at the Lodge on Wednesday evening, so that I would have a chance to spend some time with them without the complications of the whole gathering and my preoccupation with research. I spent Wednesday night in my parents' trailer and moved into my cabin Thursday forenoon, expecting to have most of the day to myself, with my parents, and contemplating fieldwork. The Swensons' eagerness to see one another and, as with myself, to get settled in so they could spend as much time as possible with everyone, changed my plans for Thursday.

Though the Swenson Family Reunion was scheduled to begin on Friday, many of the family members began to arrive at the Custer Lodge on Thursday afternoon. Locating cabins and back-and-forth visiting began immediately. When I left my cabin to visit my parents' trailer at 3:30 p.m., the campground was already set up, and the Mahlbergs were at the trailer for afternoon coffee. Norman's family arrived shortly afterward, and they were followed by part of the Forthun branch.

First meetings between relatives often took place near the Lodge as people came in to register, and some family members "staked out" near the Lodge to see kin as they arrived. Conversations included warm greetings and hugs, questions about

infirmities and illnesses, and queries about new babies and
spouses. While some family members preoccupied themselves with
setting up housekeeping and making much ado over the new babies
and new grandparents, others took advantage of Thursday afternoon
to do their sightseeing in the Black Hills before the weekend got
under way.

By Thursday evening, sections of each branch of the family had
arrived and were going through the ice-breaking of reacquainting
themselves one with the other. Cousins who hadn't seen each other
since Gordon's wedding in 1961 tried to guess who was who and
sometimes mixed branches in their guessing. In the evening, most
of the Swensons gathered at the campgrounds for coffee and conversation, which ranged from "What are you doing now?" to a discussion about overfed Swenson babies who "had to fight baby fat all
their lives."

Later in the evening, some of the second- and third-generation, particularly those of Swen's branch, gathered at the
schoolhouse where Norman and his family were staying. During
these gatherings, Twila began to distribute the T-shirts. As they
were passed around, jokes about wearing the same shirt for four
days passed around with them. Rumors also circulated about
whether or not we could have a one-hundred-percent turnout--some
members in Iowa hadn't been sure they could make it. Other topics
of conversation included "how good Grandma looked," and other
catching-up information concerning school, marriages, births,
deaths, and the like.

The first planned event of the reunion was not scheduled until
Friday night, but Friday day saw a great deal of activity throughout the Lodge area. More arrivals were happily greeted, and it
soon became known throught the network that everyone was going to
come. At breakfast on Friday, I attended one of the many
"reunions within the reunion," which were already taking place.
Margaret's branch and Christian's branch, who had grown up near
each other in Minnesota, shared breakfast at Christian's trailer
and discussed family characteristics—something particularly
interesting to Arden Mahlberg's new wife, as she was just being
introduced to the Swenson kin. Anna Marie (Christian's wife)
explained to her the amount of Swedishness in the family, noting
that her family and Mahlbergs were the only "purebloods," the
others having been tainted with Norwegianness. She and Linda then
did a run-down of the percentage of Norwegians among the spouses
(Linda is half-Swedish, half-Polish). Anna Marie also pointed out
that there were no separations in the family, perhaps because no
one (except, recently, Norris' girls) had been married before age
twenty. To which Arden Mahlberg commented: "I just assume I'm
not going to get divorced. I'm just used to that. None of the
Mahlbergs are divorced either."[15]

Spurred on by the current news that Per Gustaf had finally
hooked up the plumbing system at the homestead in honor of the
reunion, Christian recounted some stories about the homestead
bathing facilities. Arrival of Paul Mahlberg at the table stirred

up a conversation about the variety of Swedish pancake recipes
which could be found at the reunion and anecdotes about making
pancakes. This topic led to the discussion of other family
recipes and their origins, as well as the telling of anecdotes
about cooking disasters--all humorous in nature.

After breakfast, clumps of people started wandering about to
discover what was planned for the day or to form groups for sightseeing. Some of the Swensons went in to Custer to pick up people
at the airport or to shop for groceries to get them through the
weekend. The schoolhouse was open with a large coffeepot brewing
throughout the day, so many people at least stopped in there to
pause in the cool basement and say hello to whomever was around.

I took this opportunity to interview my cousin Norman in the
schoolhouse basement, where the temperature was fifteen to twenty
degrees cooler than it was outside. Other cousins and my parents
wandered in. One piece of the chatter sounded like this:

                . . .
        "Here comes the new baby."
        "Ardelle?"   [Ardelle is 32 years old]
        "How are you?"
        "Are Seattle people here?"
        "How far is Billings?"   [where Carol and Wayne
                                    Hintz live]
        "Anita and Jack just came."
        "They drove all night."
        "What's your cabin number?"
        "There's coffee upstairs."
        "My goodness, you'll have to come to my house to
            get a band-aid on it."
        "How many people have brought slides?"
        "Mahlbergs brought some films, too."
        . . .16

By Friday afternoon, the T-shirts had already made an impression
throughout the Lodge area and were drawing comments and inquiries
from non-Swensons who saw them. They served as flags. Anyone
wandering about wondering what was going on or where someone was
could spot the brightly-colored yellow, maroon, green, light blue,
orange, or navy blue shirts down the path, grouped around a table,
or sitting on a porch.

The T-shirts, as Mavis commented to me later, served to help
create "an instant identification plus a common bond and something
to talk about with strangers."[17] They certainly helped to accent
the feeling of being a group which was already becoming apparent
by Friday evening. The shirts also served as nametags and provided moments of humor. Family members would see other T-shirts
coming and turn around so they could back up to "introduce"
themselves (the names were printed on the backs of the shirts).
"Where are all the yellow shirts," one youngster was overheard
asking his mother at suppertime.

The Slide Show

Friday evening after supper, planned activities for the
Swenson reunion began with the slide show suggested by Carol
during the planning stages. This event was billed by Norman as
"Friday Night at the Movies"; each family unit had been requested
to bring ten slides for the show. Several of the North Dakota

cousins saw to it that popcorn was available, and Linnea brought
freshly-picked and cleaned strawberries and homemade doughnuts for
coffeetime following the slides.

The entire group, except for Mildred and Norris' procreative
family, who arrived Saturday morning, gathered in the basement of
the schoolhouse, sharing the discomfort of close quarters and midsummer heat. One had the feeling of being inside a bubble gum
machine--the bright colors of the T-shirts were scattered throughout the room, with some groupings of single colors, particularly
among the teenagers and young adults. Since the teenage group
consisted mainly of first cousins of the third generation in
Swen's branch, they often were a splash of yellow among more mixed
colors. The new members, most of them in Oscar's branch, also
created a color block on one side of the basement. Throughout the
evening there was a constant, distinguishable level of chatter--
these people were not hesitant to speak with one another and were,
in fact, taking advantage of the situation to catch up with one
another. The level of chatter was so constant from all parts of
the room that it is impossible to separate and understand more
than one or two comments on the tape which I ran throughout the
evening. No one person held the floor at any time.

While the slides were being set up, the Washington cousins
handed out cookbooks to each attending Swenson, and Norman in-
formed the group that $4.00 from each adult family member would
cover the organizational costs of the reunion. The cookbooks then

served as the focus of conversation here and there throughout the
room until the slides began. One small controversy arose, for
instance, between Christian and Linnea about a recipe for the
Christmas cheese, which I had recorded from Christian and submitted for the book. Recipes ranged from excerpts from Grandmother Johanna's cookbook, to personal specialities, to family
jokes, to humorous recipes gleaned from individual experiences.
Karen Gabrielson, for instance, who had lived in Africa and Saudi
Arabia, submitted a recipe for elephant stew (calling for one
whole elephant and one optional squirrel). Per Gustaf submitted
three recipes for <u>gröt</u> (mush), one that consisted of only water
and flour; Oscar submitted a recipe for <u>hundsgröt</u> (dog's mush),
which is basically inedible even for a dog. The fact that the
cookbook included a whole section for <u>gröt</u> was itself a family
joke, as mush was frequently eaten on the homestead, and even the
second generation had grown up eating an occasional bowl of milk
mush--a special treat with butter, sugar, and cinnamon. In any
case, the cookbook was appreciated by everyone in the family, and
read with relish.

Norman used the time before the slides began to make announce-
ments: the schoolhouse would be open Saturday with a coffeepot
going; the banquet Saturday would be a pay-at-the-door affair; and
we wouldn't know what plans for the Sunday service were until
Norris arrived. The only instructions for the slide show were
that whoever brought the slide had to comment on it.

Slides shown during the evening ranged in content from old
pictures taken at the Swenson homestead when the second-generation
cousins were young, to pictures of the cities wherein some of the
relatives were currently living and working. Some of the kin who
in recent years have visited the relatives in Sweden showed slides
of the Swenson-Erikson home place in Tännäs and of the surviving
family members still living on the place.

Folklorists have commented on the value of old pictures for
calling up memories, legends, and other folkloric pieces of
people's lives.[18] They serve as well to give concrete views to a
feeling of continuity within the extended kinship network. In-
laws and third-generation Swensons seemed to especially enjoy
seeing pictures of their spouses or parents as children, and the
slides most appreciated in general were those of the homestead
surroundings when the second generation was young. The cousins
from North Dakota had managed to bring a wide variety of slides
from Uncle Gus' (Per Gustaf) collection. These slides covered the
years when Erik was yet alive and his children were visiting the
homestead on a regular basis with their procreative families.
Many giggles and hoots of laughter accompanied slides of "the
kids" in winter hats out in the barn, sitting in a haystack, or
dressed up in Grandpa's oldtime swimming suit from the attic.

The slide show was as spontaneous as was the entire reunion.
No attempt was made to present a family history or to explain the
family jokes and references indicated in the slides that often

brought roars from sections of the audience. Explanation for the
uninformed newer family members presumably was left to individuals, and there was a constant level of chatter during the slides
which contained comments and explanations to spouses and children.

Some of the Swensons who had brought slides offered commentary
to their parts of the show. Norman, for instance, showed slides
of "seventeen years ago" (Gordon's wedding, when last the twenty-
one cousins had been together in one place). "As you recall," he
quipped, apologizing for the poor quality of the slide, "it was a
hot Nebraska day, and no one would stand in the sun, so, conse-
quently, none of the pictures are very good, but I brought a
couple of them anyway. You'll probably recognize yourself even if
you can't recognize anybody else."[19]

Christian showed a slide of "Uncle Gus [Per Gustaf] _trying_ to
get nieces and nephews to line up to take a picture--on the north
side of the farmhouse."[20] Commentaries such as these held "inside
jokes" for those of the audience who had been in the family long
enough to understand that they were comments on recognized
tendencies to stubbornness within the group--something purportedly
inherited especially from Erik. This slide also brought memories
of the bachelor uncle struggling with masses of nieces and nephews
--a comic situation. Innuendos such as these, though present
throughout the weekend, became particularly apparent during the
slide show, where one slide was enough to send people into howls
of knowing laughter, and you could hear unknowing newer family
members wonder why it was so funny.

Another slide from the 1961 gathering was shown by Christian;
it was of "PG, Freddy, Mr. Carlson, Oscar, Norman, and Art--look-
ing, I think, at the pigs." This comment created an uproar of
laughter, first of all because they _were_ looking at the pigs, and
then, because Norman quipped, "Or vice versa."[21]

Family anecdotes, legends, and nostalgic memories of those
deceased were all conjured up during the evening. A slide of the
mountain Brattereit in Härjedalen, Sweden, brought to mind the
story of the avalanche Erik had lived through just before he had
left Sweden--an episode for which he had received a medal of brav-
ery, but in which he had lost his best friend and cousin. Linnea
brought slides of the relatives "down in Buffalo" (South Dakota),
the offspring of Johanna's sister Anna, a tough lady who had homesteaded in utterly desolate sheep country and raised two children.
One of these children, first cousin to the first generation, had
become a legend on her own by raising twelve children in a one-
room house, also in that sheep country. Norman asked, "Does
everyone know about Buffalo?" This all led to a great deal of
giggling, as Linnea set out to identify each and every one of the
Buffalo kin on the screen, ending with: "You haven't been to
South Dakota until you've been _there_ . . ."[22]

Other slides included pictures of the first-generation's
uncles and aunts, Erik's and Johanna's brothers and sisters, with
whom the first generation had been close as they were growing up.
A few slides of Erik were shown, including one which has become

somewhat of a family icon: it was the last picture taken of him;
he is in his work clothes, sitting on the tractor mount out in the
field drinking his coffee at coffeetime.   Such pictures were a
concrete representation for the Swensons present, particularly
those who had never known Erik, and family members were conscious-
ly aware of the importance they could attach to them.   Norris, for
instance, commented to me later that it was sad that his children
and grandchildren would never have an experience of this family
founder except through such things as that picture and stories
they might hear.[23]

Two assumptions were made by the people who brought slides.
The first, most obvious was that the audience would be a group of
people who held common references and understandings.   "Seventeen
years ago" would be understood, "Brattereit" would conjure up a
family legend, and the stubbornness which prevented a good slide
from being taken would serve as apology.

The second assumption had to do with the good will and interest of the audience in other family members.   Some of the slides
portrayed the places people were presently living and things they
were doing.   Other slides showed the recent dwellings and activities of Swen previous to his death.   In general, the slide show,
coupled with the earlier greetings and meals of the day, served to
provide the means for an initial tender of recognition and shared
memories.   References and responses demonstrated during the slide
show showed an assumption that the viewing group was a composite,

linked to other groups (the relatives in Sweden, Buffalo, or Hoffman), but at the same time a separate entity.

Following the slide show, the Swensons wandered upstairs to drink coffee, talk, and partake of Linnea's doughnuts and strawberries. People were occupied with general visiting until a small crisis shook them up. I was visiting with my cousin Norris' daughter Krista, and her new husband, and some of Norman's daughters when a ripple of alarm made its way across the room. The crowd drifted to the doorway, where we'd heard Mavis Mahlberg calling for her brother Paul. The bachelor uncle, Per Gustaf, had fallen down the basement stairs as he was preparing to leave the schoolhouse. As he hadn't been in the best of health, this fall created a great deal of consternation, particularly among his nephews and nieces, since many of the first generation had already retired for the night. Paul, a medical student, and some of the nurses in the family attended to him, and he was shuttled off to the hospital in Rapid City.

After the initial shock, family members lingered in the schoolhouse worrying over Uncle Gus and discussing the problems created by the fact that he yet lived out on the home farm by himself. As I learned later, conversations during the late evening generally centered about these problems, a topic spurred on by the accident. My sister Johanna and I went to the campgrounds to inform my father, Christian, of his brother's fall, then returned to the Lodge area in order to call the hospital and see how things were. At the Lodge we met two of our first cousins who were doing the same thing. After being assured that Uncle Gus had only broken his wrist, and that he could return to the Lodge on the following day, everyone relaxed and spread the news.

This small crisis served to increase the feeling of sharedness. The accident was a shared concern: especially since Per has no children, his welfare was the business of everyone. Second-generation Swensons were concerned both for their uncle and for the effect the accident and worry would have upon their parents, his brothers and sisters. The accident also had an effect upon family interaction. Paul and the nurses were put on the spot by being asked to administer aid to a family member. During the following days, a certain amount of attention was shifted from the new babies to the injured uncle.

A Little Community

On Saturday morning the last carload of Swensons arrived from Iowa, including with them Jeremy Schlee, the one fourth-generation offspring of Erik and Johanna. This arrival brought with it a one-hundred-per-cent attendance for the reunion--something which became a source of amazement and pride for family members during the reunion and in discussions following the event. Full attendance also set a rather formidable precedent and created

speculation concerning the possibility of such a thing occurring
at future reunions.

By Saturday, a little community had been set up throughout the
Lodge grounds. Reunionites knew where everyone's cabin was and
would lounge about on porches or under the trees while others
wandered about stopping in here and there for coffee and conversation. During the morning, several carloads of Swensons went
sightseeing. Again, "reunions within the reunion" took place
throughout the day, and nuclear families spent time together as
they would have on a vacation.

Just before noon, Fred Forthun and Christian drove into Rapid
City to retrieve Per, complete with a cast on his arm. When he
returned to his cabin, Art Mahlberg moved in with him from his
camper, and other Swensons stopped over to see him during afternoon coffeetime.

Groups who went sightseeing would include anyone wearing any
color T-shirt who wished to go to see the same attractions. The
sightseers were mainly the young adults, especially those who had
never been to the Black Hills and those with young children who
had not been to the Hills, while the campgrounds and cabins were
bases during the day for older members of the family and very
young children. Space in the field by the schoolhouse was used
for whiffle ball and frisbie flying, while some Swensons went
fishing, bird watching, or just hiking.

Conversations throughout the community ranged from the mystery
about Grandmother Swenson (there had been no slides of her on
Friday night) to radial tires. I overheard two male in-laws commenting to each other about the physical similarity of the group,
specifically noticing the "well-built female cousins." Some wandering parties joined for a lunch of buffaloburgers at the inn,
some cooked in their cabins or campgrounds, and others ate at
sightseeing locations.

The T-shirts continued to make a splash in the general Lodge
area. Park rangers at Mt. Rushmore startled Mildred by calling
her name (prominently printed on her back) as she stood in line
for a hot dog. She had to go through a complete explanation of
what "all those T-shirts" were about. Wayne Hintz was interviewed
by the Rapid City radio station as he stood in a similar line, and
a gift shop clerk asked Orval how she could get one of the T-
shirts. Orval gave her a list of the unmarried males in the kinship group.

I spent the day wandering from place to place throughout the
Lodge area: looking at pictures with Uncle Oscar, visiting with
Ardelle on the porch of the Forthuns' cabin, catching up on what
was happening with Arden Mahlberg, having coffee with my sister
and her procreative family, getting some pop for Uncle Gus and
Uncle Art, and finding whomever I could to talk with. Others were
doing the same. An example of groups wandering and joining happened at noon, when my mother (Anna Marie) and I decided to walk

to the inn for a buffaloburger. At the inn we bumped into my
cousin Norris, his wife, Grayce, daughter Laurie, and grandson,
Jeremy Schlee, so we all shared a table. Norris discussed with us
his plans for the Sunday service, and we discussed the slide show,
noting the lack of pictures of Grandma Swenson. Some time was
then spent trying to decide which year she died and determine how
old her children were--wondering how they would have been affected
by her death. We also discussed the ages of Margaret and Swen
when they died. For Norris, of course, this all had bearing on
the memorial service he was planning for Sunday. We also discussed changes in the Church that had worried his father (Swen) in
his later years and worried over Uncle Gus' fall and the fact that
he was yet alone on the farm, in addition to chatting about what
each of us were currently occupying our time with.

Though most of the activities undertaken throughout Saturday
were no different from things done on any typical family vacation,
there was one main difference between the reunion as a vacation
and a vacation spent by individual nuclear families. This difference was the accessibility of kin--the planned, organized accessibility of kin. Seattle and Kansas relatives were not 3,000 miles
distant, but just down the road, in the same car on the way to the
Reptile Gardens, or sharing coffee at the campgrounds. Even the
cousins who lived in Saudi Arabia were available. The importance
of the reunion seemed to be, in fact, not that each member of the
family managed or even attempted to have a conversation with each

and every one of the relatives, but that such conversations were
possible since everyone was in the same place at the same time.
This arrangement, as mentioned in the planning stages, was a prime
reason for staging the reunion in the first place—to repeat what
had happened seventeen years earlier at a wedding in Nebraska. At
the same time that the main purpose of the event was to gather the
kin, however, the location and loose arrangements allowed family
members to include their family vacations in the weekend's activities if they so desired or needed to. This situation may have had
some bearing on the one-hundred-percent attendance, and certainly
did have bearing on the proliferation of reunions within the
reunion. The event was not a vacation that happened to be a
reunion. It was a reunion specifically planned to be at a vacation spot in order to provide group activities—much like volley-
ball serves as a group activity at a one-day reunion.

The Formal Evening

At dusk on Saturday, the Swensons disappeared into cabins and
campers to prepare for the "formal" event of the reunion: the
banquet and dance. This meal was served buffet-style at the
Lodge's inn; it was a standard roast beef dinner, chosen from the
Lodge menu by Norman because of the reasonable cost.[24] Groupings
primarily of nuclear families wandered into the inn over a period
of approximately twenty to thirty minutes and situated themselves

at tables in a less random fashion than that in which they had
grouped for daytime activities. Many people did not appreciate a
suggestion that relatives who saw each other frequently should not
sit together, and everybody ignored any possibility of seating
arrangements. Whole branches did not sit together, but nuclear
residential families did, particularly those with young children.
Other cousins scattered, but did not separate from their spouses.

On one table, the Forthun family had placed a flower arrangement brought down from their florist shop. This table, except for
Norman and his procreative family, remained empty until the last
stragglers came in and occupied the only seats available. No one,
apparently wanted to sit at what might have been considered the
"head table."

I found myself at a table with Norris, Grayce, Gordon, and
Edith. Norris proceeded to make mockery of my ever-present micro-
phone by doing an inventory of the relish tray. He then told
"Finnlander" jokes (jokes on the Finns from the Swede's perspec-
tive) from northern Minnesota. Later in the evening, Ardmore
Forthun came over from his table and swapped Norwegian jokes with
Norris.[25]

Before serving the banquet, Norman began what were to be the
only "official" proceedings of the weekend. He greeted everyone,
thanked everyone for the efforts in planning specific events, and
announced Sunday's worship service and a gathering for picture-
taking previous to it. A letter from one of the cousins in Sweden

which contained genealogical information was read, as was a letter
of greeting from the governor of North Dakota. Several people
registered surprise at the letter from the Governor, but no one
seemed overly impressed. Norman suggested that we might consider
the organization of another reunion in five years--a time period
that had been "discussed" by various family members. No action
was taken on this matter except for individual conversations
during and after dinner among various of the Swensons. This pro-
cedure followed the course of other family decisions as demonstrated in the organization of the reunion itself--large-group
interaction was a result of general agreements arrived at in a
number of smaller-group discussions. By the end of the weekend,
the "general agreement" and, indeed, understanding, was that the
next planned reunion was to be in 1983 and would be organized by
one of five or six second-generation cousins who would volunteer
at the proper time.

     When Norman had finished his announcements, Orval, who had
aided with the planning, presented Norman with a gift of apprecia-
tion from the rest of the Swensons, along with a card containing
the following "thank you":

          Norman Eric the notable scribe,
          chosen leader of the Swenson tribe,
          Has diligently strived to get us all together
          To a family reunion for worse or for better.
          We have all looked forward to a joyful time,
          But believe me it's hard to get words to rhyme.
          And so without any further ado
          Here's a great big "Thank you" from us all to You.

During dinner, conversations covered a full range of family
and current events, but there was still no attempt to relate a
family history or take care of family business. The sounds were
of genial chatter and laughter. Some family members roamed about
with cameras. Though the inn staff seemed particularly eager to
clear out the dining area, various Swensons lingered talking and
only slowly left the premises, killing time until the dance and
coffeetime would begin. Others went off to put their children to
sleep or make arrangements with baby-sitters who had come in from
Rapid City.

A slight disagreement arose over the baby-sitting arrangements
among the couples involved. Some of the North Dakota cousins had
made arrangements with cousins on the other side of their family
to sit for the various families of young children. Somehow or
other, a firm agreement had not been reached earlier with the
parents, and some did not want sitters but were obligated to pay
for them in any case. This disagreement was indirectly related to
the issue of whether or not to have a dance, which had been the
one disagreement during the planning stages of the reunion. Some
family members had wondered what parents of pre-school children
would do during the dance and did not like the idea of leaving
their children with strangers. As with the previous disagreement,
however, this argument was never blown up into an all-out quarrel
or all-family concern. Many of the young children did join the
dance; actually they were the members who got things rolling.

The dance was held in the basement of the schoolhouse. The
upstairs area was used for mingling, with a coffeepot going as
usual for the Swenson events. Here some of the younger members of
the family took advantage of the presence of the first generation
to ask questions about family stories and history, and cousins
took advantage of the gathering to discuss things ranging from the
Equal Rights Amendment to their current occupations (or my dissertation). Arden Mahlberg, for instance, took this opportunity to
have a discussion with Oscar about his mother, Margaret, who had
died when he was only twelve. He also talked with Oscar about our
grandmother Swenson, who remains a mystery to her grandchildren,
and they even discussed Arden's classification as conscientious
objector during the Vietnam era.[26] At the same time, I was in a
heated discussion with my cousin Norris about women's rights,
pacifism, and the starving in Biafra--a discussion which ended
when I dragged Norris downstairs and onto a dance floor for the
first time in his life (something for which his wife and daughters
were gratefully amused). Twila and Wayne Hintz brought in a
bottle of schnapps to put on the coffee table, but this created no
disturbance and was shared by a few other family members. The
presence of alcohol was, however, an unusual occurrence for
Swenson gatherings, as was the dance itself.

As the family members entered the schoolhouse, Per Gustaf,
with his cast and a pen, waited at the door so that each reunionite could sign the cast. His cast then became the "official guest

list" of the reunion. He and several of the other first-generation Swensons retired for the night shortly after the dance began,
so the dance was largely attended by second- and third-generation
Swensons. Some of the first generation, however, did stay for
some time and were pulled out onto the dance floor by their children, nieces, nephews, and grandchildren.

The first few minutes of the dance were rather uncomfortable.
Most family members did not know how to dance, and several of them
had not wanted a dance to be included in the reunion. As the
evening turned out, however, the dance proved to be a time enjoyed
by most of the kin. Observers reported that the dance didn't
really start until some of the younger children got out and
started "wiggling around." This broke the ice, and thereafter
there was general participation, with a great deal of joking back
and forth about someone's "first dance" or "original" step.

During the evening, splinter groups went off for conversation
and a drink up at the Lodge or dropped by cabins to visit with
other relatives who were not at the dance, but everyone stopped
into the schoolhouse for a while to spend time upstairs or downstairs with the general group.

A few second- and third-generation cousins stayed in the
schoolhouse to clean up and talk after the dance. The conversations at this late hour varied. Mark Zidon, for instance, was
curious to know why I could dance, since it didn't seem to be a
"family activity," and he quizzed me about my occupation. Others

discussed why people had come to the reunion in the first place
and who should organize the next one. That the next one should be
in five years was already tacitly understood, and speculations
about who should organize it were narrowing down to five or six of
the older second-generation cousins. Various resort areas were
discussed as possible locations.

All in all, the formal evening, though at first less comfortable than daytime activities had been, and though it carried the
possibility of family quarrels, turned out to be enjoyed by most
everyone. The dance, after the initial awkwardness, broke down a
few more of the markers of distance between the relatives by
serving as one more "we're in this together and may as well enjoy
it" event. Placing the Swensons together physically in one room
also increased the amount of contact with a wider variety of the
reunionites.

Swensons who had objected to the idea of the dance either
participated in the activities or used the time to visit. One
interesting aspect of the disagreement over the dance is the argument that it was not a "Swenson thing to do," or would not have
been approved of by the Swenson grandparents, Erik and Johanna.
Several of the family who had objected to the dance met at times
with relatives over a drink at the Lodge. Drinking is also not a
"Swenson thing to do"--especially not a thing of which Erik and
Johanna would have approved. The difference lay in that a planned
event obligated at least monetary involvement and implied an

obligation to participate with the rest of the family. Visiting
over a drink, on the other hand, was a matter of personal choice.
Another aspect to this apparent disparity of action and word is
the tendency noted earlier for Swensons to deal with small-group
interaction more freely and willingly than large-group interaction. Attitudes and modes of interaction such as these certainly
set the tone of family reunions, as they do of any gathering. In
the case of the Swenson family, the sharedness of some attitudes
and values were demonstrated and amplified by the mass gathering.

The Worship Service

> "How do we sing a song of the Lord in a foreign land?"
>   Psalm 137:4

The scheduled event on Sunday was a family worship service in
the morning. Norris, a minister as was his father, had been put
"in charge" of the service together with Mavis, a musician. Previous to the reunion, Norris had planned a memorial service but
had not contacted Mavis because he was afraid she would not want
to do that type of service. Mavis, on the other hand, wondered
just what they were going to do, so had contacted Norris just
before the reunion, and the two of them met together on Saturday
in order to organize the service and find out what facilities were
available. It is unclear why Norris worried that there would be

disagreement from his younger cousins concerning the theme of the
service; perhaps he assumed the age difference would cause differing expectations. In any case, his worry was needless, as Mavis
and a couple of the other cousins involved in the service readily
agreed with Norris' organization and worked the musical numbers
into his plan.

Before the service began, a spur-of-the-moment event took
place. It had occurred to someone on Saturday night that we
should have the opportunity to have the whole group together at
some point in order to take pictures. On Saturday night, the word
was spread that everyone should gather in their T-shirts previous
to the morning service. The entire clan gathered outside of the
chapel on Sunday morning in general pandemonium with quantities of
cameras, each wearing his "flag."

Pictures were taken of each major branch, of the first generation with and without their spouses, of the twenty-one second-
generation cousins, of people taking pictures or milling about,
and of the entire seventy-three-person ensemble. While pictures
were being taken, family members moved about laughing and talking,
picking up cameras and taking shots of whomever was posing and of
some who weren't. The mood was of a reluctance to part, a
lingering with one another.

After the photography session, Joanne's procreative family
from California left for their long drive home. The Swensons then
started to move into the chapel for the service. As the result of

a back-and-forth discussion about whether to meet inside the
rather small chapel or out in the shade of the building, the organ
was halted in mid-move and returned to the chapel through unoffi-
cial persuasion from the group to meet indoors. The family wanted
to be close together despite the beginning of a very warm day.

Norris had constructed the memorial service to the grandparents and two deceased members of the first generation, Swen and
Margaret, because he felt "that's why we're all together." The
service was built around a historical progression of hymns. The
construction followed from the strong tradition of hymn-singing
most of the Swensons had grown up with in the Swedish Lutheran
church. The congregation began with two of the old Swedish hymns
which "the forebears brought with them." Though very few, if any,
of the second- and third-generation Swensons speak Swedish, the
entire group joined in the singing.

The worship service, answering the question of the Psalmist,
"How do we sing a song of the Lord in a foreign land?"[27] proceeded
to illustrate changes in the service over the years. "The Swedish
immigrants asked the same question," Norris commented. "Their
children wanted to sing in the 'new' native tongue." Hymns from
the old Augustana (Swedish) Lutheran Church hymnal--translations
of Swedish hymns--were then sung, followed by "O Beautiful for
Spacious Skies," because "It is in this country that we make our
home. We are Americans."[28]

A solo rendition of the 23rd Psalm sung by Judy Mahlberg
(Paul's wife), a professional singer, was followed by a hymn which
had been sung by the first- and second-generation Swensons in
Sunday school. These were followed by a "hymn now characteristic
of the religious music that has developed for the third generation"--"Morning Has Broken." This "hymn" was accompanied on the
guitar by Mark Zidon.

With this historical buildup, the service of commemoration for
the "dear departed ones" began. The hymns "For All Saints Who
from Their Labors Rest," and "God Be With You Till We Meet Again"
were followed by prayer and benediction. "It has been good to be
here," Norris concluded, "God has been good to the Swenson family,
let us sing our heartfelt praises." The service ended with the
hymn, "Now Thank We All Our God. . . ."

This service was an extremely emotional time. Many tears were
shed, albeit silently, and people were reluctant to leave the
chapel. Another group was waiting to use the facility, however,
so everyone drifted out into the sun in a companionable low volume
of discussion. Christian commented that, for a group of mostly
non-Swedish-speaking people, they had done the Swedish hymns
beautifully. I heard this comment frequently in the following
months. The family was proud of it. Other comments in the
following months showed that the service had been a highlight of
the entire weekend. "It seemed to cement us, or show us common
'Swensonness' or something," Linda Mahlberg, a new in-law, told

me. Arden Mahlberg, whose mother, Margaret, passed away while he
was an adolescent, noted that those "departed souls" we were
remembering were there with us, not "departed" at all.[29]

Leave-taking

Sunday continued in this mood of togetherness and reluctance
to part. Although it had been expected that most families would
leave during the day, only a few who simply had to did. General
consensus brought the whole group together at a potluck picnic of
leftovers for the noon meal. For the remainder of the afternoon,
the group mingled about a table laden with food, including another
special treat from Linnea--her homemade lefse (a Scandinavian soft
flatbread). The weather cooperated with a warm, rainless day, so
that people sat around or slept on the grass under the trees.
Some of the younger Swensons started games of frisbie and whiffle
ball, and some of the older members went off to take afternoon
naps. One enterprising group of second- and third-generation
cousins engaged in a game of charades which was duly appreciated
by a lazier audience.

During the afternoon, one of the Buffalo, South Dakota, first
cousins to the first generation drove down to see the Swensons,
sharing the picnic lunch and visiting with whomever was still
around the table. She brought with her one of her daughters, a
son-in-law, and their children. Others in the more extended

kinship from Hoffman, Minnesota, had expressed a wish to drive
over for the afternoon (400 miles), but were unable to because of
illness. These "visitors" were welcome and greeted by any of the
relatives who knew them, but no particular attention was paid to
them; they were simply incorporated into the group relaxing around
the picnic tables.

One afternoon conversation centered around how to load all of
Gary and Karen Gabrielson's goods into Christian's and Whetstones'
cars for transportation to Lindsborg, Kansas, where they would be
stored with Gary's parents (Karen and Gary were heading back to
Saudi Arabia after a visit in Lindsborg). A cousin suggested that
they "UPS it," to which another replied, "Relatives are cheap-
er."[30] Others were discussing routes home and inviting one
another to stop by. While we were lounging under a tree under
which Norman was sleeping, Orven and I urged our Aunt Mildred to
tell us about her retirement home and what she'd been doing
lately. The game of charades brought up joking references to the
weekend and past events, such as the following interchange between
Gordon, Orven, and myself:

> . . .
> Greta--What are you doing, trying to think of all the movie
> titles you can?
> Mark Zidon--Ya, charades, you know some tough ones?
> Greta--Oh, is this one team, over here? I was wondering
> what kind of game you were playing, sitting there trying to
> think up movie titles. No, I don't want to play.
> [chatter]
> Orval--We're ready, let's go.
> [not ready on other side]
> Mark Zidon--Oh, come on Let's go we'll give you some of
> ours.

Greta--I think you should have Gordon act out "The Last
Waltz"--or "Tango in Paris" maybe.
Gordon--I got your mother out there dancing!
Greta--I know you did, that was nice.
Gordon--I get a few points for that.
Greta--You get a lot of points for that--course, you already
had points. You were points ahead before you started.
Gordon--I see.
Greta to Orven--Gordon carried me up Spring Butte on his
shoulders once.
Orven--Is that right?
Greta--That's right.
Gordon--Orven was along too, but he was walking.
Orven--Nobody ever carried me up!
Greta--I didn't have any shoes on, as I recall.
Gordon--That was a weak excuse.
[laughter]
Orven--That was a pretty good excuse not to walk up a butte
. . .
Greta--I think that was the same time that I'd been out at
the farm and you [Orven] and I went out and . . . There was
a dust storm and we'd gone out with those big hooks to get
tumbleweed off the fence.
Orven--Oh, I remember that, ya . . .
Greta--I remember, we came in and all you could see was, you
know, black. There must have been two inches of dust on our
faces. And your mother wouldn't let me go out in the afternoon. She didn't think a girl should be out doing that
[laughter]. You had to go out though . . .[31]
. . .

Sunday supper was an individual affair, and many nuclear
families used the time to begin preparations for their leave-
taking. By dark, everyone remaining had gathered at the campgrounds for a campfire. The groups lingered there, singing and
laughing until late into the night, again reluctant to leave one
another. They dispersed finally when someone voiced the opinion
that they may be disturbing other campers occupying the area.
Assuming that everyone would take off early in the morning, fare-
wells and well-wishing were exchanged.

Monday morning, people were yet reluctant to leave. Despite
plans to leave early for the long drives home, everyone lingered
for breakfast together and to stop by for goodbyes and coffee at
the campgrounds where a stove was still available. Sunday morning, the siblings and spouses of the first generation had gotten
together without "the children," a traditional event, which took
place whenever they were all together and served to celebrate all
of the wedding anniversaries in one fell swoop. I was not allowed
at this gathering and, in fact, didn't even hear about it until
later. Monday, however, was a mixed day. I breakfasted at the
Lodge with Forthuns, Norman's family, Aunt Mildred, and Uncle Gus.
Others were at the campgrounds or in a cabin. The morning was
slow, with the tail-end of the Swenson family leaving sometime
after noon.

As my Uncle Per and I were signing out at the reservation
desk, Mrs. Meyer, the manager of group arrangements at the Lodge,
said to me, "You're writing this thing on reunions. Well, yours
has been one of the nicest we've had around here, and we're real
pleased to have you. You can write that down, too." I did. I'm
certain the entire family agreed with her. As Norris commented
during the service, it had been good to be there.[32]

CHAPTER 7

SHAREDNESS

Without a conscious effort, the Swenson family reunion followed the general patterns found in other documented reunions:
people related through a blood bond gathered together to share
time in a common space; they visited, played, and shared food.
The gathering was not one of happenstance, but highly organized,
even planned two years in advance. As demonstrated, the Swenson
reunion and family development share even more specific patterns
with other families in Adams County, North Dakota. These reunions
adhere closely to the historical maturation of the seventy-year-
old county, beginning to occur at a point in time when the
families were able to travel to meet one another, and when the
generation which had homesteaded the county together had reached
the status of elders. The Zimmerman, Stedje-Hjelle, and Swenson
reunions varied only in specifics. The families emphasized different shared religious, ethnic, and, primarily, homesteading
heritages, but they did so in similar patterns.

As pointed out, the Adams County families structurally
approximate the "modified extended family" suggested by Litwak on
the basis of a study in a Connecticut community. This study,
concerned with geographic mobility, first of all postulated that

220

such a family structure would support geographical mobility
economically, socially, and psychologically; that geographic
distance did not destroy extended family aid and interaction, but
simply modified it.[1] The out-migration from Adams County during
the Depression was regretted by the inhabitants, but not frowned
upon. It was and, indeed, is yet expected. The following
generations move for employment, school, military service, or
emotional reasons, and their extended families do not try to
prevent such mobility. In the Swenson family, Norman jokes each
Christmas about all the new addresses for his younger cousins, and
the reunion was truly a group of geographically far-flung people.

Information from the Swenson reunion further supports Litwak's
hypothesis. I have indicated that facilitation of transportation
and communication spurred on the reunions of Adams County families. Litwak hypothesized that advances in communication aided
extended family social relations over distances. This is certainly the case with the Swenson family. Contact is maintained with
selected family members who, in turn, maintain contact with other
selected members. The kin network is one of communication and
aid. The studies, such as Vance Packard's Nation of Strangers,
which bewail the lack of long-term proximic relations in a neighborhood or community have not sufficiently taken into consideration the considerable traffic in long-distance communication and
visiting undertaken by Americans.[2] Packard's study was based in
part upon the telephone disconnect rates in the United States. He

did not, however, consider the volume of long-distance calling in
the evenings and on weekends, nor the overloaded telephone
circuits during holidays.

Litwak further hypothesized that the moving extended family
does not create financial difficulties because the families
coalesce when they are at a peak earning capacity.[3] Movements of
the Swenson kin tend to be of elementary families or individuals,
not extended networks. There is, however, a historical tendency
to follow a type of chain migration, particularly among adult
siblings. Individuals who left Dakota during the 1930s were often
followed by or accompanied by siblings, as illustrated by the
movements of the first generation away from the homestead, developing the North Dakota, Minnesota, and Washington groupings. The
second-generation Washington branch, though widely dispersed
during military service and college years, has also gradually
relocated near each other, one grouping in the northwest, another
in Iowa. Other second-generation Swensons are yet in career and
family formation stages, but show tendencies to group near siblings. This tendency was made apparent with the "reunions within
the reunion."

In terms of the chain migrations and the groupings at the
reunion, again and again in the history of the Swenson family the
importance of life-long sibling bonds emerges. The immigrant and
homesteading generations maintained patterns of social, economic,
and emotional aid and contact throughout their lives, extending

this tradition to the following generations. These patterns were
demonstrated with the living and eating arrangements at the reunion and are revealed more formally in such things as the choice
of siblings as godparents for offspring. Such continuing bonds
belie the scholastic and media focus upon the marriage bond and
the nuclear residential family unit outlined in Chapter 1.

Being structured as a modified extended family, however, is
not sufficient motivation for the organization of a family reunion. In addition to the historical timing of family maturation,
two other situations are necessary for the organization and continuation of family reunions. One is the organizing personality.

We see with the Swenson reunion that the mode of the reunion
was determined to a certain extent by the personality of Norman.
He is a self-professed "family person," and has always been interested in keeping in contact with his and his father's cousins (his
mother has only one unmarried sister). Norman was the first of
the American Swensons to visit the relatives in Sweden, and in his
adult life with his children has visited each of his aunts and
uncles as well as the great aunts and uncles. Feeling the lack of
cousins as a young boy, he later kept track of his young cousins
as we were growing up, making efforts to attend weddings and send
greetings for other important events. Norman was the obvious,
undisputed organizer, nonpartisan, the eldest of eldest, i.e., the
next head of the family. Being a Certified Public Accountant
increased his suitability in terms of facilities available for the

lengthy planning correspondence with family members and general
organizational abilities. His age and status as a long-estab-
lished non-transient Swenson further enhanced the suitability of
his choice, since the majority of the second-generation adults in
the kin network are yet unsettled or have very young children.

Similar personalities in the other families I documented also
proved to be the driving forces in reunion organization and continuity (see Chapter 4). In very plain terms, organizing a large
family reunion is a big job, and whoever undertakes the coordination of such an effort has to be interested in seeing the reunion
continue and be enjoyed by the family.

The other necessity for the continuation of family reunions
is, of course, participation by eligible members. In cases where
reunions have phased out, people simply quit joining committees
and coming; often this has occurred when the organizing force or
the founding grandparents have died. What will happen to the
Swenson reunion is uncertain. Members have already discussed the
possible demise of the reunion because the force in common, the
Swenson grandparents, are unknown to the third and fourth generations. Indications from other reunions and from Swenson family
history and interaction point to a splintering of the reunion into
reunions of the descending branches, taking on different pinnacles
of descent, for instance, Swen's descendants reuniting unto themselves.

In addition to the importance of the adult sibling bonds, one other aspect of the family reunions I studied stands out: this was the intense interest family members displayed in shared family characteristics, shared blood.

As noted earlier, rather than family history, conversations at the Swenson reunion more often circulated around family character- istics or the characteristics of one family member. Not only the Swensons, but each person with whom I spoke over the course of my research had something to say about "family characteristics," physical, emotional, or mental attributes which they had decided had come to them through the bloodline and were shared by most, if not all of their relatives.

The Svihovecs, for instance, were struck by the physical sim- ilarities of their lost New York cousins.[4] While discussing her husband's family reunion, the spouse of a Kansas Mennonite de- scribed him as someone who "had inherited the work ethic, but that's about it."[5] Evelyn Haag explained the regular choir prac- tice and performance at the Stedje-Hjelle Reunion as a natural activity, since ". . . we're all real, very musical."[6] Others commented upon shared traits such as stubbornness or being good cooks. "There is something unnerving about all this resemblance, as though we all wore masks," one academic commented after attend- ing his family reunion.[7]

In the Swenson family, several traits were observed before, during, and after the reunion. In fact, the reunion time served

as a proving-ground for some of the ideas about family characteristics. When something happened that a particular family member
didn't want to happen, he or she wrote it off as a product of the
"stubbornness" or some other trait recognized throughout the
family (see the discussion of the slide show in Chapter 6).

Two or three things seem to stand out for the Swensons as
shared characteristics. One is a unique, idiosyncratic sense of
humor. I myself, long before the reunion was planned, would find
myself often chuckling or laughing in situations where no one else
was amused. My pat response and consolation would be, "If one of
my cousins (or sisters) were here now, they'd laugh." I've never
had a doubt that they would, indeed, find amusing the same things
I do. These humorous situations are difficult to record. When I
asked him to give me an example, my cousin Orven commented, "You
can't think up a Swenson joke; they just happen, otherwise it
wouldn't be funny." Another cousin just laughed.[8] Whether or not
this shared aspect of worldview is Swenson or can be partially or
wholly attributed to other shared regional or ethnic cultures is
not important here, though regional cultures are not shared by all
of the Swenson cousins. It is important that family members
themselves consider this to be a marker of membership in that
specific family. The Swenson humor is part of the family self-
image, and also of the image presented to the outside world.

I found that the in-laws talked about this Swenson "trait"
more than did the Swensons themselves. Living with what they

considered to be Swenson characteristics was a theme they all had
in common as non-Swensons, a shared struggle they could all rally
around. One evening prior to the reunion, Renee commented that
she and Orval had confounded the people in the hospital because
they went into the delivery room for their first child "cracking
Swenson-type jokes." After she had related this anecdote, someone
in the room immediately asked of her husband, "You'd initiated her
already?" And he replied, "A long time ago." That was humorous
too.

At the reunion there were several comments about or whole
conversations about the Swenson humor, and these continued in
conversations following the reunion. The North Dakota branches
had a discussion over dinner at the homestead when they returned
from the reunion; this conversation was primarily for the benefit
of Orven's new wife, Debbie, as a means of explaining some of what
went on at the reunion. Oscar's wife, Norma (Debbie's mother-in-
law), told her: "Ya, they say it without cracking a smile and you
don't know whether they're . . . serious or if they're kidding . .
. I still get caught, [laughs] after all these years!"[9] Another
new spouse mentioned to me after the reunion that she was disap-
pointed there hadn't been a written family history so that she
could have been in on all the jokes.[10]

A second characteristic discussed by the Swenson in-laws and
by the Swensons when they were disgusted with someone was a tendency to stubbornness. When asked about family characteristics,

this particular one often is mentioned by many families. People
are proud of being stubborn. They also use the "characteristic"
as an excuse for not getting something accomplished.

When I asked Norman if he'd noticed any Swenson characteristics as he planned the reunion, he responded: "Oh, nothing new .
. . The characteristics, whether they are or they aren't, they're
--blamed--on the Swensons. I think some of them have come out
[during the course of planning the reunion] . . . Oh, the
stubbornness . . . just a little--depends on whose spouse you're
talking to."[11]

Such a response is not specific to the Swenson family. If a
spouse is unhappy with the conduct of his or her mate, they do not
attribute "stubbornness" to the mate himself as an individual
characteristic, but attribute it to his bloodline--something over
which he or she has no control.

Looking at family characteristics is part of a search. Several cousins during the reunion had wanted to find out something
about Grandmother Swenson (Johanna), a mystery figure to the
second generation. My sister Anita related to me one of the many
discussions which took place about Johanna. Oscar had told some
second-generation cousins that his mother ". . . apparently had a
fear of cancer. She worried more than necessary." The cousins
decided that this "trait" (worrying) had been handed down
generously.[12]

My research reveals my own curiosity about this family mystery. As shown in this interchange with Linnea, during interviews with my aunts and uncles, I always asked about Grandmother:

> . . .
> GS--Did you pick up any things that you remember from her, such as preparations in the kitchen?
> LF--OK. Going to her cooking, she was an extremely good cook. Dad always used to say, if you learn to cook like your mother, why then you'll get along fine [laughs]. And, well, I can remember how he used to talk about, this was at the time before they were married, how he used to be able to tell when Johanna had made the bed, 'cause she was very meticulous with what she did. And she used to go down and help with the chores. And she was also a very modest person. As I remember, extremely modest. She used to go down and help milk. And separate. Feed the chickens; pick the eggs.
> . . .
> GS--Did she encourage you to go to high school?
> LF--Oh, yes, they wanted us to go to high school. The only thing he said was I couldn't go--let's see that's when I was a junior I couldn't go, they did not have money. And if they couldn't find a place for me to work for my room and board, why I couldn't go. Well then she stepped out, and she did find a place. Well, a telephone man came. That was when we first had the telephone. And, I don't know just how he happened to stop out there, but somehow things got started.
> . . .[13]

Such questions were also asked by some of the other cousins during the reunion. Arden Mahlberg, for instance, considered information about Grandmother to be important for getting to know more about her daughter Margaret, his mother.[14] Betty Svihovec attributed the same importance to contact with relatives at their reunion:

> . . .
> And I learned more about my dad. You see, my oldest sister was only twelve when he died. And, you can learn things about other people from someone who was a little bit more removed from the family [her sibling group]. For instance,

a cousin can relate things of my dad's younger life that
even the older kids in our family wouldn't remember. And it
was fun for me to find these things out.[15]

Norman expressed the same belief when I asked him what he remem-

bered of Grandmother Swenson:

> . . .
> GS--Any impressions of what Grandma was like? [remembers
> seeing her only once]
> Norman--. . . derives more from knowing some of her sisters.
> When I think of Grandma, I think of Aunt Amanda, because, to
> me they kinda looked alike. And I don't know whether they
> acted alike or not, but that's the relationship I put on.
> . . .[16]

Another cousin, Twila Zidon, seemingly frustrated by the gen-

eral spontaneity of the event commented that "Swensons don't make

decisions." When frustrated by the fact that most of the family

returned to their cabins or campers right after the band quit on

the night of the dance, she commented that "Swensons seem to abide

by the clock too closely."[17] This was her means of expressing

frustration that people didn't want to do what she wanted to do

without insulting any one person or being too personal about it.

What can you do about something that is in your blood?

Though in a very real sense proud of their humor and stubborn-

ness, in several situations Swensons conjured up characteristics

that were derogatory--family inheritances that explained what they

perceived to be faults in their own characters. When Swen printed

his "Swen and Mildred Swenson Family Tree" in 1968, he introduced

the endeavors by lauding the heritage:

> Let it be known that our forebears were all humble folk.
> They were peasants, share-croppers and laborers in their
> ancestral environment. They were also honest, industrious,

frugal and deeply religious. No one can ask for an inheritance of greater worth. I have for some time planned to
record in summary the data in my possession, in order that
it may become the common treasury of our family, lest the
memory of these worthy people be entirely lost. With such
a purpose in mind, this "Family History" is affectionately
dedicated to our beloved children and grandchildren.[18]

He included a section on "Family traits" in this work, because:

Heridity [sic] and environment shape the individual. Genes
may lie dormant for one or more generations and then reappear. No special traits of weakness or predisposition to
certain illnesses are apparent in our hereditary line.
Certain trends are evident.[19]

Despite pride in the inheritance, however, the traits he chose to

list for the Swensons and Eklofs cannot be considered as compli-

mentary:

     The Eklofs: Tendency to obesity,
                   Determined temperament tending
                     to stubbornness.
     The Swensons: Allergies.
                   Easily triggered temper.
                   Early baldness.
                   Some ability in artistic
                     expression.
                   Aptness in mathematics and
                     mechanics.[20]

Spouses responded with more complimentary attributes for the

Swenson family. Linda Mahlberg, one of the new spouses, for

instance, noted that everyone she met at the reunion seemed to be

basically honest and trustworthy, not trying to pull anything over

on her. She felt that this entered into the fact that there are

no divorces in the kin network. When her husband, Arden, bewailed

the "trait" of needlessly worrying about things, Linda retorted

that that was part of being "careful people."[21] Others noted that

Swensons seemed to be subdued, and expressive only in small
groups, characteristics valued by some and bemoaned by others.

All such observations were, in a very concrete way, self-
examinations. Information about Grandmother Johanna Swenson and
Swen and Margaret, the two deceased members of the first generation, was actively sought by their direct descendants. What kind
of people they had been, how they had affected the family character, and what were the physical problems causing their early
deaths were basic concerns for many reunionites. As Arden
Mahlberg commented after the reunion, it was comforting to learn
that other people have had the traits you have.[22]

Until approximately twenty years ago, adoption agencies in the
United States had a policy which prevented the natural parents and
adoptive parents from knowing anything about one another. This
policy is changing because adopted children embark upon long
searches to discover their natural parents. The blood bond is
both more mysterious and more concrete for them than are social
and cultural bonds. It is for all of us. We are always searching
to find out why we are who we are, and we look to our genetic pool
for the answers.

The emphasis placed upon family characteristics--intellectual,
physical, and emotional--during the Swenson Family Reunion and in
conversations with other reunionites illustrates the intensity of
this bonding. No matter how little kin may share socially and
culturally, there is no escaping the genes. Membership in the

group cannot be denied, and, indeed, a motivating force for
attending reunions was often curiosity about the shared charac-
teristics--or characteristics believed to be shared.

The Swenson reunion also served as a forum for exchanges of
other shared folkloric forms, including shared values and beliefs.
The chosen mode of interaction (relaxed small-group interchange),
the enthusiasm for the church service, and the willingness to go
along with unclear majorities showed trust and shared values among
the Swensons. As demonstrated, such folklore items as recipes,
jokes, and allusions to family anecdotes and other stories were
exchanged during the weekend.

As a folkloric function, the Swenson Family Reunion can be
viewed as an indigenous festival, perhaps the only truly indigenous type of festival, one which cannot be organized by a non-
member. The occasion is a reaffirmation of identity. As a powwow
asserts one's Indianness, attendance at a reunion reaffirms membership in one's kin group.[23] It is an occasion for "men to
rejoice" together--to interact in an ambience of acceptance and
conviviality."[24] No one whom I interviewed, and no article I
unearthed, reported that their reunions were anything but enjoyable.

Festivals, whether school homecomings or pioneer fests, emphasize shared experience for the participants. "By participating .
. . we say something about who and what we are . . ." Susan Kalčik
has noted.[25] But it is a selective statement. A pioneer

festival, such as that described by Warner in The Living and the
Dead, celebrates a shared, selective history of events. The
town's 300th anniversary celebration consists of "delayed
interpretation" of past events.[26] Those interpretations and what
is selected to be presented as history reflect the conceptual
realities of, at least, and maybe only, the festival organizers.
Such festivals celebrate the past in the same way that high school
or college homecomings consist of a recollection of a historically
limited period of shared experience.

Community festivals, such as Turtle Days in Churubusco,
Indiana investigated by John Gutowski, emphasize another sharedness: that of a "locally significant event, belief, tale, or
legend."[27] What is shared here is not the memory of concrete
historical experience, but a shared knowing that is part of a
social-community identity. Community festivals emphasize shared
social and/or historical experience.

Ethnic festivals emphasize a shared concept of historical and
cultural experience, ordinarily celebrating a community social
sharedness as well. The Lindsborg pioneer festival studied by
Larry Danielson demonstrated that community and social identity
were as important, and perhaps even more important, than was the
Swedish heritage highlighted in the town's biannual festival.[28]
Recently, Linda Dégh, investigating a Hungarian community fest in
Louisiana, found that the community social concept of sharedness
far outweighed any actual shared heritage.[29]

What makes the Swenson family reunion and other family
reunions distinctive as celebrations of sharedness is that the
emphasis placed on the events is not shared historical or social
experience, but relatedness, shared characteristics and blood. As
demonstrated, the Swensons and other families investigated do not
share social lives except on an occasional basis. Kin who had
never socially interacted were included; though historical events
such as the homesteading were recognized as common heritage, they
also were not the emphasis. The family reunion as a celebration
of shared identity emphasized the "enduring diffuse solidarity"
introduced by Schneider as an aspect of American families. Smith
describes festivals as a time when "One lives for a period of time
in another world in which the premises of reality are different
from those of ordinary reality."[30] The reality suspended during
the Swenson reunion was that of a dispersed kin group: for three
days, the Swensons were accessible one to the other as a small
community, indulging in the luxury of interacting with persons
whom they considered to be like themselves. "It is comforting to
know that so many people share your traits," Arden Mahlberg had
told me at the end of the reunion. That was the solidarity being
celebrated.

CONCLUSIONS

The reunions discussed here show that American families are
not of a dying species, but are vital, emergent forms. Patterns
of contact and aid among broadly spread-out kin networks are
celebrated and demonstrated by means of planned contact--people
put forth extra effort to organize and attend family reunions.

To a great extent, the effort expended in planning family
reunions can be attributed to the distinguishing mobility of the
American population from its very beginnings. You reunite only if
you have first been separated. It is entirely possible that some
cultures would not even conceive of planning and organizing such a
family gathering. The worldview simply may not contain this idea
of organizing into a group a bunch of people that is by definition
already a group. Reactions from Bretons, Jugoslavs, Swedes,
Ugandans, and other non-American colleagues and friends were of
amazement when I outlined to them the American reunions. When
everyone lives in the same village, or near by, reunions are
unnecessary. We see similar events in the patronal fiestas of
South America, where villagers who have moved to the cities return
once a year to reaffirm their identity with a village/family, but
this, again, is an identity tied to place as well as blood.[31]

The city workers in South America return for the patronal
fiesta in order to reaffirm identity to the patron saint, locality, and family. For North Americans, the identity celebrated in

reunions is not normally a geographically located one. Our neighborhoods are flexible and, as demonstrated with the Swensons, some
of us move hundreds of miles for jobs and careers more than once
during our lifetimes; we marry outside the village and state,
often outside the ethnic group. What has this done to our feeling
of belongingness?

     Vance Packard told us that we were rootless and falling to
pieces. Research with family reunions indicates another possibility. Even when reunions are held at the family farm, people
organize, not to visit the home place, but to see their relatives.
The claim to belonging as a family, not community, is brought to
the fore. This may be a compensation or adaptation, pinpointing
the unreliability of one key identity resource--place--and shift-
ing to an emphasis upon an ultimately reliable resource--blood.
Felix Oinas recently pointed out to me that similar psychological
transfer seems to be happening in areas, such as Estonia, under
Soviet rule. Families gather together more frequently and in a
much larger grouping than they used to. The blood bond is
ultimate security.[32]

     The Macedonian sobor recently investigated by Timothy Rice is
another event similar to the patronal fiestas and family reunions,
but one also tied to place. Rice claims that with this yearly
event, villagers who are now pulled apart by "conflicting
loyalties to state, job, school, money, and family," are able to
stage a tightly bounded event which reestablishes social ties.

When the <u>sobor</u> celebrations cease, he postulates, the villagers
will then have "lost the battle to new and different loyalties."[33]
It is entirely possible that the loyalties will not be "new" at
all, but perhaps, as they seem to be with some American families,
blood bonds may play an even greater role in identity.

Indeed, increasing mobility and transiency may spur on events
such as family reunions in other parts of the world. "An ideal
community," Keyes concluded in his study, <u>We, the Lonely People</u>,
"would be like a good family: the group from which one can't be
expelled."[34] An event in West Germany similar to our family
reunions has already been related to me by a professor from
Germany. Members of the von Bismark family gathered one summer at
a resort castle from all over West Germany. This reunion was made
up of the dispossessed members of the family who had fled the
family land holdings in Prussia during the war. Their reunion is
of the immigrant branches, as are the American reunions.[35] And
Hermann Bausinger has recently declared that now is the time to
study the change from <u>Heimat</u> as a cultural orientation to whatever
orientation will be the result of mobility within Germany and
Western Europe in general.[36]

All of this points out the futility of studying the nuclear
family in isolation from the kin network, or a kin network as a
geographically located group. When we consider family folklore,
we must take into consideration the overall structure and contact
of the kinship network. At reunions, this structure moves from

the posited to the apparent. The past and future of a line is
gathered and underlined with the focus of attention on the point
of shared descent and the curiosity about new members.

NOTES

CHAPTER 1

1.   C. W. von Sydow, "On the Spread of Tradition," in Selected
Papers (Copenhagen, 1948), p. 12.

2.   Ibid., p. 13.

3.   The list of such recognition is long. See, e.g., Jack
Goody, ed., The Developmental Cycle of Domestic Groups, Cambridge
Papers in Social Anthropology no. 1 (Cambridge: The University
Press, 1962); Herbert J. Gutman, The Black Family in Slavery and
Freedom, 1750-1925 (New York: Pantheon Books, 1976); Margaret
Mead and Ken Heyman, Family (New York: The Macmillan Company,
1965); Margaret Mead, And Keep Your Powder Dry (New York: W.
Morrow & Co., 1942; reprint, 1965); Charles E. Rosenberg, ed., The
Family in History (Philadelphia: University of Pennsylvania
Press, 1975); Lloyd W. Warner, The Family of God (Westport, Conn.:
Greenwood Press, 1959; reprint, 1975); Ingeborg Weber-Kellerman,
Die Familie (Frankfurt: Insel Verlag, 1976).

4.   Barre Toelken, The Dynamics of Folklore (Boston: Houghton
Mifflin Company, 1979), p. 82.

5.   See especially Stephen Stern, "The Sephardic Jewish Commu-
nity of Los Angeles: A Study in Folklore and Ethnic Identity,"
(Ph.D. diss., Indiana University, 1977); Clara Bianco, The Two
Rosetos (Bloomington: Indiana University Press, 1974); Larry Wm.
Danielson, "The Ethnic Festival and Cultural Revivalism in a Small
Midwestern Town" (Ph.D. diss., Indiana University, 1972); Barbara
Kirshenblatt-Gimblett, "Traditional Storytelling in the Toronto
Jewish Community: A Study in Performance and Creativity in an
Immigrant Culture" (Ph.D. diss., Indiana University, 1972); E. K.
Francis, "The Nature of the Ethnic Group," The American Journal of
Sociology 52:393-400; Richard Bauman, "Differential Identity and
the Social Base of Folklore," in Toward New Perspectives in
Folklore, ed. Americo Paredes and Richard Bauman (Austin:
University of Texas Press, 1972), pp. 31-41.

6.   Alan Dundes, Folklore Theses and Dissertations in the United
States (Austin: University of Texas Press for the American
Folklore Society, 1976).

7.   There has been an emphasis on the personality of the teller
in Russian folklore study since the collections of Rybnikov and
Gil'ferding in the mid- and late nineteenth century. See Y. M.
Sokolov, Russian Folklore, trans. Catherine Ruth Smith (Detroit:
Folklore Associates, 1971) for a discussion of this emphasis.
Also see, Mark Asadowsky, Eine sibirische Märchenerzählerin,
Folklore Fellows Communication 68 (Helsinki, 1926). For more
recent examples of this approach, see Linda Dégh, Folktales and
Society, trans. Emily M. Schossberger (Bloomington: Indiana
University Press, 1969); and Juha Pentikainen, Oral Repertoire and
World View: An Anthropological Study of Marina Takalo's Life
History, Folklore Fellows Communication 219 (Helsinki:
Suomalainen Tiedeakatemia, 1978).

8.   Laurel Doucette, Skill and Status: Traditional Expertise
within a Rural Canadian Family, National Museum of Man Mercury
Series, Canadian Centre for Folk Culture Studies no. 28 (Ottawa:
National Museum of Man, 1979).

9.   Lois Karen Baldwin, "Down on Bugger Run: Family Group and
the Social Base of Folklore," Ph.D. diss., University of
Pennsylvania, 1975.

10.   Bob Copper, A Song for Every Season: A Hundred Years of a
Sussex Farming Family (London: William Heinemann Ltd., 1973).

11.   Jean Ritchie, Singing Family of the Cumberlands (New York:
Oxford University Press, 1955).

12.   Carl Fleischhauer and Alan Jabbour, eds., The Hammons
Family: A Study of a West Virginia Family's Tradition
(Washington: Library of Congress, 1973).

13.   Millicent R. Ayoub, "The Family Reunion," Ethnology 5
(1966):415.

14.   Ibid., pp. 415-16.

15.   Baldwin, p. 304.

16.   Gwen Kennedy Neville, "Kinfolks and the Covenant: Ethnic
Community among Southern Presbyterians," in The New Ethnicity,
Perspectives from Ethnology, ed. John W. Bennett, Proceedings of
the American Ethnological Society 1973 (St. Paul: West Publishing
Co., 1975), pp. 258-74.

17.   See note 5.

18.   See Gerald R. Leslie, The Family in Social Context, 4th ed.
(New York: Oxford University Press, 1979) for a historical
account of family studies in the United States.

19.   Mead, Powder, pp. 27-37.

20.   Ibid., p. 37.

21.   Ibid., pp. 37-53.

22.   Ibid., p. 84.

23.   Ibid., p. 91.

24.   Ibid., p. 85.

25.   Talcott Parsons, "The Kinship System of the Contemporary
United States," in Essays in Sociological Theory, rev. ed.
(London: The Free Press of Glencoe, 1954 and 1949), pp. 177-96,
186.

26.   Talcott Parsons, "The Stability of the American Family
System," in A Modern Introduction to the Family, ed. Norman W.
Bell and Ezra F. Vogel (New York: The Free Press, 1960),
pp. 93-97, 96.

27.   Warner, The Family of God.

28.   Ibid., p. 21.

29.   Ibid., p. 22.

30.   Carle C. Zimmerman, Family and Civilization (New York:
Harper & Brothers, 1947).

31.   For a cogent account of these developments within the discipline of sociology, see Gerald R. Leslie, The Family in Social
Context, 4th ed. (New York: Oxford University Press, 1979).

32.   Vance Packard, A Nation of Strangers (New York: David
McKay Company, Inc., 1972), p. 4.

33.   Ralph Keyes, We, the Lonely People, Searching for Community
(New York: Harper & Row, Publishers, 1973).

34.   Ibid., p. 9.

35.   See Stephen R. Graubard, "Preface," The Family, ed. Stephen
R. Graubard, Daedalus (Spring 1977); Tamara K. Hareven, "Family
Time and Historical Time," Daedalus, Spring 1977, pp.57-70; E.
Anthony Wrigley, "Reflections on the History of the Family,"
Daedalus, Spring 1977, pp. 71-85; Tamara K. Hareven, ed., Family
and Kin in American Urban Communities, 1780-1920 (New York, 1977);
John Demos, A Little Commonwealth: Family Life in Plymouth Colony
(New York, 1970); Philip Greven, Four Generations: Population,
Land, and Family in Colonial Andover, Massachusetts (Ithaca, N.Y.,
1970).

36.   Leslie, p. 189.

37.   Ibid., pp. 190-91.

38.   Claude Lévi-Strauss, "The Family," in Man, Culture, and
Society, ed. Harry L. Shapiro, rev. ed. (London, Oxford, New York:
Oxford University Press, 1971), p. 339.

39.   Pooles's Index to Periodical Literature, 1802-1906, 5 vols.

40.   The American Family, vol. 1, 1942.

41.   Ibid., vol. 1, no. 6 (April 1943), p. 2.

42.   K. Eby, "We Have No Roots!" Christian Century 58 (13 August
1941):1000-02.

43.   Advertisement from James Robison television special, TV
Guide, 10 July 1979, emphasis added.

44.   Bloomington Herald-Telephone, Bloomington, Indiana,
Saturday, 21 July 1979.

45.   See also James West's study, Plainville, U.S.A. (New York
and London: Columbia University Press, 1945).

46.   David M. Schneider, American Kinship: A Cultural Account,
University of Chicago Anthropology of Modern Societies Series
(Englewood Cliffs, N.J., 1968), p. v.

47.   David M. Schneider and George C. Homans, "Kinship Terminology and the American Kinship System," in Bell and Vogel,
p. 480-81.

48.   Sheila R. Klatzky, Patterns of Contact with Relatives
(Washington, D.C.: The American Sociological Association, 1973),
p. 84.

49.   James H. S. Bossard and Eleanor S. Boll, Ritual in Family
Living (Philadelphia: University of Pennsylvania Press, 1950),
p. 87.

50.   Bernard Farber, Comparative Kinship Systems, A Method of
Analysis (New York, London, Sydney: John Wiley & Sons, Inc.,
1968), p. 33.

51.   Ibid., p. 29.

52.   Ibid., p. 33.

53.   Mary Jo Bane, Here to Stay: American Families in the
Twentieth Century (New York: Basic Books, 1977), p. xiv.

54.   See note 35 and Leslie. The works we have investigate
family life in the northeastern sections of the United States. It
is highly likely that the coresidential extended family is more
prevalent in the southern mountains.

CHAPTER 2

1.   David M. Schneider, American Kinship: A Cultural Account,
University of Chicago Anthropology of Modern Societies Series
(Englewood Cliffs, N.J., 1968).

2.   Raymond Firth, Jane Hubert, Anthony Forge, et al., Families
and their Relatives, Kinship in a Middle-Class Sector of London
(London: Routledge and Kegan Paul; New York: Humanities Press,
1969).

3.   This program was begun during the 1975 Festival of American
Folklife and is currently a separate section of the Smithsonian
Institution's Folklife program. See Kin and Communities, ed.
Allan J. Lichtman and Joan R. Challinor for an account of their
activities. Their publications include a brochure designed to
teach people how to interview family members. I am grateful to
Steven Zeitlin for providing me with information about this
program.

4.   Following Litwak, see Norman W. Bell and Ezra F. Vogel, ed.,
A Modern Introduction to the Family (New York: The Free Press,
1960), p. i.

5.   From taped interview with Evelyn Haag, 13 July 1978,
Hettinger, North Dakota.

6.   Schneider, Cultural Account.

7.   Gwen Kennedy Neville, "Kinfolks and the Covenant: Ethnic
Community among Southern Presbyterians," in The New Ethnicity,
Perspectives from Ethnology, ed. John W. Bennett, Proceedings of
the American Ethnological Society 1973 (St. Paul: West Publishing
Co., 1975), p. 26.

8.   Schneider, p. 53.

9.   Joan Barthel, "Family Reunions," Ladies' Home Journal,
August 1978, p. 71.

10.   Millicent R. Ayoub, "The Family Reunion," Ethnology
5(1966):419-22.

11.   Such principles are set forth in various field guides for
collectors of folklore. See, for example, Kenneth Goldstein, A
Guide for Field Workers in Folklore (Hatboro, Penn. and London:
Folklore Associates and Herbert Jenkins, 1964); or Edward D. Ives,
"A Manual for Field Workers," Northeast Folklore 15(1974).

12.   See especially George Carey, "The Storyteller's Art and the
Collector's Intrusion," in Folklore Today, A Festschrift for
Richard M. Dorson, ed. Linda Dégh, Henry Glassie, and Felix J.
Oinas, pp. 81-92.

13.   Lois Karen Baldwin, "Down on Bugger Run: Family Group and
the Social Base of Folklore" (Ph.D. diss., University of Pennsylvania, 1975), p. 57.

14.   Firth et al., p. 57.

CHAPTER 3

1.   Alex Haley, Roots (New York: Doubleday, 1976).

2.   "Family reunion: Help Stamp out the generation gap," Better
Homes and Gardens, 1970, pp. 38-39, 76, 80-81.

3.   "How to Plan an Old-fashioned Family Reunion," Better Homes
and Gardens, November 1977, pp. 56-58.

4.   Joan Barthel, "Family Reunions," <u>Ladies' Home Journal</u>,
August 1978, cover.

5.   All information concerning the Kiwanis International Family
Reunion Day is from a personal interview with Mr. John L. McGehee,
Director of Public Relations, Kiwanis International, 12 May 1978,
Chicago, Illinois.

6.   From materials given to me by Mr. McGehee.

7.   I later met Governor Link and discovered that his family
also reunited during the summer of 1978 in an event similar to
that of the Swenson family.

8.   Bill Weeks, "America's Happiest Family Reunion," <u>Colliers</u>, 6
October 1951, p. 76.

9.   Ibid., p. 75.

10.   Barthel.

11.   From personal interview, 21 June 1978.

12.   Millicent R. Ayoub, "The Family Reunion," <u>Ethnology</u>
5(1966):426.

13.   Weeks, p. 18.

14.   "Boy Meets 416 Cousins," <u>Look</u>, 1 September 1959, p. 84.

15.   Chapman J. Milling, "Reunion in Georgia," <u>South Atlantic
Quarterly</u> 35(1936):42-49.

16.   Allen W. Porterfield, "In Patriarchal Fashion," <u>The
Saturday Review of Literature</u>, 13 August 1932, p. 45.

17.   <u>Lindsborg NewsRecord</u>, 16 August 1979.

18.   Ibid., 14 June 1979.

19.   From taped interview with Allen Johnson, 3 May 1978, St.
Paul, Minnesota.

20.   From taped interview with Lee Becker, 2 February 1978,
Lindsborg, Kansas.

21.   From taped interview with Mrs. Harley Erickson, 28 June
1978, Hettinger, North Dakota.

22.   From personal interview with Joel Levenberg, 22 February 1978, Bloomington, Indiana.

23.   From transcription of tape recorded during the Festival of American Folklife. Supplied by Steve Zeitlin.

24.   From taped interview with Allen Johnson, 2 May 1978, St. Paul, Minnesota.

25.   See Barthel article.

26.   Weeks, p. 76.

27.   From personal interview with Roy Hahner, 16 December 1977, Kansas City, Kansas.

28.   Weeks.

29.   "Boy Meets 416 Cousins," Look, 1 September 1959, pp. 84-88.

30.   Information from member of the Gish family, fall 1978, Lindsborg, Kansas.

31.   When Old Country relatives visit they, of course, are invited, but they are not considered as pieces of the reunion normally; they are guests.

32.   Several of the persons I interviewed indicated to me that they went to reunions in order to see their cousins and aunts and uncles. Some families had a core group who attend every year.

33.   Weeks, p. 75.

34.   Personal interviews, mostly with affines to families who have large reunions.

35.   Ayoub, pp. 415-16.

36.   Carter Walker Craigie, "A Movable Feast: The Picnic as a Folklife Custom in Chester County, Pennsylvania, 1870-1925" (Ph.D. diss., University of Pennsylvania, 1976), p. 119.

37.   Ibid., p. 124.

38.   "Keagle Descendants Hold 33rd Reunion," Lindsborg NewsRecord, Thursday, 16 August 1979.

39.   Information supplied by Steven Zeitlin of the Smithsonian Institution Family Folklore Program.

40.   From personal interview with Joel Levenberg, 22 February
1978, Bloomington, Indiana.

41.   From taped interview with Wayne Hintz, 25 June 1978, Custer
Lodge, Custer, South Dakota.

CHAPTER 4

1.   For an account of this development, see Walter Prescott
Webb, The Great Plains (Boston: Ginn and Co., 1931); see also
Elwyn B. Robinson, History of North Dakota (Lincoln: University
of Nebraska Press, 1966).

2.   Harold E. Briggs, "The Great Dakota Boom, 1879–1886," North
Dakota Quarterly 4(1929–30):78–108.

3.   Robinson, p. 238.

4.   Mrs. Harley Erickson and Mrs. Dan Merwin, eds., Prairie
Pioneers: A Story of Adams County, Dakota Buttes Historical
Society publication (Bismarck, N.D.:   Taylor Publishing Company,
1976).

5.   In 1930, a government study determined that 160 acres in wet
woodlands (east of the Mississippi River) had the productive capa-
city of 2,560 acres on the semi-arid High Plains. The Enlarged
Homestead Act of 1909 allowed a homesteader 320 acres. See K.
Ross Toole, The Rape of the Great Plains (Boston and Toronto:
Little, Brown and Company, Atlantic Monthly Press, 1976), p. 134.

6.   Demographic maps are supplied in J. M. Gillette, "North
Dakota Weather and the Rural Economy," North Dakota Historical
Quarterly 12(1945):12–98.

7.   Ibid., p. 52.

8.   Ibid., p. 86.

9.   Elwyn Robinson, "The Themes of North Dakota History," North
Dakota Historical Quarterly 23(1959):5–24.

10.   From taped interview with D. J. Shults, 5 July 1978,
Hettinger, North Dakota.

11.   From taped interview with Per Gustaf Swenson, 28 June 1978, Hettinger, North Dakota.

12.   See Robinson and Gillette.

13.   Information from the Adams County Clerk, personal conversation, 21 June 1978, Hettinger, North Dakota; see also Robinson, Gillette, and Erickson and Merwin, eds.

14.   From taped interview, 5 June 1978, Hettinger, North Dakota.

15.   From a survey of the Adams County Record and conversations with D. J. Shults.

16.   James West, Plainville, U.S.A. (New York and London: Columbia University Press, 1945), p. 58.

17.   Ibid., p. 59.

18.   From taped interviews with Betty Svihovec, 29 June 1978; and conversations with Rudolph Svihovec, 1 July 1978, Hettinger, North Dakota.

19.   Interviews, 1 July 1978, Hettinger, North Dakota.

20.   From taped interview with Betty Svihovec, 29 June 1978, Hettinger, North Dakota.

21.   From personal interviews and observation during June 1978, Hettinger, North Dakota.

22.   As I observed the picnic, many Zimmermans asked me "who I belonged to" and encouraged me to join them in the food line. In this situation, it was helpful to have Hettinger connections, thus not be a total outsider. My father and his siblings had been schoolmates of some of the Zimmermans.

23.   From taped interview with Evelyn Haag and her daughter, Caroline, 13 July 1978, Hettinger, North Dakota.

24.   From taped interview with Pauline Olson, 11 July 1978, Hettinger, North Dakota.

25.   From taped interview with Mrs. Harley Erickson, 28 June 1978, Hettinger, North Dakota.

CHAPTER 5

1.   Information concerning the Swenson family background is
gleaned from some written records, personal knowledge, and extensive interviews with Per Gustaf Swenson, 15-16 July 1978, Adams
County, North Dakota; Oscar F. Swenson, 16 June 1978, Adams
County, North Dakota; Christian N. Swenson, 29 and 31 December
1975, 28-29 April 1979; Linnea Forthun, 11 and 13 July 1978;
Norman Swenson, 23 June 1978; Mildred Swenson, 28-29 June 1978;
and from personal conversations with various Swensons and Swenson
spouses over the past few years.

2.   Erik's oldest son, Swen, recorded this family saga in 1968
for his children and grandchildren. Each of Swen's siblings and a
majority of the second-generation Swensons know some variant of
this story. During the reunion in 1978, slides were shown of the
avalanche mountain (see Chapter 6).
          It was Saturday morning, February 1, 1895. Two young
     men, Erik Swenson and Erik Jonasson, cousins, were
     crossing the snowy slope of Brattriet, a mountain in the
     province of Hdrjedalen, Sweden. They had set snares in
     the ptarmigan trails and were checking their catch. It
     was legal at that time to hunt and sell ptarmigan commer-
     cially. Deep snow on a steep incline is treacherous and
     the tapping of the skiis that sunny morning loosened a
     massive avalanche. When the holocaust finally ceased,
     Erik Swenson found himself lying on his back, firmly
     packed in snow and ice. His feet were securely anchored
     by the skiis which were tied on with leather thongs. He
     thought that possibly his cousin had escaped the ava-
     lanche and was looking for him. Hence he called loudly
     several times. There was no reply. He then calmly
     assayed his situation and determined to try to escape.
     His body heat softened the snow around him. By closing
     his hands he could compact the snow and secure more room.
     Finally he was able to reach the hunting knife in his
     belt. With this he slit his boots and freed his feet.
     Then he began to inch his way through the snow and ice.
     When he reached the surface it was again morning and the
     snow glistened in the bright sunlight. It was cold, he
     had four or five miles to go to the nearest habitation
     and he was barefoot. Youth and determination prevailed
     and he reached home once again. His feet were badly
     frozen, face and hands were raw from abrasion, his hip
     badly bruised and he was thoroughly exhausted. It was
     seven weeks before he could stand on his feet again, but
     after that recovery was rapid and complete. The sport
     association of his native land awarded him a medal for

demonstrated stamina and valor. But there was sorrow in
his soul. Erik Jonasson was killed in the avalanche and
his body was not found until the snow melted in the
spring. This grief and the mountains which continually
reminded him of the dangers he had faced no doubt
crystalized his resolve to leave his native land.
Strange as it may seem, he overcame completely the
injuries he had suffered and enjoyed rugged health almost
til the day of his death. But to him the open prairie
was home. He never again felt at ease in the mountains.
From Swen L. Swenson, "Family Tree," 13 September 1968
(mimeographed).

3.   Ibid.

4.   After homesteading 160 acres of land, a homesteader was
allowed to occupy more land by planting a percentage of the
acreage in trees and showing improvement after five years.
Hoffman is located in a relatively treeless area of Minnesota:
western Minnesota on the eastern edge of the Plains.

5.   Northern Minnesota and Wisconsin are called "cutover"
because of the devastation caused by lumberers who moved through
before the land opened for homesteading. The loggers "over cut"
the area, causing ecological imbalance and consequent erosion.

6.   From taped interview with Per Gustaf Swenson, 15 July 1978,
Adams County, North Dakota.

7.   Related to Per Swenson in Hoffman, Minnesota, during a
family funeral in the early 1970s; personal communication.

8.   See Elwyn B. Robinson, History of North Dakota (Lincoln:
University of Nebraska Press, 1966).

9.   From taped interview with Christian N. Swenson, 31 December
1975, Lindsborg, Kansas.

10.   From taped interview with Christian N. Swenson, 28-29 April
1979, Lindsborg, Kansas.

11.   See quotation concerning the family's move to Cuba from
taped interview with Per Gustaf Swenson, 15 July 1978 (note 6
above).

12.   From taped interview with Linnea Forthun, 11 July 1978,
Hettinger, North Dakota.

13.   From taped interview with Christian N. Swenson, 29 April
1979, Lindsborg, Kansas.

14.   From taped interview with Christian N. Swenson, 29 December 1975, Lindsborg, Kansas.

15.   Ibid.

16.   From taped interview with Oscar F. Swenson, 16 June 1978, Adams County, North Dakota.

17.   A fact I was reminded of by my cousin Orven Swenson, who noted that as a child, anytime any of his siblings complained about having to share beds or bedrooms, they heard the full account of how the boys all had to sleep in one shed during that celebration. Personal communication, 28 June 1980, Bloomington, Indiana.

18.   See accounts of other Adams County families in Chapter 4.

19.   From taped interview with Oscar F. Swenson, 16 June 1978, Adams County, North Dakota.

20.   From taped interview with Christian N. Swenson, 29 April 1979, Lindsborg, Kansas.

21.   From taped interview with Per Gustaf Swenson, 15 July 1978, Adams County, North Dakota.

22.   From taped interview with Oscar F. and Norma Swenson, 16 June 1978, Adams County, North Dakota.

23.   From private conversation with Mildred Swenson, 26 June 1978, South Dakota.

24.   Personal communication from Anna Marie Swenson, spring 1980.

25.   From taped interviews and personal conversations.

26.   Personal communication.

27.   Personal communication.

28.   Private conversation with Orven Swenson, 28 June 1980, Bloomington, Indiana.

29.   From taped interview with Frederick Forthun, 11 July 1978, Hettinger, North Dakota.

30.   From taped interview with Norman Swenson, 23 June 1978, State Game Lodge, Custer, South Dakota.

31.   Gerald Leslie, <u>The Family in Social Context</u>, 4th ed. (New York: Oxford University Press, 1979), p. 408.

32.   Ibid., p. 251.

33.   Eugene Litwak, "Geographic Mobility and Extended Family Cohesion," <u>American Sociological Review</u> 25(1960):385-94.

34.   Leslie, p. 252.

35.   Ibid., p. 253.

36.   Ibid., pp. 252-57.

37.   Mrs. Harley Erickson and Mrs. Dan Merwin, eds., <u>Prairie Pioneers: A Story of Adams County</u>, Dakota Buttes Historical Society publication (Bismarck, N.D.: Taylor Publishing Company, 1976).

CHAPTER 6

1.   From taped interview, 23 June 1978, State Game Lodge, Custer, South Dakota.

2.   Norman kept a detailed log of correspondence, telephone calls, and discussions with relatives during planning stages of the reunion. This information was shared with me by Norman for my study.

3.   All of these letters were available to me in Norman's file.

4.   From complete file kept by Norman during the two years of reunion preparation.

5.   Personal communication previous to the reunion.

6.   Letter from Carol Hintz to Norman Swenson, Christmas 1977.

7.   From taped interview, 23 June 1978, State Game Lodge, Custer, South Dakota.

8.   Personal communication previous to the reunion.

9.   Personal communication from Norman Swenson prior to the reunion.

10.   According to 1970 statistics, North Dakota population was
38% Catholic and 47.8% Lutheran; 36.9% of the Lutheran population
were members of the American Lutheran Church (ALC), indicating
Norwegian or German heritage. Cited in Robert P. Wilkins and
Wynona Huchette, North Dakota: A Bicentennial History (New York:
Norton and Company; Nashville: American Association for State and
Local History, 1977), p. 65.

11.   From taped interview, 23 June 1978, State Game Lodge,
Custer, South Dakota.

12.   Correspondence from Twila Zidon, fall 1978.

13.   Correspondence from Mavis Mahlberg, fall 1978.

14.   From taped interview, 25 June 1978, State Game Lodge,
Custer, South Dakota.

15.   From field notes, 23 June 1978.

16.   From tape, 23 June 1978, State Game Lodge, Custer, South
Dakota.

17.   Correspondence from Mavis Mahlberg, fall 1978.

18.   See especially, Steven Ohrn and Michael E. Bell, eds.,
Saying Cheese, Folklore Forum Bibliographic and Special Series 13
(Bloomington, Ind.: Folklore Forum, 1975).

19.   From tape of the event, 23 June 1978, State Game Lodge,
Custer, South Dakota.

20.   Ibid.

21.   Ibid.

22.   Ibid.

23.   Private conversation, 23 June 1978, State Game Lodge,
Custer, South Dakota.

24.   Personal communication.

25.   From field notes. The tape from this event was not usable
due to a noise overload.

26.   Personal communication.

27.   Psalm 137:4.

28.   This and the following from a tape of the service, 25 June 1978, State Game Lodge, Custer, South Dakota.

29.   From taped discussion following the reunion.

30.   From tape of afternoon conversations.

31.   Ibid.

32.   From field notes.

CHAPTER 7

1.   Eugene Litwak, "Geographical Mobility and Extended Family Cohesion," American Sociological Review 25(1960):385-94.

2.   Vance Packard, A Nation of Strangers (New York: David McKay Company, Inc.: 1972).

3.   Litwak, p. 386.

4.   From taped interview with Betty Svihovec, June 1978, Hettinger, North Dakota.

5.   From taped interview with Lee Becker, 2 February 1978, Lindsborg, Kansas.

6.   From taped interview with Evelyn Haag, 13 July 1978, Hettinger, North Dakota.

7.   Leslie H. Farber, "Family Reunion," Commentary 57(1974):38.

8.   Personal conversation with Orven Swenson, 28 June 1980, Bloomington, Indiana; with Arden Mahlberg, 27 July 1980.

9.   From taped dinner conversation, 27 June 1978, Adams County, North Dakota.

10.   From post-reunion taped discussion with Arden and Linda Mahlberg.

11.   From taped interview, 23 June 1978, State Game Lodge, Custer, South Dakota.

12.   From notes from Anita Berg received after the reunion.

13.   From taped interview with Linnea Forthun, 11 July 1978, Hettinger, North Dakota.

14.   Personal communication.

15.   From taped interview with Betty Svihovec, June 1978, Hettinger, North Dakota.

16.   From taped interview with Norman Swenson, 23 June 1978, State Game Lodge, Custer, South Dakota.

17.   From notes from Twila Zidon received after the reunion.

18.   Swen L. Swenson, "The Swen and Mildred Swenson Family Tree," 13 September 1968, mimeographed.

19.   Ibid.

20.   Ibid.

21.   Post-reunion taped conversation with Linda and Arden Mahlberg.

22.   Personal communication.

23.   David McAllester, "A Paradigm of Navajo Dance," Parabola 4(1979).

24.   Robert J. Smith, "Festivals and Celebrations," in Folklore and Folklife, ed. Richard M. Dorson (Chicago: University of Chicago Press, 1972).

25.   Susan Kalčik, "The Good, the Bad, and the Questionable," Center for Southern Folklore Magazine (summer 1979), p. 3.

26.   W. Lloyd Warner, The Living and the Dead, A Study of the Symbolic Life of Americans, Yankee City Series vol. 5 (New Haven: Yale University Press, 1959), pp. 214-15.

27.   John A. Gutowski, "American Folklore and the Modern American Community Festival: A Case Study of Turtle Days in Churubusco, Indiana" (Ph.D. diss., Indiana University, 1977).

28.   Larry Wm. Danielson, "The Ethnic Festival and Cultural Revivalism in a Small Midwestern Town" (Ph.D. diss., Indiana University, 1972).

29.   Unpublished manuscript.

30.   See Robert J. Smith, The Art of the Festival, University of
Kansas Publications in Anthropology 6 (Lawrence, Kans., 1975),
p. 9.

31.   Ibid.

32.   Personal communication from Felix Oinas.

33.   Timothy Rice, "A Macedonian Sobor: Anatomy of a Celebration," Journal of American Folklore 93(1980):128.

34.   Ralph Keyes, We, the Lonely People, Searching for Community
(New York: Harper & Row, Publishers, 1973), p. 168.

35.   From personal conversation with Magrit Dorsch, fall 1978,
Lindsborg, Kansas.

36.   Hermann Bausinger et al., Grundzüge der Volkskunde
(Darmstadt: Wissenschaftliche Buchgesellschaft, 1978).

SELECT BIBLIOGRAPHY

Adams County Record. 1915--.

Aeschbacher, W. D. "Historical Organization on the Great Plains." *North Dakota History* 34(1967):93-100.

The American Family. 1940--.

Ariès, Philippe. "The Family and the City." *Daedalus*, spring 1977, pp. 227-35.

Armstrong, F. H. "The Family: Some Aspects of a Neglected Approach to Canadian Historical Studies." *The Canadian Historical Papers*, 1971, pp. 112-23.

Asadowskij, Mark. *Eine sibirische Märchenerzählerin*. Folklore Fellows Communications 68. Helsinki, 1926.

Ayoub, Millicent R. "The Family Reunion." *Ethnology* 5(1966): 415-33.

Baldwin, Lois Karen. "Down on Bugger Run: Family Group and the Social Base of Folklore." Ph.D. dissertation, University of Pennsylvania, 1975.

Bane, Mary Jo. *Here to Stay: American Families in the Twentieth Century*. New York: Basic Books, 1977.

Barclay, D. "Family Folklore." *New York Times Magazine*, 25 December 1955, p. 21.

Barthel, Joan. "Family Reunions." *Ladies' Home Journal*, August 1978, pp. 71-82, 120-31.

Bauman, Richard. "Differential Identity and the Social Base of Folklore." *Journal of American Folklore* 84(1971):31-41.

Bausinger, Hermann; Jeggle, Utz; Korff, Gottfried; and Scharfe, Martin. *Grundzüge del Volkskunde*. Darmstadt: Wissenschaftliche Buchgesellschaft, 1978.

Bell, Norman W., and Vogel, Ezra F., ed. A Modern Introduction to the Family. New York: The Free Press, 1960.

Bern, Enid, ed. "They Had a Wonderful Time: The Homesteading Letters of Anna and Ethel Erickson." North Dakota History 45(1978):4-10.

Berry, Wendell. The Unsettling of America: Culture and Agriculture. San Francisco: Sierra Club Books, 1977.

Bieder, Robert E. "Kinship as a Factor in Migration." Journal Of Marriage and the Family 35(1973):429-39.

Bolton, K. "Genealogy and History." American Historical Association Report 1912:206-16.

Bossard, James H. S., and Boll, Eleanor S. The Large Family System. Philadelphia: University of Pennsylvania Press, 1956.

_____. Ritual in Family Living. Philadelphia: University of Pennsylvania Press, 1950.

"Boy Meets 416 Cousins." Look, 1 September 1959, pp. 84-88.

Brandes, Stanley H. "Family Misfortune Stories in American Folklore." Journal of the Folklore Institute 12(1975):5-18.

Briggs, Harold E. "The Great Dakota Boom, 1879 to 1886." North Dakota Historical Quarterly 4(1929-30):78-108.

Brinsmade, Ellen. "A North Dakota Pioneer." Western Folklore 11(1952):38-40.

Buechler, Hans C. "The Ritual Dimension of Rural-Urban Networks: The Fiesta System in the Northern Highlands of Bolivia." In Peasants in Cities, edited by William Mangin, pp. 62-71. Boston: Houghton Mifflin Company, 1970.

Burgess, Ernest W., and Locke, Harvey J. The Family. New York: The American Book Company, 1945.

Carey, George. "The Storyteller's Art and the Collector's Intrusion." In Folklore Today: A Festschrift for Richard M. Dorson, edited by Linda Dégh, Henry Glassie, and Felix J. Oinas, pp. 81-92. Bloomington, Ind.: Indiana University, 1976.

Cavan, Ruth S. The American Family. New York: Thomas Y. Crowell Co., 1969.

Chrisman, L. H. "Chasing Ancestors." Scribners Magazine, August
    1936, pp. 120-21.

Copper, Bob. A Song for Every Season: A Hundred Years of a
    Sussex Farming Family. London: William Heinemann Ltd.,
    1973.

Craigie, Carter Walker. "A Movable Feast: The Picnic as a
    Folklife Custom in Chester County, Pennsylvania, 1870-1925."
    Ph.D. dissertation, University of Pennsylvania, 1976.

Cross, F. C. "Hobbyhorse Hitching Post: Ancestor Hunting."
    Rotarian, June 1936, pp. 52-53.

Cumming, Elaine, and Schneider, David M. "Sibling Solidarity: A
    Property of American Kinship." American Anthropologist
    63(1961):498-507.

Cutting-Baker, Holly, comp. "Family Folklore Bibliography."
    Mimeographed. Washington: The Smithsonian Institution,
    Folklore Programs.

Dégh, Linda. Folktales and Society: Story-telling in a Hungarian
    Peasant Community. Translated by Emily M. Schossberger.
    Bloomington, Ind.: Indiana University Press, 1969.

Dick, Everett. The Sod-House Frontier. New York: D. Appleton-
    Century Company, 1943.

Dike, S. W. "The Family in the United States." Contemporary
    Review 64(1892-95):724.

Dober, Virginia. "We'll Tell 'Em." North Carolina Folklore
    4(1956):15-22.

Doucette, Laurel. Skill and Status: Traditional Expertise within
    a Rural Canadian Family. National Museum of Man Mercury
    Series, Canadian Centre for Folk Culture Studies, no. 28.
    Ottawa: National Museum of Man, 1979.

Drache, Hiram M. The Challenge of the Prairie. Fargo: North
    Dakota Institute for Regional Studies, 1970.

_____. "The Economic Aspects of the Northern Pacific
    Railroad in North Dakota." North Dakota History
    34(1967):320-72.

Dundes, Alan. "The American Concept of Folklore." Journal of the
    Folklore Institute 3(1966):226-49.

_____. "Folk Ideas as Units of World View." Journal of American Folklore 84(1971):92-103.

_____. Folklore Theses and Dissertations in the United States. Austin: University of Texas Press for the American Folklore Society, 1976.

Dundes, Alan. "Thinking Ahead: A Folkloristic Reflection of the Future Orientation in American Worldview." Anthropological Quarterly 42(1969):53-72.

Eilers, H. K. "Your Family Tree." Hobbies, December 1958, p. 126.

Eliot, T. S. "The Family Reunion." London: Faber and Faber Limited, 1939.

Engler, Richard E., Jr. The Challenge of Diversity. New York: Harper and Row, 1964.

Erickson, Mrs. Harley, and Merwin, Mrs. Dan, ed. Prairie Pioneers: A Story of Adams County. Bismarck: Taylor Publishing Company for Dakota Buttes Historical Society, 1976.

The Family. Daedalus, spring 1977.

Family Folklore: Collected by the Family Folklore Program of the Festival of American Folklife. Washington: The Smithsonian Institution, 1976.

Family Heritage. 1978--.

Family History Newsletter. 1962--.

"Family Reunion: Help Stamp Out the Generation Gap." Better Homes and Gardens, 1970, pp. 38-39, 76, 80-81.

Family Ties. 1976--.

Family Weekly. 1953--.

Farber, Bernard. Comparative Kinship Systems, A Method of Analysis. New York, London, and Sydney: John Wiley & Sons, Inc., 1968.

Farber, Leslie H. "Family Reunion." Commentary 57(1974):38-42.

Firth, Raymond et al. Families and Their Relatives: Kinship in a Middle-Class Sector of London. London: Routledge & Kegan Paul; New York: Humanities Press, 1969.

Fleischhauer, Carl, and Jabbour, Alan, ed. The Hammons Family: A
    Study of a West Virginia Family's Tradition. Washington:
    Library of Congress, 1973.

Fox, Dixon Ryan. Sources of Culture in the Middle West. New York
    and London: D. Appleton Century Co., 1934.

Furer, Howard B., ed. The Scandinavians in America, 986-1970.
    Dobbs Ferry, N.Y.: Oceana Publications, Inc., 1972.

Fury, K. D. "Family Reunion: Southeastern Newlin Association."
    Redbook 141:98.

Gallagher, Dorothy. Hannah's Daughters: Six Generations of an
    American Family: 1876-1976. New York, 1976.

Garland, John H., ed. The North American Midwest: A Regional
    Geography. New York: John Wiley, 1955.

Gastil, Raymond D. Cultural Regions of the United States.
    Seattle and London: University of Washington Press, 1975.

Gerlack, L. R., and Nichols, M. L. "Mormon Genealogical Society
    and Research Opportunities in Early American History."
    William and Mary Quarterly 32(1975):625-29.

Gillette, J. M. "North Dakota Weather and the Rural Economy."
    North Dakota Historical Quarterly 12(1945):2-98.

Gillin, June Jacobi. "Lore from a Swedish Grandfather." New York
    Folklore Quarterly 9(1963):268-72.

Goffman, Erving. Behavior in Public Places: Notes on the Social
    Organization of Gatherings. London: The Free Press of
    Glencoe, Collier-Macmillan Ltd., 1963.

_____. Encounters: Two Studies in the Sociology of
    Interaction. Indianapolis and New York: The Bobbs-Merrill
    Company, Inc., 1961.

_____. Interaction Ritual: Essays in Face-to-Face
    Behavior. Chicago: Aldine Publishing Company, 1967.

_____. The Presentation of Self in Everyday Life.
    Woodstock, N.Y.: The Overlook Press, 1973.

_____. Strategic Interaction. Philadelphia: University
    of Pennsylvania Press, 1969.

SELECT BIBLIOGRAPHY

263

Goode, William J.; Hopkins, Elizabeth; and McClure, Helen M.
Social Systems and Family Patterns, A Propositional
Inventory. Indianapolis and New York: The Bobbs-Merrill
Company, Inc., 1971.

Goody, Jack. Comparative Studies in Kinship. London: Routledge
& Kegan Paul, 1969.

Goody, Jack, ed. The Developmental Cycle in Domestic Groups.
Cambridge Papers in Social Anthropology, no. 1. Cambridge:
The University Press, 1962.

Greven, Philip J., Jr. Four Generation. Ithaca and London:
Cornell University Press, 1970.

Gustafson, Philip. "Climbing the Family Tree: Ella Hecksher
Describes her Methods in Searching out Forgotten Ancestors."
The American Swedish Monthly 32(1938):10-12.

Gutman, Herbert G. The Black Family in Slavery and Freedom, 1750-
1925. New York: Pantheon Books, 1976.

Haimowitz, Morris L., and Haimowitz, Natalie Reader. Human
Development: Selected Readings. 3d ed. New York: Thomas
Y. Crowell Company, 1973.

Haley, Alex. Roots. New York: Doubleday, 1976.

Hall, Edward T. Beyond Culture. Garden City, N.Y.: Anchor
Press/Doubleday, 1976.

Hamsun, Knut. The Cultural Life of Modern America. Edited and
translated by Barbara Gordon Morgridge. Cambridge, Mass.:
Harvard University Press, 1969.

Hareven, Tamara K. "Family Time and Historical Time." Daedalus,
spring 1977, pp. 57-60.

Hareven, Tamara K., ed. Themes in the History of the Family.
Worcester: American Antiquarian Society, 1978.

Hendrickson, Gordon Olaf, ed. Peopling the High Plains:
Wyoming's European Heritage. Cheyenne: Wyoming State
Archives and Historical Department, 1977.

Henke, Warren A. "Imagery, Immigration and the Myth of North
Dakota, 1890-1933." North Dakota History 38(1971):413-91.

Herrick, C. A. "Family Trail Through American History."
Minnesota Historical Bulletin 3(1920):489-505.

Hijiya, James A. "Roots: Family and Ethnicity in the 1970s."
    American Quarterly 30(1979):548-56.

"How to Plan an Old-fashioned Family Reunion." Better Homes and
    Gardens, November 1977, pp. 56-58.

Howard, Jane. Families. New York: Simon and Schuster, 1978.

Hsu, Francis L. K. "Roots of the American Family: From Noah to
    Now." In Kin and Communities, Families in America, edited by
    Allan J. Lichtman and Joan R. Challinor, pp. 219-36.
    Washington: Smithsonian Institution Press, 1979.

Humphrey, Linda T. "Small Group Gatherings." Journal of the
    Folklore Institute 16(1979):190-201.

Huntington, Gale, ed. "Folksongs from Martha's Vineyard: Some
    Songs of the Singing Tiltons of Chilmark." Northeast
    Folklore 8(1966):1-88.

Ives, Edward D. "A Manual for Field Workers." Northeast Folklore
    15(1974):38-45.

Irish, Donald P. "Sibling Interaction: A Neglected Aspect in
    Family Life Research." Social Forces 42(1964):279-88.

Journal of Comparative Family Studies. 1970--.

Journal of Family History. 1976--.

"Joys of Genealogy." Independent, 2 November 1911, pp. 996-97.

Kelly, Jill. "The Finlinson Family Reunion Tradition." AFFword
    4(spring 1974):37-39.

Keyes, Ralph. We, the Lonely People, Searching for Community.
    New York: Harper & Row, Publishers, 1973.

Kinship. 1961--.

Klatzky, Sheila R. Patterns of Contact with Relatives.
    Washington: The American Sociological Association, 1973.

Klein, D. B. "Why Worry about Your Family Tree?" Science Digest,
    July 1944, pp. 43-44.

Köngas, Elli Kaija. "A Finnish Schwank Pattern. The Farmer-
    Servant Cycle of the Kuusisto Family." Midwest Folklore
    11(1961-62):197-211.

Kraenzel, Carl Frederick. The Great Plains in Transition.
    Norman: University of Oklahoma Press, 1955.

Larson, Lyle F. The Canadian Family in Comparative Perspective.
    Scarborough: Prentice-Hall of Canada Ltd., 1976.

Leinbach, P. P. "Family Reunion: Our Annual Watering of Roots."
    Farm Journal, August 1971, p. 34.

"Les 'Américains' reviennent au pays: Dans les familles
    gourinoises on 'tue le veau gras.'" La Bretage à Paris 1695,
    29 June 1979, p. 8.

Leslie, Gerald R. The Family in Social Context. 4th ed. New
    York: Oxford University Press, 1979.

Lévi-Strauss, Claude. "The Family." In Man, Culture, and
    Society, edited by Harry L. Shapiro, rev. ed., pp. 333-57.
    London: Oxford University Press, 1971.

Lesy, Michael. Wisconsin Death Trip. New York: Pantheon, 1973.

Lichtman, Allan J., and Challinor, Joan R., ed. Kin and Communi-
    ties, Families in America. Washington: Smithsonian
    Institution Press, 1979.

Lindberg, John S. The Background of Swedish Emigration to the
    United States. Minneapolis: University of Minnesota Press,
    1930.

Litwak, Eugene. "Geographical Mobility and Extended Family
    Cohesian." American Sociological Review 25(1960):385-94.

Lowenthal, David, and Bowden, Martyn J., ed. Geographies of the
    Mind, Essays in Historical Geosophy in Honor of John Kirtland
    Wright. New York: Oxford University Press, 1976.

Luebke, Frederick C., ed. Ethnicity on the Great Plains.
    Lincoln: University of Nebraska Press, for the Center for
    Great Plains Studies, 1980.

Lumpkin, Ben Gray. "Folksongs from a Nebraska Family." Southern
    Folklore Quarterly 36(1972):14-35.

Lynd, R. "Looking for an Ancestor." Living Age 15 March 1924,
    pp. 518-21.

Mahlberg, Mavis. "The Family Bedtime Ritual: Its Implications
    for Family Therapy." Unpublished paper.

McAllester, David. "A Paradigm of Navajo Dance." Parabola
     4(1979):28-35.

McKee, Russell. The Last West: A History of the Great Plains of
     North America. New York: Thomas Y. Crowell Co., 1974.

Mead, Margaret. And Keep Your Powder Dry: An Anthropologist
     Looks at America. New York: W. Morrow & Co., 1942.

_____. Blackberry Winter. Austin, Tex.: Touchstone
     Books, 1973.

_____. World Enough: Rethinking the Future. Boston and
     Toronto: Little, Brown, and Company, 1975.

Mead, Margaret, and Heyman, Ken. Family. New York: The
     Macmillan Company, 1965.

Milling, Chapman J. "Reunion in Georgia." South Atlantic
     Quarterly 35(1936):42-49.

Moberg, Vilhelm. "A Wheat Field in North America." American-
     Scandinavian Review 37(1949):243-46.

Mogey, John. "Residence, Family, Kinship: Some Recent Research."
     Journal of Family History 1(1976):95-105.

Morgan, Kathryn. "Caddy Buffers: Legends of a Middle Class Negro
     Family in Philadelphia." Keystone Folklore Quarterly
     11(1966):67-88.

Neville, Gwen Kennedy. "Kinfolks and the Covenant: Ethnic
     Community among Southern Presbyterians." In The New
     Ethnicity, Perspectives from Ethnology, edited by John W.
     Bennett, pp. 258-74. Proceedings of the American Ethno-
     logical Society 1973. St. Paul: West Publishing Co., 1975.

North Dakota Historical Quarterly. Formerly North Dakota History.
     1926--.

Ohrn, Steven, and Bell, Michael E., ed. Saying Cheese: Studies
     in Folklore and Visual Communication. Folklore Forum
     Bibliographic and Special Series 13. Bloomington, Ind.:
     Folklore Forum, 1975.

Ostergren, Robert C. "Prairie Bound: Migration Patterns to a
     Swedish Settlement on the Dakota Frontier." In Ethnicity on
     the Great Plains, edited by Frederick C. Luebke, pp. 73-91.
     Lincoln: University of Nebraska Press, 1980.

Osterreich, Helgi. "Geographical Mobility and Kinship: A
    Canadian Example." International Journal of Comparative
    Sociology 6(1965):131-45.

"The Painters: Reunion for Far-flung Family." Life, November
    1968, pp. 131+.

Packard, Vance. A Nation of Strangers. New York: David McKay
    Company, Inc., 1972.

Parsons, Talcott. "The Kinship System of the Contemporary United
    States (1943)." In Essays in Sociological Theory. Rev. ed.
    London: The Free Press of Glencoe, 1954.

_____. "The Stability of the American Family System." In
    A Modern Introduction to the Family, edited by Norman W. Bell
    and Ezra F. Vogel. New York: The Free Press, 1960.

Pearce, Helen. "Folk Sayings in a Pioneer Family of Western
    Oregon." California Folklore Quarterly 5(1946):229-42.

Peattie, L. R. "Your People." Good Housekeeping, April 1949, pp.
    15+.

Pentikäinen, Juha. Oral Repertoire and World View: An Anthro-
    pological Study of Marina Takalo's Life History. Folklore
    Fellows Communications 219. Helsinki, 1978.

Piddington, Ralph, ed. Kinship and Geographical Mobility.
    Leiden: E.J. Brill, 1965.

Porterfield, Allen W. "In Patriarchal Fashion." The Saturday
    Review of Literature, 13 August 1932, p. 45.

"Quest for Identity. Americans Go on a Genealogy Kick." U.S.
    News, 29 July 1974, pp. 41-42.

Ribbe, Wolfgang, and Henning, Eckart. Taschenbuch für
    Familiengeschichtsforschung. Neustadt an der Aisch: Verlag
    Degener & Co., Inh. Gerhard Gessner, 1975.

Rice, Timothy. "A Macedonian Sobor: Anatomy of a Celebration."
    Journal of American Folklore 93(1980):113-28.

Ritchie, Jean. Singing Family of the Cumberlands. New York:
    Oxford University Press, 1955.

Roberts, Leonard W. Song Branch Settlers: Folksongs and Tales of
    a Kentucky Mountain Family. Publications of the American
    Folklore Society, Memoir Series, vol. 61. Austin: Univer-
    sity of Texas Press, 1974.

Robinson, Elwyn B. History of North Dakota. Lincoln: University
    of Nebraska Press, 1966.

_____. "An Interpretation of the History of the Great
    Plains." North Dakota History 41(1974):5-19.

_____. "The Themes of North Dakota History." North Dakota
    History 26(1959):5-24.

Rölvaag, O. E. Giants in the Earth. Translated by Lincoln
    Colcord and O. E. Rölvaag. New York: Harper & Row, 1927.

Rosenberg, Charles E., ed. The Family in History. Philadelphia:
    University of Pennsylvania Press, 1975.

Sauer, Carl O. Land and Life. Berkeley and Los Angeles: Univer-
    sity of California Press, 1963.

Schell, Herbert S. "Official Immigration Activities of Dakota
    Territory." North Dakota Historical Quarterly 7(1932-33):
    1-24.

Schneider, David M. America Kinship: A Cultural Account.
    University of Chicago Anthropology of Modern Societies
    Series. Englewood Cliffs, N.J., 1968.

_____. "Kinship, Community, and Locality in America." In
    Kin and Communities, Families in America, edited by Allan J.
    Lichtman and Joan R. Challinor, pp. 155-74. Washington:
    Smithsonian Institution Press, 1979.

Schneider, David M., and Cottrell, Calvert B. The American Kin
    Universe: A Genealogical Study. Chicago: University of
    Chicago Press, 1975.

Schneider, David M., and Homans, George C. "Kinship Terminology
    and the American Kinship System." In A Modern Introduction
    to the Family, edited by Norman W. Bell and Ezra F. Vogel,
    pp. 465-81. New York: The Free Press, 1960.

Schneider, David M., and Smith, Raymond T. Class Differences and
    Sex Roles in American Kinship and Family Structure.
    Englewood Cliffs, N.J.: Prentice-Hall, Inc., 1973.

Selden, Charles A. "The Family Reunion, A Vacation Fantasia."
    Harpers Weekly, 16 June 1906, pp. 841-43.

Shapiro, Harry L., ed. Man, Culture, and Society. Rev. ed.
    London: Oxford University Press, 1971.

"The Science of Genealogy." Spectator 96(1902-06):414.

Smith, M. "So You Want to Know Who You Are!" Good Housekeeping,
    December 1942, pp. 43+.

Smith, Robert J. The Art of the Festival, As Exemplified by the
    Fiesta to the Patroness of Otuzco: La Virgen de la Puerta.
    University of Kansas Publications in Anthropology 6.
    Lawrence, Kans., 1975.

Stack, Carol B. All Our Kin. New York: Harper & Row, 1974.

Stern, Stephen. "The Sephardic Jewish Community of Los Angeles:
    A Study in Folklore and Ethnic Identity." Ph.D. disserta-
    tion, Indiana University, 1977.

von Sydow, Carl Wilhelm. Selected Papers on Folklore. Selected
    and edited by Laurits Bødker. Copenhagen: Rosenkilde and
    Bagger, 1948.

Taube, Kristi. "Family Folklore with a German Flair." Journal of
    the Ohio Folklore Society n.s. 3(1974):17-19.

Toelken, Barre. The Dynamics of Folklore. Boston: Houghton
    Mifflin Company, 1979.

_____. "Folklore, Worldview, and Communication." In
    Folklore: Performance and Communication, edited by Dan Ben-
    Amos and Kenneth Goldstein, pp. 265-86. The Hague and Paris:
    Mouton, 1975.

Toole, K. Ross. The Rape of the Great Plains: Northwest America,
    Cattle and Coal. Boston and Toronto: Little, Brown and
    Company, 1976.

Tufte, Virginia, and Myerhoff, Barbara, ed. Changing Images of
    the Family. New Haven: Yale University Press, 1979.

Tudor-Craig, A. "In Pursuit of a Pedigree." Saturday Evening
    Post, 21 March 1936, pp. 24-25.

Voegelin, Eric. Anamnesis. Translated and edited by Gerhart
    Niemeyer. Notre Dame and London: University of Notre Dame
    Press, 1978.

"Want to Look Up Your Family Tree?" Changing Times, November
    1954, pp. 15-17.

Warner, W. Lloyd. America Life, Dream and Reality. Rev. ed.
    Chicago: University of Chicago Press, 1953.

_____. The Family of God. Westport, Conn.: Greenwood
    Press, 1959. Reprint. New Haven: Yale University Press,
    1975.

_____. The Living and the Dead: A Study of the Symbolic
    Life of Americans. Yankee City Series, vol. 5. New Haven:
    Yale University Press, 1959.

Webb, Walter Prescott. The Great Plains. Boston: Ginn & Co.,
    1931.

Weber-Kellermann, Ingeborg. Die Familie. Frankfurt: Insel
    Verlag, 1976.

Weeks, Bill. "America's Happiest Family Reunion." Collier's, 6
    October 1951, pp. 18+.

Wells, R. V. "Family History and Demographic Transition."
    Journal of Social History 9(1975):1-19.

West, James. Plainville, U.S.A. New York: Columbia University
    Press, 1945.

Wiggins, William H. Jr. "'Free at Last!': A Study of Afro-
    American Emancipation Day Celebrations." 3 vols. Ph.D.
    dissertation, Indiana University, 1974.

Wilkins, Robert P., and Huchette, Wynona. North Dakota, A
    Bicentennial History. New York: W.W. Norton & Company,
    Inc.; Nashville: American Association for State and Local
    History, 1977.

Wills, Bernt Lloyd. North Dakota: The Northern Prairie State.
    Ann Arbor: Edward Brothers, Inc., 1963.

Woiwode, Larry. Beyond the Bedroom Wall: A Family Album. New
    York: Avon Books, 1965.

Wrigley, E. Anthony. "Reflections on the History of the Family."
    Daedalus, spring 1977, pp. 71-85.

Wyman, Walker D., ed. Frontier Woman: The Life of a Woman on the
    Dakota Frontier. River Falls: University of Wisconsin,
    River Falls, Press, 1972.

Zeitlin, Steven et. al. Family Folklore. Washington: Smith-
    sonian Institution, 1976.

Zimmerman, Carle C. Family and Civilization in the East and West.
    New York: Harper & Brothers, 1947.

INDEX